The Social Thought of
Karl Marx

Social Thinkers Series

Series Editor
A. Javier Treviño
Wheaton College, Norton, MA

Published
The Social Thought of Georg Simmel
By Horst J. Helle

The Social Thought of Karl Marx
By Justin P. Holt

The Social Thought of Émile Durkheim
By Alexander Riley

The Social Thought of C. Wright Mills
By A. Javier Treviño

Forthcoming
The Social Thought of Erving Goffman
By Michael Hviid Jacobsen and Søren Kristiansen

The Social Thought of Talcott Parsons
By Helmut Staubmann

The Social Thought of
Karl Marx

Justin P. Holt
New York University

Los Angeles | London | New Delhi
Singapore | Washington DC

Los Angeles | London | New Delhi
Singapore | Washington DC

FOR INFORMATION:

SAGE Publications, Inc.
2455 Teller Road
Thousand Oaks, California 91320
E-mail: order@sagepub.com

SAGE Publications Ltd.
1 Oliver's Yard
55 City Road
London EC1Y 1SP
United Kingdom

SAGE Publications India Pvt. Ltd.
B 1/I 1 Mohan Cooperative Industrial Area
Mathura Road, New Delhi 110 044
India

SAGE Publications Asia-Pacific Pte. Ltd.
3 Church Street
#10-04 Samsung Hub
Singapore 049483

Copyright © 2015 by SAGE Publications, Inc.

Library of Congress Cataloging-in-Publication Data

Holt, Justin P.

The social thought of Karl Marx / Justin P. Holt, The Gallatin School of New York University.

pages cm.—(Social thinkers series)
Includes bibliographical references and index.

ISBN 978-1-4129-9784-3 (pbk. : alk. paper)

1. Marxian economics. 2. Marxian school of sociology. 3. Marx, Karl, 1818–1883—Political and social views. I. Title.

HB97.5.H5774 2015
335.4′1—dc23   2014006295

Acquisitions Editor: Jeff Lasser
Editorial Assistant: Nick Pachelli
Production Editor: David C. Felts
Copy Editor: Kim Husband
Typesetter: C&M Digitals (P) Ltd.
Proofreader: Victoria Reed-Castro
Indexer: Karen Wiley
Cover Designer: Gail Buschman
Marketing Manager: Erica DeLuca

14 15 16 17 18 10 9 8 7 6 5 4 3 2 1

For Alise

Contents

Series Editor's Foreword

T he SAGE Social Thinkers series is dedicated to making available
compact, reader-friendly paperbacks that examine the thought of
major figures from within and beyond sociology. The books in this series
provide concise introductions to the work, life, and influences of the most
prominent social thinkers. Written in accessible and provocative prose, these
books are designed for advanced undergraduate and graduate students of
sociology, politics, economics, and social philosophy, as well as for scholars
and socially curious general readers.

The first few volumes in the series are devoted to the "classical" thinkers—
Karl Marx, Émile Durkheim, Max Weber, Georg Simmel, George Hebert
Mead, Talcott Parsons, and C. Wright Mills—who, through their seminal
writings, laid the foundation for much of current social thought. Subsequent
books will feature more "contemporary" scholars as well as those not yet
adequately represented in the canon: Jane Addams, Charlotte Perkins
Gilman, Harold Garfinkel, Norbert Elias, Jean Baudrillard, and Pierre
Bourdieu. Particular attention is paid to those aspects of the social thinker's
personal background and intellectual influences that most impacted his or
her approach in better understanding individuals and society.

Consistent with SAGE's distinguished track record of publishing high-
quality textbooks in sociology, the carefully assembled volumes in the Social
Thinkers series are authored by respected scholars committed to disseminating the discipline's rich heritage of social thought and to helping students
comprehend key concepts. The information offered in these books will be
invaluable for making sense of the complexities of contemporary social life
and various issues that have become central concerns of the human condition: inequality, social order, social control, deviance, the social self, rationality,
reflexivity, and so on.

These books in the series can be used as self-contained volumes or in
conjunction with textbooks in sociological theory. Each volume concludes

with a Further Readings chapter intended to facilitate additional study and research. As a collection, the Social Thinkers series will stand as a testament to the robustness of contemporary social thought. Our hope is that these books on the great social thinkers will give students a deeper understanding of modern and postmodern Western social thought and encourage them to engage in sociological dialogue.

Premised on Newton's aphorism, "If I have seen farther, it is by standing on the shoulders of giants" (an aphorism, incidentally, that was introduced into sociology by Robert K. Merton, himself a towering figure in the discipline), the Social Thinkers series aims to place its readers on the shoulders of the giants of 19th- and 20th-century social thought.

Acknowledgments

First and foremost, I would like to thank A. Javier Treviño, the Social Thinkers series editor and the author of the volume on C. Wright Mills. If Javier had not contacted me about writing an introductory book on Marx, I would have never attempted it. But, thankfully, he provided me with the opportunity, and I'm glad he did. His comments and criticisms were always helpful and made this book much better than the initial drafts. I'm quite happy with the outcome, and I hope he is too. The six readers of a draft—Benjamin F. Hadis, Fatmir Haskaj, Alexa Trumpy, Daniel Egan, Kristopher Kohler, and Ernesto Castañeda—devoted a considerable amount of time in providing insightful commentary, which made this book clearer and more accessible. I thank them for their commitment and candor. Finally, my beautiful and talented girlfriend, Alise Wallis, has helped me in countless ways over the years. If it wasn't for her intelligence, compassion, and insight, this book would never have been completed.

Introduction

Karl Marx's influence on the social sciences and philosophy has been one of emulation, disgust, horror, and praise. Many students are taught about Marx in an introductory sociology, political science, philosophy, or economics course, but usually they do not learn the complexity of his work. His ideas appear as an influence in many contemporary theories, either as a supporting or detracting basis. In addition, Marx occupies a notable place in the popular imagination as a social analyst and feared revolutionary. As of late (this book was finalized in 2013), Marx has received some renewed interest due to people suffering from the worst economic downturn since the Great Depression of the 1930s. This coverage indicates that people are buying Marx's books again. Shocked by the economic downturn, people are seeking to understand why and how capitalism can fail to grow and maintain employment. In this media coverage of Marx and his ideas, little attention is given to those scholars that attempt to analyze our economic shortcomings with the achievements of Marx and those who have further developed his theories. All this influence, hysteria, and notoriety does not inform us of the actual work that Marx did.

This book is about Marx's work including his philosophy, sociology, economics, and politics. My intention in writing this book is to explain what Marx said and to examine if it still makes any sense. I think that Marx's work has a cogency that can be presented clearly and systematically. What specifically is Marx's work about? Marx's work was an attempt to understand the social processes of capitalism. Capitalism is discussed at greater length in the first chapter. For now, we can simply describe capitalism as a social system with the following features: people are free to sell their labor, they are able to accumulate property as their own, and market transactions are commonplace. Marx became interested in capitalism because he found that these features resulted in misery for the majority of people who live in capitalist societies and societies affected by capitalism. Marx also found this outcome of mass misery to be profoundly irrational. Thus, he wanted to understand how such an irrational system of social organization could exist when its members have the power of reason. In simple terms, Marx's social scientific project is an attempt to answer the question: "How can capitalism exist when it produces results that are detrimental for the majority of humanity?" Marx answered this question via the use of various categories of analysis he developed. Chapters 3 through 9 of this book explain the various categories of analysis utilized by Marx and his theoretical and empirical results.

In review, this book is about the *work* of Karl Marx. Marx's work was an attempt to understand the social processes of capitalism. He was interested in understanding capitalism because he found the social outcomes common within capitalism to be detrimental for the majority of humanity. This book will discuss Marx's examination of capitalism by explaining the various categories he used in his work.

Outline of the Book

This book is composed of two introductory chapters, six chapters on Marx's categories of social analysis, one chapter devoted to applying Marx's work to environmental problems, and a final chapter on suggested readings.

Chapter 1 is an overview of the topics and influences of Marx's work and a presentation of the general themes of this work. This chapter begins with an introduction to capitalism, which provides a historical and an analytical presentation of capitalism. Included in this introduction is a consideration of some of the social problems of capitalism including inequality, poverty, and unemployment. The second section builds on the presentation of capitalism to consider why Marx's ideas can still be regarded as important. The third section gives a detailed presentation of the general themes of the work of Karl Marx: the influence of technological development and industrialization on human social organization; the influence of social organization and technological development on human behavior; and the potential for human civilization to produce nonantagonistic social relationships. The remainder of the first chapter considers the intellectual climate and influences on Marx's life and gives a brief biography of his life.

Chapter 2 is an overview of Marx's materialism, a consideration of Marx's conception of the interrelation of individuals and society, and a discussion of Marx's method. Materialism has become so commonplace in today's natural and social sciences people no longer know what it means not to be a materialist. On one hand, materialism is the theory that all natural and social occurrences are explained by material causes as opposed to supernatural or spiritual causes. An example of the difference between a material explanation and a spiritual explanation is that the Earth orbits the sun due to the forces of gravity and inertia as opposed to God's intervention. On the other hand, materialism is the theory that human societies are shaped by natural and technological causes and not the result of ideas, which are intrinsic to the human mind. Marx accepts both definitions of materialism, but the second one is very important to understand the groundbreaking nature of his work. Marx's method will be presented in light of his materialist theory. Marx attempts to develop explanations of the social world that identify simple causal determinations of social events. Chapter 2 reviews and analyzes Marx's statements on method and considers some examples.

Chapter 3 is devoted to Marx's theory of alienation. Alienation is when an object or a person is detrimental, hostile, or unaccepting of someone. Marx finds that people who have no control over the means of production due to class antagonisms suffer from alienation. People become alienated when they lose control over the means of production because the products of their labor are owned by others, they have little to no control over the labor process, they are unable to develop their abilities, and they are in antagonistic relationships with others. Marx finds that this has to be the case since people who don't own any amount of the means of production themselves have to sell their labor to survive. The people who hire them own what they produce and thereby enjoy the revenue that is generated from selling these goods and services. People who are hired are subject to the authority of their employers in regard to product creation and development. Since workers don't make decisions regarding the use of the means of production at their firm level, at the local level, or at a national level, they can't make decisions that will allow for their abilities to develop. Finally, people are in competition with one another when the means of production are scarce. Since people are in competition with one another for employment and market share, their relations are antagonistic.

Chapter 4 is on Marx's class theory. Class is the social position of a person in respect to other people's social positions. In particular, class is a social position designated by a person's economic relationship to others. For example, a class position can be determined according to income, wealth, profession, training, or education. Many contemporary class theories utilize income to designate class position, but Marx thinks class should be designated by whether one owns the productive resources of a society or not. The first section of Chapter 4 is an analytical reconstruction of Marx's theory of class. This presentation includes a discussion of how the ownership of the productive forces structurally determines class position. Next is a consideration of what are objective class interests and subjective class consciousness. Then there is a discussion of class alliances and ideology. The second section discusses Marx's analysis of class in *The Communist Manifesto*. Special importance is placed on determining the class position of the middle classes.

Chapter 5 is an overview of Marx's theory of historical materialism. Historical materialism is a theory of the social development of civilization. Marx's theory conjectures that material events as opposed to ideas or supernatural occurrences cause a society to develop. This chapter begins with an examination of the classical statement of historical materialism found in the preface to *A Contribution to the Critique of Political Economy*. This statement is expanded by utilizing Marx and Engels's comments from *The German Ideology*. The materialist dynamics of social development and revolution are elaborated. Special attention is paid to the problem of fettering. Fettering is when a given mode of production is no longer able to effectively develop the forces of production. The various modes of production and their causes of transition are analyzed. Last is a consideration of the possibility of free will and predetermination in Marx's theory of history.

Chapter 6 is on Marx's economics. The chapter begins with a discussion of the difference between exchange value and use value. Why Marx finds that commodities exchange at their labor values is analyzed. Next is a presentation of Marx's theory of surplus value and exploitation. Building on these categories, the chapter finishes with a consideration of Marx's theory of unemployment and his analysis of economic crisis.

Chapter 7 is on Marx's theory of ideology. This chapter begins with a discussion of why Marx's theory of ideology is a materialist theory. There is an exposition of the origin of ideology and the origin of ideologists. Next is a discussion of the kind of ideological notions Marx found to be common in the orthodox social scientific conception of capitalism. The chapter ends with a brief section on how Marx thought ideology could be demystified by social scientific critique and class formation.

Chapter 8 is on Marx's theory of communism. Communism is a society in which a sizable amount of society's productive resources are publicly owned and individuals cannot exploit others economically. This chapter has three parts. The first part is a presentation of what Marx found to be the ills of capitalism. The second part is an overview of the various aspects of Marx's vision of communism. The final part is a discussion of how Marx thought his vision of communism addressed and corrected the ills of capitalism.

Chapter 9 is on Marx's hypothesis that the dynamics of capitalist accumulation are not environmentally sustainable. First, this chapter reviews the dynamics of capitalist accumulation. This review examines how the goal of accumulation is to achieve further accumulation. Next comes a consideration of some of Marx's explicit environmental statements. Finally, there is a brief consideration of whether communism can be environmentally sustainable.

Finally, Chapter 10 is a short presentation of further readings. The chapter has been divided into sections on the topics of Marx's writings, online sources, and journals devoted to the study of Marx's ideas.

Each chapter ends with some questions for thought. These questions are provided for the reader to further reflect on the topics of the chapter. Many of the questions do not have answers that can be explicitly found in the preceding discussions, but these discussions should help the reader think about how to answer these questions. The questions have also been written to challenge the reader to think about contemporary critiques of Marx's work and contemporary applications of his work.

It is my hope that this work will provide a thorough introduction to the work of one of the great social theorists of the modern period. It has been written with a broad audience in mind, including students, scholars, and interested laypeople. Not all of the themes of Marx's work have been discussed, but the general categories and topics of his social thought have been touched on. These will, I believe, provide groundwork for readers to pursue Marx's ideas in greater depth.

1

The World of Karl Marx

Capitalism and the Enlightenment Legacy

Marx's working life was spent analyzing, criticizing, and attacking capitalism theoretically and politically. In order to understand his social thought, it is important that we learn what capitalism is, his personal background, and his intellectual influences. This opening chapter will begin with a section that provides a more detailed presentation on capitalism. Next will be a brief consideration of why Marx's ideas can still be regarded as important. Third, there will be a discussion of the general themes of this book. Fourth, there will be a consideration of Marx's place within intellectual history, in particular his relationship to the Enlightenment. The fifth section will be a brief biography of his life. The final section is a discussion of his influences.

What Is Capitalism?

The majority of Marx's social scientific work was an attempt to analyze what **capitalism** is and identify its tendencies for further development. Many readers may not understand exactly what capitalism is. Before we begin a discussion of Marx's analysis of capitalism, we should provide a brief overview of the features of capitalism. Capitalism will be defined here in two complementary ways: historically and analytically.

Capitalism Historically

Historically, capitalism began during the late European Renaissance (approximately the 16th and 17th centuries) and continues to the present. Capitalism's historical development has a geographical range as well. During its beginning, capitalism was contained in small Italian city-states, Holland, and England. From this small beginning, capitalism extended outward, encompassing essentially the entire globe by the early 20th century.

Historical periods other than capitalism have also existed. Previous to capitalism, **feudalism** existed in Europe from the fall of the Roman Empire until the complete dominance of capitalism (in approximately the mid-19th century). Marx's term for delineating different periods of technological, economic, and social activity is **mode of production**. For example, capitalism is a mode of production that is different from feudalism. This means that feudalism is also a mode of production.

An Analytical Description of Capitalism

Capitalism is a historical period, but it is also a term to describe a particular set of economic and social activities. Capitalism can be distinguished from other ways of describing the activities of people's economic and social lives. This means that the economic and social activities people perform within capitalism will be different from the activities that were performed within feudalism. There will be strong similarities, of course, but there is a divergence that makes the two modes of production different. For now, an analytical description of what constitutes the unique economic and social activities of capitalism will suffice. Later sections in this book will discuss the distinction between capitalism and other ways people's social and economic lives can be organized.

Capitalism has the following characteristics: (1) People are free to sell their labor and unemployment is commonplace, (2) private property is a common form of property and inequalities in wealth holdings have no limit, and (3) people exchange commodities in a market and markets are prone to economic slumps. Many other characteristics can be attributed to capitalism, but these three will suffice for an introduction. These three characteristics describe the kinds of activities and common economic results indicative of capitalism and thereby distinguish it from other periods such as feudalism. Each characteristic is explained below.

The Free Selling of Labor and Unemployment

First, people are free to sell their labor within capitalism. This means that people can choose to sell their labor to whoever is willing to buy their labor. This distinguishes capitalism from **feudalism** and **slavery**. Within feudalism,

serfs were not free to sell their labor to whomever they wished. Serfs within feudalism were legally required to provide a certain amount of labor to their feudal lords on projects the lords selected. They could not become employed by another lord if they wished. Within slave societies, slaves were not free to sell their labor. Their labor was owned by another person, the slave owner. The ability to sell one's labor is a fundamental characteristic of capitalism and distinguishes it from other periods of history.

There are many instances in the history of capitalism in which some people were able to sell their labor and some were not. For example, slavery existed within capitalism as a legal institution in the Americas until the 19th century. In addition, some kinds of labor bondage exist within capitalism even though they are illegal. For example, people are forced into slavery within contemporary capitalist countries, or some people are smuggled into contemporary capitalist countries to work as slave laborers.

The free selling of labor also means that people are free to hire whomever they wish within capitalism. People can select who they wish to perform a certain task. This also means that there is no obligation that people must be hired within capitalism. From the perspective of the employer, this is desirable. They can choose the candidates who best suit their preferences. From the perspective of society as a whole, the free hiring of labor is also desirable. People will compete for positions, and only those seen as exhibiting the desirable characteristics will be hired.

From the perspective of those who seek employment, the unemployed, this is not necessarily a beneficial result. The unemployed suffer from many problems beyond lack of income. They also have poorer health and higher rates of suicide than the employed. The unemployed miss opportunities for training and experience. Unemployment has also been positively correlated with crime (Feldstein, 1978; Hagan, 1994; Philpott, 1994). The problem of unemployment is unique to capitalism. In other modes of production, such as feudalism, people's indenture as serfs prevented them from losing their gainful work. In contradistinction, people are free to sell their labor within capitalism, but this does not mean they will find employment. When this book was written, there were approximately 200 million people worldwide who were unable to find work (ILO, 2012, p. 10). The free selling of labor is for many people only an abstract right. If there are no jobs available then one cannot exercise one's right to freely sell one's labor.

In review, within capitalism, people are free to sell their labor and people are free to buy labor. There are no obligations for people to work for others. In addition, there is no obligation for private individuals to provide people with jobs. The free selling and buying of labor supposedly leads to people being selected for a position who have the desired characteristics. The free selling of labor results in the phenomena of unemployment. People are unemployed when they cannot find anyone who wishes to employ them. The results of unemployment are poverty, poor physical and mental health, poor training and experience opportunities, and an increase in crime.

Private Property and Inequality of Wealth

Second, people can own **private property** within capitalism. Private property is when a person or persons own money, land, buildings, tools, machines, raw materials, and other objects exclusively. This is in contradistinction to **public property**, where objects are owned collectively and managed by a political body, such as a town, city, state, or nation.

When property is privately owned, those who own it can decide how it will be used and by whom. The owners of private property can rent it, sell it, use it, or let it lie idle according to their desires. Private property is a regular form of property ownership within capitalism.

The ownership of private property can produce incentives for people to use their property in productive pursuits. People might use their property productively to increase their own wealth and well-being. From the perspective of society, this is beneficial since new goods and services will be offered for sale when people productively use their private property.

A distinctive negative result of private property ownership is that there is no guarantee that people have ownership of certain amounts of property to provide for their subsistence. The possibility for some people to have exclusive ownership of property means that some people can own no property other than their personal effects. The result is that large inequalities in the ownership of property may occur. Inequality in property ownership can prevent many people from starting their own business or being able to afford certain goods and services (Burczak, 2006; Hill, 1998).

Also, private property ownership conveys the right of use to owners only. This means that the owners of a firm will make decisions on how property is used as opposed to the nonowner workers of a firm. If ownership conveys the right of use, then nonowners will be unable to express their interests at their jobs. Nonowners will have to follow instructions as opposed to creatively participating in the production process. Since property can be difficult if not impossible for many people to acquire, the right of use conveyed to owners effectively excludes the majority of people within capitalist nations from creatively participating in the production process.

As will be discussed at many points and at length in the chapter on economics, Marx finds that inequality in wealth holdings allows for workers to be exploited. **Exploitation** is when one person gains at the expense of another. Marx defines exploitation as when a person produces more value during the production process than she or he is paid for. Workers are subject to exploitation because they have insufficient wealth of their own to productively employ. Workers are effectively forced to work for capitalists due to the inequity of wealth holdings within capitalism.

In review, private property ownership occurs when individuals can have exclusive control over money, land, buildings, tools, machines, raw materials, and other objects. Private ownership of property can encourage people to use their property productively for their own gain. These productive uses may increase the well-being of others in society. The private ownership of property may result in inequalities of property ownership. Inequalities in the ownership of property can thus limit people's ability to start businesses, purchase certain goods and services, and creatively participate in the production process and allows for the exploitation of workers.

Market Transactions and Market Slumps

Third, transactions between people are self-regulating within capitalism. These transactions are called market transactions. A market transaction occurs when people willingly enter into agreements for the buying and selling of goods and services, usually for money instead of barter. When a person goes to the supermarket to buy potatoes or lottery tickets, she is conducting a market transaction.

Market transactions can be distinguished from transactions based on tradition or transactions that are the result of command. Transactions based on tradition occur when people exchange goods and services according to the mores and expectations of their society. For example, when Native Americans met to exchange items in a potlatch, they were exchanging items according to tradition. Command transactions occur when individuals and parties exchange goods and services according to authority. For example, when serfs provided labor to their lords, this was done according to the authority of their lord (Heilbroner & Galbraith, 1990, p. 442; Polanyi, 1944).

Market transactions are a distinguishing characteristic of capitalism. They are the dominant kind of transaction that occurs within capitalism. Market transactions are not coordinated by an external authority. Each group of people conducting transactions does so according to its own assessment of its preferences. This means that many groups of people can be transacting for the same purpose. For example, suppose there is an increase in demand for tin. If people have a preference to make money, they will enter into transactions with tin producers, the desired result being that they can hopefully sell the tin at a profit.

The result of an increase in tin purchases can be that the demand for tin is met, the demand for tin is not met, or the demand for tin is exceeded. If the demand for tin is met, then all buyers and all sellers have their preferences met regarding the exchanging of tin. If the demand for tin is not met, there will be people with an unmet preference to purchase tin. If the demand for tin is exceeded by the amount of tin supplied, then there will be people who cannot sell their tin but would prefer to do so.

Market transactions are an important characteristic of capitalism because the lack of coordination of the various transactions within capitalism causes economic expansions and contractions. Market transactions allow people to enter into economic competition with others. This competition supposedly results in innovation and economic growth. The lack of coordination between market participants can also result in the overproduction of goods and services. Overproduction occurs when there are too many items for sale and not enough buyers. The result of overproduction is an economic contraction, which is also called an economic crisis, a recession, or sometimes a depression. Economic growth slows or stops during a contraction. When an economic crisis occurs, businesses go bankrupt and unemployment and poverty increase (U.S. Census Bureau, 2011, p. 14). The effects of recessions are particularly detrimental for young workers, as their lifetime earnings are adversely affected (Oreopoulos, Von Wachter, & Heisz, 2012).

It is important to point out that the profits capitalists gain from the production process allow them to accumulate wealth holdings that are greater than individual workers' holdings. When economic slumps occur, these wealth holdings allow capitalists to enjoy higher and more comfortable incomes than do workers who have become unemployed or whose wages have been reduced. The dynamics of production within capitalism result in outcomes wherein the ill effects of economic turbulence are unequally shared, with workers in the more precarious position.

In review, market transactions are the dominant form of transactions within capitalism. A market transaction is when people freely buy and sell items. The result of this freely chosen buying and selling can be an economic expansion or an economic contraction. An economic expansion results in economic growth. An economic contraction results in a slowing or stopping of growth, the bankruptcy of businesses, and increases in unemployment and poverty. Also, due to inequalities of wealth within capitalism, workers are in a more vulnerable position during an economic slump.

Why Read Marx?

The previous section on capitalism hinted at some of the problems that affect people within capitalism: unemployment, inequality, poverty, exploitation, and economic crises. These problems still exist even within advanced industrialized countries. The current economic malaise, which began in 2008, is a severe but not a unique outcome within capitalism. The world has gone through several economic contractions since Marx's day. Even before the Great Depression of the 1930s, there were the Great Depression of the 1890s and numerous other contractions (Kindleberger & Aliber, 2005).

The ills of capitalism can be minimized by using welfare state transfers, macroeconomic intervention, and coordination between industry and the state. Even though it is possible to reduce unemployment and poverty to negligible degrees and minimize inequality or its effects on opportunity, capitalist nations still have large segments of their populations that are unemployed, in poverty, or unable to take advantage of opportunities. If these problems can be corrected but are not, many people may ask why this is the case. Why do the economic ills of capitalism persist when their cures have been known for several decades? Is there something about capitalism that prevents these problems from being solved?

Marx would answer the last question by stating that the social dynamics of capitalism are intrinsically antagonistic. He finds that the measures that would eliminate the listed ills of capitalism are contrary to the interests of the dominant class within capitalism, which are the **capitalists**, also called the **bourgeoisie**. Thus, Marx's analysis of the social and political dynamics of capitalism advances a hypothesis about the continued persistence of economic ills within capitalism. Marx conjectured that unemployment, poverty, and restricted opportunity are unavoidable results within capitalism and cannot be eliminated without actually changing the fundamental characteristics of capitalism. Stated in a more Marxian fashion, the ills of capitalism cannot be corrected without changing the mode of production from capitalism to communism.

It is useful to restate the heading of this section as a question: Why should people in the 21st century be interested in learning about Marx? People should be interested in what Marx wrote because the capitalism of the 21st century still has not solved many of the same problems that existed in the capitalism of the 19th century. One would be hard pressed today to find a child who has died from overwork in an advanced industrialized country. One can find many children who live in poverty in these advanced countries (Mishel, Bernstein, & Shierholz, 2009, p. 384). In the United States, the number of job seekers can exceed the number of job openings. This had been the case even before the start of the recession in 2008 (Shierholz, 2013). Poverty has increased during the recession even though cash transfers exist to mediate its effects (U.S. Census Bureau, 2011). Also, one doesn't have to look far to find current factory conditions in China and Mexico or the mines of Africa that are surprisingly similar to the workplace conditions of the 19th century (Malkin, 2005; Robson & Ward, 2012; UN News Center, 2012).

People in the 21st century may wish to read about the possible reasons a social system that has and still does produce amazing wealth does not distribute its gains in a fashion that allows people to move out of poverty and unemployment. Why can opulence and squalor coexist? A short version of Marx's answer to this question is that the motivations and social structures that allow for such amazing growth also prevent the gains from this growth from being shared throughout society. The very social dynamics that allow for capitalism to grow also produce the ills as a necessary result of this growth. The reasons Marx lists for these outcomes are numerous and detailed; they will be discussed at length in later chapters.

If capitalism cannot be reformed, then what other social forms are there? Marx infamously postulated that capitalism would be superseded by communism, a society in which the antagonisms of capitalism will be absent. The most pronounced features of communism are the conversion of the majority of private property into public property and the democratic coordination of economic development and the workplace. Marx seeks not only an elimination of unemployment and poverty but also an expansion of democracy into areas that are currently unheard of. Marx's theory of communism not only confronts the problems of unrewarding work and authoritarian workplaces but also argues for expanding people's engagement and voice into areas few people have direct access to. If people of the early 21st century feel disenfranchised and alienated by politics and their work, Marx speaks directly to these problems.

In review, many of the problems and ills people face around the world have been discussed by Marx in his writings. He tried to show why these problems exist, why they cannot be solved within capitalism, and what he found to be real solutions to these problems. His ideas are fascinating and still address problems that haunt our current societies.

General Themes

This work will focus on the following general themes in the work of Karl Marx:

1. The influence of technological development and industrialization on human social organization

2. The influence of social organization and technological development on human behavior

3. The potential for human civilization to produce nonantagonistic social relationships

These are abstractions of the concrete work that Marx conducted. These general themes are an after-the-fact appraisal of Marx's lifetime of work. These themes are complicated conjectures about our social world, but we can start to explain what they are and how they are interrelated now.

Theme 1: Technological Development and Human Social Organization

The first theme of this book on Marx is the causal influence of technological development and industrialization on human social organization. There is a causal connection between the two that is not simply unidirectional. This means that technological development causes changes in human social organization and also that human social organization causes changes in technological development. There is thus a codevelopment between the two. This relationship can also be called a feedback process. A feedback process occurs when a change in object A causes a change in object B and then this change in object B causes another change in object A.

It must be stressed that even though Marx thinks that human technological ability and human social organization are coemergent, he finds technological development to be the ultimate and not the proximate cause of this feedback process (Marx & Engels, 1978, pp. 155–157). It is beneficial to point this out now since it is an important part of Marx's social theory and it separates him from writers who take the representation of human social organization to be the ultimate and not the proximate cause.

Examples will help to demonstrate the codevelopment/feedback causal process of technological development and human social organization. To demonstrate the feedback process, we can use the technological activity of food procurement and the social organization of work tasks. We can begin with the abstract example of settled agriculture, with no different work tasks between people. At this starting point, all people perform the same activities of farming. All people plant, harvest, and store food plants. If we introduce a technological development such as irrigation, we can see how this causes changes in the organization of work tasks. In particular, how will technological development affect the amount of direct labor used in farming and the total amount of produced output? After an irrigation system has been built, we will assume that this increases the production of food plants. The result of the irrigation is that the amount of labor required to grow a certain amount of food is reduced. The upshot of this technological change of irrigation is that labor is freed from farming and can be utilized for other tasks. A society utilizing this freed labor develops the new tasks of irrigation operator and food warehouse worker. Over time, other tasks may develop, perhaps because of increased production and labor saving due to the new specializations. For example, the development of the new specialization of the animal handler could increase agriculture output due to the use of animal power. This example demonstrates the feedback effect.

In review, a technological change, such as the implementation of irrigation, allowed for less labor to be used in the production of food. This reduction in the use of labor allowed for changes in social organization, which was the development of new specializations. One particular change in social organization was the development of animal handlers. The new social position of animal handler resulted in a new technological development, the application of animal power to farming. This application of animal power allowed for greater food output. As we can see, an initial technological change brought about a change in social organization. This change in social organization resulted in further technological change.

A current example of the codevelopment/feedback causal process of technological development and human social organization is the use of computers for communication. The introduction of computers has allowed groups to take advantage of the labor-saving features that resulted in the computerization of typing, publication, and communication. Groups that were previously unable to communicate information due to the cost of professional typists, printers, and distribution can now do so easily. The technological development of computers allows for nonspecialized groups to perform functions that took several different specialists in the past. These developments have changed the nature of communication from a machine-intensive and costly enterprise to a relatively simple and inexpensive process. Small and nonprofessional groups may attempt to develop and disseminate their ideas and opinions. This change in the social organization of communication dissemination was driven by technological development and the changing nature of the work tasks.

This relationship between technological development and social organization is important for Marx. In many ways, it forms the basis of his outlook of social development (Marx & Engels, 1978, p. 4). This feedback process has been identified by many other authors before Marx, including Plato, Aristotle, Locke, and Rousseau. In addition, this notion of technological development bringing about social development and vice versa is now standard in social science literature, such as Diamond (1997), Service (1975), Sen (1999), Jones (2002), and Blanchard (2002).

The idea that there is a causal feedback process between technological development and social organization in Marx's writings has been termed **historical materialism**. It has been given this name because it is a theory of the development of human societies that considers the material objects of technological change and social organization as decisive causes. Marx started writing about this notion in an unfinished work that is now called the *1844 Manuscripts*. In this work, he describes industry as the actual history of humans as opposed to a spiritual or moral conception of human development (Marx & Engels, 1978, p. 90). Later, Marx developed with Engels their theory of historical materialism in the unpublished *The German Ideology* in 1845 and 1846 (Marx & Engels, 1978, p. 182). They presented a thorough version of historical materialism in *The Communist Manifesto* in 1848 (Marx & Engels, 1978, p. 474). The seminal version of historical materialism, which is commonly cited, appears in the preface to Marx's *A Contribution to the Critique of Political Economy*, which was written in 1859 (Marx & Engels, 1978, p. 3).

We will discuss Marx's conception of historical materialism in greater detail in Chapter 5. For now, a brief overview will suffice based on our previous examples and comments. The examples discussed earlier were developed in order to introduce Marx's theory of historical materialism. Marx understands that human technological activity develops over time, making not only new technologies but also new kinds of societies possible. In the broad scope of human societal development, Marx finds that human civilization moves through the main epochs of an egalitarian society, slave society, feudalism, and capitalism, and there is a strong chance (some readings of Marx find that it is inevitable) that civilization will develop into communism.

Why society moved from an egalitarian society into a slave society and a slave society into feudalism and so forth is due to the effects of technological development. In particular, the reduction of direct labor time and the increase in the products of subsistence (food, shelter, and clothing) caused a change in social organization. The reduction of labor for a particular activity frees up people to work on other tasks. This process, according to Marx, explains the development of human civilization.

Marx is interested in studying the origins of capitalism within feudalism. He studied this change not only to understand the dynamics of capitalism but also to understand how human civilization will move beyond capitalism and into communism. The previous examples of how the development of new technologies makes new work tasks possible contains the germ of how Marx understands the formation of capitalism. During feudalism, the increased ability of people to produce allows for items to be sold and not directly consumed. This in turn allows for trade and production for sale to become increasingly common. Also, the development of technology results in the emergence of new **classes**. Not only do new classes arise, but the old ones become antiquated because they are from a period of technological development and social organization that has been surpassed by these new formations. New types of human societies replace the old ones (Marx & Engels, 1978, pp. 473–483).

In review, the first theme of this work is that technological development and social organization are in a relationship of codevelopment. Marx finds that technological development is the ultimate cause of this codevelopment. This does not mean that social organization has no effect on the development of technology. Rather, Marx finds that social organization can effect change in the development of the technological processes of a society. The codevelopment of technology and social organization occurs through labor-saving technologies and new forms of social organization that take advantage of these labor-saving technologies. Historical materialism is the common term used to describe Marx's theory of human social development.

Theme 2: Social Organization, Technological Development, and Human Behavior

Marx's materialist understanding of how society developed does not stop at the technological and organizational level. Marx also considered how technological and organizational development causes human behavior to change and how human behavior causes technological development and organizational development to change. This brings us to the second theme of this book. To simplify matters, we can discuss social organization and technological development as a single term: the **mode of production**. The mode of production is the combined social, economic, and technological aspects of a society. Human behavior represents the actions of individuals and the legal, political, philosophic, religious, and moral representations of their actions. We can now analyze how a mode of production can be in various causal relationships with human behavior.

First, human behavior can be affected by a mode of production. This means that people can change from one set of behaviors to another set of behaviors due to the influence of a mode of production. For example, increased pay and desirable working conditions may cause people to accept the goals of the firms they work for as their own goals. Instead of seeing their work as separate from their own long-term plans, people begin to see their work as part of their own plans (Galbraith, 1967).

Another example is when people accept the goals and outcomes of their society. If people accept the goals and outcomes of their society, they will not find these outcomes to be detrimental or unjust. For example, if it is common for people within a society to think that the cause of unemployment is laziness, then people will find that the outcome of unemployment is the result of individual behavior and not the result of social processes beyond an individual's control. Thus, unemployment is a problem for the unemployed person alone and it is not understood as a social problem. Unemployment could be considered an acceptable and just outcome since it is an outcome of a person's own efforts. If this is the common understanding of people within a particular society, then the social processes of one's society are not understood as unjust regarding unemployment. Also, an individual's actions are understood as the cause of their unemployment.

Second, people's behaviors can affect the development of a mode of production. For example, people may decide that they wish to make more money. In order to achieve this goal, they decide to go to school to receive additional training. This additional training will in turn allow a mode of production to change, since a better-trained workforce can utilize different machinery than in the past and workers can be organized in new ways. Thus, the behaviors of an individual can cause changes in a mode of production.

Let's take the example of unemployment again. If workers become aware that unemployment is actually due to the economic shortcomings of their society, these workers may attempt to lessen unemployment through political action. Their behavior could bring about changes in the mode of production.

The two types of causal relationships discussed are both analyzed by Marx. The development of the technological and social factors of a mode of production can bring about changes in people's behaviors. The classic example is when the normal operations of capitalism cause an economic crisis to occur. The result of this crisis is a change in worker behavior from being favorable to capitalism to being unfavorable to capitalism. The second causal relationship, when behaviors bring about changes in the mode of production, could be the result of this new change in worker behavior. Their new unfavorable opinion of capitalism could result in revolutionary actions that bring about a change in the mode of production (Marx & Engels, 1978, p. 480).

Once again, there is a causal feedback process that is between a mode of production and human behavior. The examples attempt to show that developments in technology and in social organization can change human behavior, and developments in human behaviors can bring about changes in technology and social organization. In Marx's theory of historical materialism, the most important kind of change is when people's behaviors develop and this brings about changes in the social organization of society by altering the class structure. This change in the class structure of society can further technological development. In addition, this process can operate in another way when technological development causes changes in the form of social organization and this changes people's behaviors.

In review, the mode of production and human behaviors are codeterminate. Each can cause changes in the other. Additionally, a mode of production and human behaviors can be involved in a casual feedback loop. Marx's theory of historical materialism hypothesizes that changes in a given mode of production can alter people's behaviors from a favorable assessment to an unfavorable assessment of this mode. When this happens, people's behaviors may prompt them to take revolutionary action and alter the mode of production.

Theme 3: The Possibility of Nonantagonistic Social Relationships

Now let us examine the third general theme: the potential for human societies to produce nonantagonistic social relationships. Before we can understand what nonantagonistic social relationships are, antagonistic social relationships need to be defined. An antagonistic social relationship is when one social actor benefits at the expense of another social actor. In other words, the gains for some people in society come at the expense of other people in society.

The well-known occurrence of slavery will suffice to demonstrate an antagonistic social relationship. The institution of slavery is premised upon the labor of a person kept in bondage being performed for the benefit of another person who owns the person in bondage. The slave owner must gain proportionally more than the slave benefits or the institution of slavery is pointless. If the labor performed by slaves was beneficial to them, there would be no reason to hold them in bondage. They would freely commit themselves to the tasks desired of them. As we can see, the institution of slavery is antagonistic according to its definition, for if it were not, there would be no need for the bondage of slavery.

Now, based on this example, we might want to define a nonantagonistic social relationship as one in which people would freely choose to engage in the relationship on the terms offered. This actually is not sufficient due to the problem of choice under dire necessity, called *voluntarium imperfectum* (Ryan, 1996, p. 103). Choice under dire necessity is the situation in which there is a substantial fear for the loss of life, limb, or health of oneself and one's dependents that influences the decision. Under the conditions of dire necessity, choice is in fact voluntary but is profoundly questionable under all circumstances other than general and widespread dire necessity for a society. This means that one cannot call a choice truly voluntary under the conditions of dire necessity if these conditions are not general and widespread for a given society.

For example, recently freed slaves are still in an antagonistic social relationship if their choice is arduous labor at bare subsistence wages for themselves and their dependents when their employer can afford to pay them more without dooming themselves to loss of life or health. The freed slave has a choice to accept low wages or starvation, but this is a choice that is unnecessarily dire.

Now, we can say that a nonantagonistic social relationship is one in which people freely choose outcomes in which subsistence is not in jeopardy. This may not be enough since human life is about more than mere subsistence. People find fulfillment not only in meeting their subsistence requirements but also in forming relationships with others and accomplishing long-term goals (Staub, 2004). This means that if the current distribution of resources within a society does not allow people to fulfill their desires for social relationships and the accomplishment of long-term goals, then this society should still be classified as having antagonistic social relationships. Added to this definition is the caveat that these resources can be redistributed without generally reducing the potential for people to fulfill their desires for relationships and accomplishments.

For example, a societal member is in an antagonistic social relationship with others if he is unable to reasonably pursue relationships and accomplish his long-term goals (if these relationships and accomplishments can be pursued without harming the prospect for others to fulfill these same ends). There is a lot to be said about what it means to be able to reasonably pursue one's long-term goals and relationship with others. We do not have the space to pursue this point in depth. What is important to the matter at hand is to stress that what constitutes a nonantagonistic society is from the perspective of what can be fulfilling for people given the current conditions. This means that a person has a reasonable claim to alter the social and economic outcomes in her society if these outcomes can be altered without limiting the minimal fulfillment of others.

It is true that employers lose out if they pay their employees more or that men lose out if they no longer can enjoy the free labor of their wives and children or White people may lose economic and social benefits if people of color are treated equitably or that slave owners lose opportunities for gaining profits if their slaves are emancipated. Redistribution of gains should occur up to the point at which reasonable fulfillment of one's long-term accomplishments can still be met. This means that a nonantagonistic social relationship occurs when an optimal mutual benefit is possible. This is a society in which all individuals receive benefits from participating in society and no individual gains at the expense of another individual.

This rule of redistribution is not simply a conclusion derived from the distributive justice literature. It is also a rule of redistribution, which Marx endorses but not as explicitly as it has been stated here. Marx's critique of capitalism is that the control and enjoyment of resources should be redistributed to improve the chance of fulfilling a person's long-term goals while also not lessening the lives of others in any meaningful way. For example, this means that redistribution of capitalists' resources and control over society's wealth should occur, and the loss that the capitalists would suffer is justified (Marx & Engels, 1978, pp. 484–491).

The justification of this particular amount of loss for capitalists and the requisite gain that would occur to other classes in society will be the subject of many of the discussions contained in this book. Marx thought that it was entirely reasonable to assume that people would seek to alter the distribution of resources in their society to obtain optimum mutual benefit. Marx notes in many places that when a society does not provide a distribution of resources at a possible level of optimum mutual benefit, this society will be subject to revolutionary actions by those who are losing out (Marx & Engels, 1978, pp. 4, 483).

In review, an antagonistic society is one in which one person gains at the expense of another person. A nonantagonistic society is one in which all individuals receive benefits from participating in society and no individuals gain at the expense of another individual. If in the creation of a nonantagonistic society some individuals lose certain benefits while others gain certain benefits, this is justified if no one is reduced to a situation in which her or his reasonable long-term goals are affected. Marx thinks that a nonantagonistic society of mutual benefit is possible. Marx called this society communism.

General Themes Overview

The development of technological activities changes the social organization and the behavior of humans. In turn, human behavior and social organization can cause technological development. In addition, human behavior can alter patterns of social organization. The expectations of humans to have a level of fulfillment that is possible for society to maintain for everyone will lead to political action that alters what kinds of social organization exist. This political action will bring about a change in human behavior and further development of technology. Marx thinks humans innately desire to meet their needs and achieve higher levels of fulfillment (Marx & Engels, 1978, pp. 115, 476, 531). Thus, technological development brings about changes in people's expectations, and these expectations bring about desires to change human social organization. This in turn changes human behaviors and continues to develop humanity's technological abilities.

Marx's position is that societies develop to meet the expectations of their members. This is where all three themes of this book intersect. Societal change is brought about to fulfill unmet needs. Interestingly, the reason these needs are unmet is because society has changed technologically and these new needs have developed. Even though these needs have been created by society, the distribution of resources within this society does not allow a significant number of people to satisfy their needs. People will, according to Marx, attempt revolutionary action to bring about the fulfillment of their new needs by creating a new society.

In review, the three general themes of this book are causally interrelated, but the ultimate cause for change within Marx's system of social development is technological development. Technological development creates the new needs, which people seek to satisfy through the creation of a new society. Marx's discussion of the history of social dynamics, his analysis of current social formations, and his consideration of possible future states of affairs all have their root in technological development.

The Enlightenment and Capitalism

Marx's critique of capitalism is an extension of the values of the Enlightenment and a criticism of the procapitalist reading of these values. The Enlightenment was centered in Europe from the 17th century to the early 19th century. This period was characterized by the notion that reason can improve the human world through political reforms and the use of science. Some notable thinkers of the Enlightenment period are Isaac Newton, Leonhard Euler, Jean-Jacques Rousseau, Pierre-Simon Laplace, and John Locke.

Two movements within the Enlightenment were of particular interest to Marx: (1) the defense of political freedom and equality as natural law and (2) the theory of the social contract, which considers the individual as the basic economic unit. This section will present a general overview of these two enlightenment movements and will provide Marx's critique.

Rights as Natural

The natural freedom and equality of humans has been famously argued by many early and late Enlightenment thinkers such as Hobbes, Locke, Rousseau, Kant, and Hegel. In the late 18th century, the idea of the naturalness of political rights was stated in a number of political documents such as

The Declaration of Independence and *Declaration of the Rights of Man and of the Citizen*. A small excerpt from *Declaration of the Rights of Man and of the Citizen*, which was drafted by the National Assembly of France on August 26, 1789, can help demonstrate these notions and values:

> [T]he National Assembly doth recognize and declare, in the presence of the Supreme Being, and with the hope of his blessing and favour, the following *sacred* rights of men and of citizens:
>
> 1. Men are born, and always continue, free and equal in respect of their rights. Civil distinctions, therefore, can be founded only on public utility.
>
> 2. The end of all political associations is the preservation of the natural and imprescriptible rights of man; and these rights are Liberty, Property, Security, and Resistance of Oppression.
>
> 3. The Nation is essentially the source of all sovereignty; nor can any individual, or any body of men, be entitled to any authority which is not expressly derived from it.
>
> 4. Political Liberty consists in the power of doing whatever does not injure another. The exercise of the natural rights of every man, has no other limits than those which are necessary to secure to every *other* man the free exercise of the same rights; and these limits are determinable only by the law. (National Assembly of France, 1789/2003)

As can been see in this quote, the notion of the naturalness of human freedom and equality is clearly stated. People are naturally entitled to be at liberty, to have property, to be secure, and to be free of oppression. In addition, people are their sovereign authority, at least, existing as a nation. If we ask what any of these rights entail, what are their limits, and how they support or conflict with one another, we are left with few answers.

For example, let us take equality. The excerpt states that people are born equal and that unequal distinctions will only be allowed due to public utility. This appears to mean that people will only be treated unequally if it is of benefit to the public. Exactly what is of benefit to the public? Does public utility entail democracy or technocracy—that is, the rule by experts? A technocracy may come up with solutions to problems that people may dislike, but is the benefit to the public the people's enjoyment of the solution? As we can see, there are possible conflicts among equality, public utility, and sovereign self-rule.

Another example is the relationship among liberty, equality, and property. Is the holding of property to be equal? If the holding of property is equal, does this increase or decrease liberty? A person exclusively holding a piece of property may decrease another person's liberty by his no longer being able to use this particular piece of property. Does the limitation of liberty as "whatever does not injure another" include injury to economic well-being or only to physical well-being?

These two examples of conflict between these rights were perceived by people during the 18th century such as Pierre-Sylvain Maréchal in his *Manifesto of the Equals* written in 1796:

> Equality! First need of nature, first demand of man, and chief bond of all legitimate society! French people! You have not been more favoured than the other nations that vegetate on this wretched globe! Always and everywhere poor humanity, in the hands of more or less adroit cannibals is the tool of every ambition, the pasture of every tyranny. Always and everywhere men were lulled by fine phrases; never and nowhere did they receive the fulfillment with the promise. From time immemorial we have been hypocritically told: *Men are equal;* and from time immemorial the insolent with the most degrading and most monstrous inequality has weighed down the human race. Since civilized society began, this finest possession of humanity has been unanimously recognized, yet not once realized; equality was only a fair and sterile fiction of the law. To-day when it is more loudly claimed, we are answered: Silence, wretches! Real equality is but a chimera: be content with the constitutional equality: you are all equal before the law. *Canaille,* what more do you want? What more do we want? Legislators, governors, rich proprietors, listen in your turn. (Maréchal, 1796/2003)

In this quote, there is a presentation of the conflict between the professed natural equality of the age and the unequal social distinction of officials and property holders. Maréchal shows the unresolved tensions that existed between the various political values of the Enlightenment. He also points out the dominant means of solving these tensions: a reading that privileges a certain meaning of the values. In the passage, Maréchal mentions that equality is only to be considered equality before the law, which means that people will have the law applied to them equally. Thus, all people will have, for example, the right to legal action or the right to express their opinion publicly. This equality of trial and public expression does not take into consideration the differences in means to exercise these equal rights. Certain people will be more effective in advocating for their desires through the courts because they can hire more or better lawyers. Alternatively, people will have a greater chance of expressing their opinions publicly because they can afford to take out ads in publications, start universities and research foundations to support their opinions, or donate to political campaigns. All people have the right to legal action and public expression within this understanding of Enlightenment values, but they do not have the same substantive equality to utilize these rights.

Marx realized, like Maréchal before him, that the dominant understanding of the democratic and universal political values of the Enlightenment favored the ruling group of his time, which was the capitalists. Marx went further to conclude that the dominant ideas of any age will be those of the dominant class (Marx & Engels, 1978, p. 172). In several different works, Marx attempted to show that the current understanding of Enlightenment values does favor the preservation of the current class structure. He notes in *On the Jewish Question:*

> None of the supposed rights of man, therefore, go beyond the egoistic man, man as he is, a member of civil society; that is an individual separated from the community, withdrawn into himself, wholly preoccupied with his private interest and acting in accordance with his private caprice. (Marx & Engels, 1978, p. 43)

Marx finds that the rise of capitalism and the ascension of capitalists as the new ruling class resulted in an understanding of the rights of man, which takes individual interests as the correct reading of the conflict between the various rights. Thus, an individual's advantage will be given preference over the public good or preference will be given to those who own private property instead of those individuals who have no private property to defend. Marx further clarifies the dominant reading of the rights of man as one that serves not all private interests but the interests of the new capitalist class. Capitalists are "the *true* and *authentic* man" (Marx & Engels, 1978, p. 43). He shows that the dominant interpretation of rights theory in Europe during the mid-19th century uses the capitalist as the definition of what a free and equal person is. In addition, this dominant interpretation of rights theory defends the interests of capitalists by stating that these interests are the natural and authentic rights of man.

Marx further examines this dominant interpretation of rights theory, which defends capitalists' interests in *The Communist Manifesto* when he discusses the right of freedom: "By freedom is meant, under the present bourgeois conditions of production, free trade, free selling and buying" (Marx & Engels, 1978, p. 486). The capitalist, or bourgeois, society's conception of freedom takes a particular position on the conflict between property and freedom. There can be a conflict since the freedom of a person depends on her ability to utilize material resources to achieve her desires. Marx finds that all actions require a material basis to actualize. People require the material means of life (food, clothes, shelter, etc.) to live their lives. They require materials to strive toward their goals, to work, to have a family, or just for any activity. Even leisure requires the use of resources to be alive and to be at rest. To be a person means to exist as a living being, which entails that one must have the resources to survive. Freedom requires the access to resources so one can be free to perform a desired action.

Marx finds that the closure of the debate over the meaning of Enlightenment values precludes attaining the actuality of the Enlightenment vision as noted in the *Declaration of the Rights of Man and of the Citizen*, where people are able to rule themselves and their societies and not be ruled by others according to rank, birth, religion, or wealth. Marx does believe in the political values of the Enlightenment. He advocates the values of freedom, liberty, equality, property, and sovereignty. If one considers just one well-known work by Marx and Engels, *The Communist Manifesto*, one can find passages advocating for each of these Enlightenment political values and how these values will be achieved within communism.

In review, Marx overall agrees with the professed values of the Enlightenment. He thinks that there is no simple, natural reading of these values and their relationship. Marx advocates a communist reading of Enlightenment values because he thinks this reading would benefit all members of society and not just particular people and particular classes.

Social Contract Theory

A distinctive break that Marx had with the Enlightenment political tradition is his criticism of the social contract doctrine. The social contract is the idea that humans exist alone as individuals in their natural state. They form groups only by choice. This idea can be found in the work of Hobbes (1994, p. 109), Locke (2003, p. 141), and Jefferson (1774/2003).

Marx finds the social contract doctrine to be not only a historical fiction; it also has political consequences that are dangerous. Marx's critique of the social contract doctrine is twofold. First, he dispels the notion of people existing alone and independent in a natural state. Later, he provides a history to support his critique (Marx & Engels, 1978, p. 222). Humans by nature exist in groups and reproduce their social and economic lives as a society. Social reproduction is not an isolated occurrence of a single individual; it engages all members of a community. Second, Marx wants to show that the idea of humans existing with no relationship to resources to provide for their needs is a result of the social contract doctrine. This theory that people in their natural state live isolated and alone gives birth to the idea that people are naturally and always isolated economic actors. It can be argued that it follows from this assumption that economic outcomes should always be considered as the result of people's own efforts. As we discussed earlier, if people live in societies in which their well-being can be affected by others, then the rewards from their work are not what they could be, free from the antagonisms of their society.

The orthodox political economy of Marx's time utilizes the assumptions of the social contract doctrine to support the political conclusion that capitalism is a just arrangement. This is the case because the economic outcomes of capitalism are supposedly due to each individual's effort and are not the result of violence, coercion, or *voluntarium imperfectum*. Marx criticizes this myth of just exchange with his theory of **primitive accumulation**. Since humans are physical beings and require the natural world to provide for their existence, Marx hypothesizes that the only way people could be turned into isolated individuals with no resource other than their labor is if they were forced into this condition (Marx & Engels, 1978, p. 433).

Marx accepts one element of the Enlightenment political tradition that the social contract doctrine was used to justify: the right to rebel. The social contract doctrine concluded that if societies could be made by choice, they could be unmade by choice also. In contradistinction to the social contract method, Marx finds that the history of the world is the history of class struggles (Marx & Engels, 1978, p. 473). This means that it is part of the ordinary process of social development for new modes of production to replace old modes of production that no longer allow for the development of society (Marx & Engels, 1978, p. 5). Marx tries to demonstrate that revolution is a part of human social development. Social revolutions allow for further development of human abilities and their technological capacities.

In review, the social contract doctrine is the idea that humans live isolated and alone in their natural state. They form societies by choice. The social contract doctrine forms the basis for the concept of economic man in mainstream social theory. Economic man is not dependent on others and only enters into transactions with others for their own benefit. Marx found the social contract doctrine to be historical fiction and a notion that precluded the possibility of natural interdependence within economic arrangements. Marx analyzed the social contract doctrine with his theory of primitive accumulation. Marx found that people were forced into unequal economic positions instead of their economic situation being the result of their uncoerced actions. Marx accepted one notion that was part of social contract doctrine, the right to rebel. Marx thought that revolutions were a means for the development of human societies.

Biography

Karl Heinrich Marx was born in Trier, a town in the Rhineland, on May 5, 1818, to a Jewish family. Marx's paternal grandfather, Marx Levi, was the rabbi in Trier. Marx's father Hirschel was born in 1782. His mother, Henrietta Presburg, came from a rabbinical family in Holland. Even with such strong Jewish roots, Marx's father changed his name to Heinrich and converted to Protestantism in 1824. The main reason appears to be the anti–Semitic spirit of the time, which made public life for Jewish people extremely difficult. Heinrich Marx was an advocate in Trier and eventually became *Justizrat*, which is equivalent to becoming a Queen's council. Heinrich was a staunch defender for Prussia and disliked the Napoleonic reforms. His patriotism was due primarily to his Enlightenment view, which he perceived in the actions of Frederick the Great (Mehring, 1936, pp. 1–2).

Karl was fond of his father, and his father's letters show that Heinrich loved his son greatly. Even though Marx's father died while Karl was still at university, Marx always had dear thoughts for him and carried his picture with him even in his later years. Heinrich was optimistic for his son since Karl demonstrated great intellectual ability in his youth. Nonetheless, Heinrich was worried that Marx was driven by a passion that might consume his life. It appears that Heinrich was correct, since Marx lived a life mainly in poverty devoted to a cause that brought him little notoriety when he was alive.

In 1830, Marx enrolled at the Trier Gymnasium and completed his studies in 1835. It seems he was interested in contributing to the assistance of humanity even at this early age. The progressive outlook of the young Karl Marx is captured in what he wrote during the summer of 1835:

> If we have chosen the position in life in which we can most of all work for mankind, no burdens can bow us down, because they are sacrifices for the benefit of all; then we shall experience no petty, limited, selfish job, but our happiness will belong to millions, our deeds will live on quietly but perpetually at work, and over our ashes will be shed the hot tears of noble people. (Marx & Engels, 1975, pp. 8–9)

In October of that year, Marx enrolled as a law student at Bonn University. His father's letters at the time contained great concern about Marx studying too hard and ruining his health (Marx & Engels, 1975, pp. 645–655). When Marx wasn't consuming books, he was trying his hand at poetry; some of his poems were even published. Heinrich found Marx's early artistic attempts confused and urged him to find a profession other than being a poet. His concern was perhaps driven by Karl's inability to manage his finances. This was a problem that Marx was never able to overcome, for he was always in need of money throughout his life.

Marx was a born bookworm, which is why his father's concern over his health due to overwork was well justified. He also had a reckless side that is noted in his certificate of release from the Bonn University:

> In regard to his behavior, it has to be noted that he has incurred a punishment of one day's detention for disturbing the peace by rowdiness and drunkenness at night; nothing else is known to his disadvantage in a moral or economic respect.

Subsequently, he was accused of having carried prohibited weapons in Cologne: "The investigation is still pending" (Marx & Engels, 1975, p. 658). This recorded youthful folly did not affect his studies since the comment for most of the lectures he attended was "diligent and attentive."

Marx left Bonn University to continue his studies at Berlin University in 1836. Heinrich Marx was happy for the change, hoping that Marx's boisterous and spendthrift ways could perhaps be abated at the more conservative and serious institution in the Prussian capital. Heinrich's worry about Karl's tendency to overwork was again realized. He continued his study of law in Berlin. He even tried to develop a philosophy of law. He gave this up after writing several hundred pages and turned his attention to philosophy. He did this all in his first term! Thus, his pace of work was again extreme. He rested in the village of Stralau between terms. Marx returned to university for the second term and recommenced with a feverish pace of work.

He soon discovered the work of Hegel while back at school. Hegel was a German philosopher who lived during the late 18th and early 19th centuries. The philosophic system he developed was extremely influential and was still being taught in Berlin (Hegel is discussed in greater detail in what follows). Marx disliked what he initially found, which is often the case for students of Hegel even today. He became intrigued by Hegel's work even if he still had reservations about it (Marx & Engels, 1978, pp. 7–8).

After Marx began to read Hegel, he became associated with the Young Hegelian club, which was a hotbed of anti-establishment ideas. Critiques of religion and Prussian authority were commonplace. The Young Hegelians were interested in reforming and liberalizing Germany. They thought that intellectual critique was the means to break the chains of superstition and conservatism. Marx was greatly influenced by his discussions with the Young Hegelians, and the result was his dissertation titled *Difference Between the Democritean and Epicurean Philosophy of Nature*. This work was an analysis of the ancient atomist systems of Democritus and Epicurus. Atomism is a theory in which the world is understood as only atoms and not composed of spiritual or supernatural entities. This seemingly dry topic was actually an attempt by Marx to learn from the radical ideas of the ancient world. In particular, Marx was intrigued by atomic theories that showed that free choice was possible at the smallest level of matter. Marx's dissertation, while extremely technical, is an attempt to show that freedom of movement for matter is possible. The political implications from such a doctrine lend themselves to reform efforts and not to naturalistic arguments for conservatism.

After receiving his doctorate, Marx attempted to become a lecturer of philosophy in Bonn. The anti–Left Hegelian government made it difficult for him to obtain a position. He thereby entered into journalism to voice his reformist notions about German society. Marx's attempts to avoid government censorship and control were briefly realized when he worked as a contributor and eventually the editor-in-chief for the new liberal paper *Rheinische Zeitung*. During his time at the *Rheinische Zeitung*, Marx wrote his famous piece concerning a new wood theft ordinance. This piece was a critique of the recently established law, which prohibited the collection of wood from forests. Many peasants depended on this collected wood as a source of fuel. The recently established law prohibiting this collection was a limitation of the traditional rights of the peasants. This law protected the property rights of those who owned the forests. Marx was critical of the law since it was a detriment to people with little means to support themselves. The paper was subject to censorship and finally was forced to shut down.

In 1843, Marx married Jenny von Westphalen at Kreuznach in the Rhineland. Marx became engaged to Jenny von Westphalen while he was still at Bonn University. Her father was Privy Councilor Ludwig von Westphalen, who served as a governmental adviser in Trier. While at university, Marx dedicated a book of poems to his fiancée (Marx & Engels, 1975, pp. 521–522). Jenny was 4 years his senior and had a great intellect. Karl's father was quite happy after the announcement of Jenny and Karl's marriage since he felt that Marx's burning desire to assist humanity could best be supported by a brilliant companion. These laudable characteristics were not what the townspeople of Trier remember of Jenny after Karl and she had long left. In 1863 when Karl returned to Trier for his mother's funeral, people still asked him about the most beautiful woman in Trier that he had married. Married life for Jenny and Karl was difficult due to Marx's inability to secure a dependable income as well as their frequent relocation for political reasons. For almost the first decade of their marriage, they moved from country to country in Europe. Several times Marx was exiled due to his political work and writings. Eventually in the early 1850s, they settled in London. They had six children together. Five of them were born before they moved to London. Tragically, Marx lived to see four of his children die.

After marrying Jenny, Karl began working on *Contribution to a Critique of the Hegelian Philosophy of Law* while they were still in Kreuznach. One can find Marx developing his materialist critique of Hegel in this work and the earliest forms of his philosophy of history. In October of that year, the newlyweds moved to Paris, where Marx indented to publish the journal *Deutsch-Französische Jahrbücher.* Only one issue was printed due to difficulties in distributing it in Germany without the knowledge of the authorities. Marx became acquainted with Frederick Engels through their correspondence for work on the *Deutsch-Französische Jahrbücher.* Marx and Engels became lifelong friends and wrote several books together.

The year 1844 was a profound one for Marx in Paris. He worked on a set of manuscripts, which are today called the *1844 Manuscripts.* These writings contain one of his first forays into political economy. They also contain his seminal writings on alienation and a rather exact critique of Hegel's philosophy. One can see a definite shift in his thinking toward attempting to understand human action in a materialist fashion. In August of 1844, Engels and Marx began work on their first cowritten work, *The Holy Family.* This is the first work in which they analyzed the Young Hegelians from a materialist perspective.

During this time, Marx contributed to a German newspaper published in Paris called *Vorwärts!* The critical nature of the newspaper toward the Prussian government caused the French to capitulate to demands to have Marx exiled. In 1845, Marx moved to Brussels. His young family and Engels followed him shortly. While in Brussels over the years 1845 and 1846, Marx and Engels worked on the manuscript called *The German Ideology.* This work was a continuation of their materialist critiques of the Young Hegelians. This work contains one of the most detailed attempts by Marx and Engels to construct a materialist theory of history. It also contains his seminal theoretical treatment of ideology.

In 1847, Marx wrote *The Poverty of Philosophy,* a critique of Proudhon. This is Marx's first sustained work on political economy. Marx and Engels joined the League of the Just, which later changed its name to the Communist League. They worked on and published *The Communist Manifesto* during the French Revolution of 1848. On March 3, 1848, the King of Brussels ordered Marx to leave. He arrived in Paris on March 5. By this time, the revolution had spread throughout Europe. In April, Marx and Engels went to Germany to take part in the German Revolution. He began to publish a daily newspaper in Cologne called the *Neue Rheinische Zeitung.* The publication was a troubled affair with financial difficulties and pending censorship by the government.

The year 1849 was a turbulent one for Marx. Early in the year, Marx was put on trial for insulting the authorities in his publication of the *Neue*

Rheinische Zeitung. He was eventually found not guilty. Even with all this disruption occurring, Marx published *Wage Labor and Capital* in the *Neue Rheinische Zeitung.* This was another early political economic critique that did not contain the advances of his later works. He was eventually exiled from Germany on May 16. He returned to Paris with the expectation of an imminent workers' uprising, but none emerged. He was again exiled from France and moved to London, which became his family's home for the remainder of his life.

In the early period of Marx's new life in London, he published *The Class Struggles in France* in 1850 and *The 18th Brumaire of Louis Bonaparte* in 1852. Both of these works were attempts to interpret the 1848 French Revolution from a materialist perspective. They were also works that developed many conjectures about the nature of class consciousness, class alliances, and ideology. Marx provided a thorough class analysis of the counterrevolution that occurred in France. In addition, during his early years in England, Marx became the London correspondent for the *New York Daily Tribune*; this generated a meager income for his family. He contributed articles until the time of the United States Civil War. In the early 1850s, Engels moved to England to work in Manchester's industry. He started to provide dearly needed material support for Marx and his family. This support continued throughout Marx's lifetime.

The 1850s were a time of study for Marx. Other than writing articles for the *New York Daily Tribune*, he studied economics and utilized the resources at the library of the British Museum. In 1857, Marx worked on a series of notebooks that have become known as the *Grundrisse*. This work contains not only fascinating economic examinations but also some detailed statements concerning method and the social nature of humans. The *Grundrisse* was never published, but in 1859, Marx published *A Contribution to the Critique of Political Economy*. This work began to demonstrate many of his mature economic positions. This work contains the seminal statement on historical materialism in the preface.

The 1860s were a period of continued work on economics for Marx; this was the decade when the first volume of *Capital* was published. In the early 1860s, Marx worked on a series of manuscripts that are now called *Theories of Surplus Value*. These documents contain critiques of other economists' positions and many details on economic crises. In 1865, Marx wrote *Value, Price and Profit*, which is a short statement of his mature economic ideas including a discussion of exploitation. In addition, *Value, Price and Profit* contains an important refinement of Marx's understanding of the tendency of wages to fall within capitalism. As opposed to his earlier statements on the topic, he discusses how wages can fluctuate due to several factors.

Finally, after years of study and writing, Marx published the first volume of *Capital* in 1867. Marx's ideas about economics are quite complex, and the corpus of his economic writings spans greatly beyond the first volume of *Capital*. In the first volume of *Capital*, Marx provides a detailed account of the labor theory of value, the origin of surplus value, the necessity of exploitation within capitalism, the nature of commodity fetishism, the factors that determine fluctuations in employment, and the theory of primitive accumulation, which is a conjecture of how the working class came to exist.

Marx continued his work on the remaining two volumes of *Capital* for the rest of his life. They were never completed, but Engels edited the manuscripts and published them after Marx's death. Volume 2 was published in 1885 and Volume 3 in 1894. After the publication of the first volume of *Capital*, Marx was busy with political work and became sick in his later years. One of his great post–1860s writings is *The Civil War in France*, published in 1871. This work analyzes the proletarian revolution in France, which eventually failed. *Critique of the Gotha Program* was written in 1875 and was published by Engels in 1891. This is one of Marx's few statements regarding the problems of remuneration within communism. Marx also discusses the possibility of communist societies having developmental stages.

Jenny Marx died on December 2, 1881. Karl's health declined after his wife's death and he died on March 14, 1883. He was buried on March 17 in Highgate Cemetery in London. Engels gave a speech at his funeral in which he discussed his social scientific accomplishments and his political work. He concluded with these words: "His name will endure through the ages, and so also will his work" (Marx & Engels, 1978, p. 682).

Influences on His Work

As noted, Marx received a doctorate and wrote his dissertation on ancient philosophical theories of atomism. His intellectual interests spanned beyond his university education and encompassed three main influences: Hegel, Feuerbach and other Young Hegelians, and the classical economists. Each of these thinkers and groups of thinkers was read and criticized by Marx in his published and unpublished writings.

Hegel

Georg Wilhelm Friedrich Hegel was a philosopher of the German Idealist school who lived from 1770 to 1831. Hegel was a famous and renowned philosopher during his lifetime, a feat enjoyed by few philosophers. He produced a number of important works of great influence, including *The Phenomenology of Spirit*, *The Encyclopedia of the Philosophical Sciences*, *The Science of Logic*, and *The Philosophy of Right*. Hegel's philosophy has been of tremendous influence during the 19th and 20th centuries. As with Marxism, many philosophical schools have developed as a response to Hegel's work, including existentialism, phenomenology, and even analytical philosophy. Hegel's philosophy is of incredible complexity, so only a fraction of his work can be discussed here.

Hegel's work is influenced by the German Idealist thinker Immanuel Kant (1724–1804). Kant developed an idealist understanding of epistemological and moral phenomena. An idealist philosophy basically finds that not all concepts that people have of the world are derived from their sensations. This means that people have concepts about the world that are innate to the structure of their minds. For example, Kant argued that the concept of cause and effect is not derived from our observation of objects. Say one sees a white billiard ball move across a snooker table, which collides into a red billiard ball, and then this red billiard ball falls into a side pocket of the table. The event of the sinking of the red ball by force exerted by the white ball is not an observation. Rather, idealists find that the event of the sinking of the red ball is the organization of sensations by our mind. This means that our minds organize sensory data into events, which we classify as cause-and-effect occurrences. Other concepts that Kant argued were idealist in origin include quantity and quality.

Hegel developed these idealist theories about how the mind organizes sensory data in new directions. He found that the mind not only organizes sensory data, it also contains all possible permutations of physical and social events. He applied this theory to the development of human history. Hegel theorized that human history must move through certain stages of development, which culminates in a fully developed culture. A fully developed culture understands what necessary social interactions are and why they must be this way. Hegel argued that this culture is one in which people have become truly free (Hegel, 1991, pp. 35, 189). The values of freedom, equality, and property defended by Enlightenment theorists are accepted by Hegel, but he finds that these values would not be properly understood in a natural state unimpeded by society. The full realization and full understanding of these Enlightenment values comes about by the process of cultural evolution. People realize after centuries of cultural development what it means to be truly free and why private property should be valued. The past mistakes of a culture affect the refinement of its valuations.

It is important to note that Hegel understands each stage in the development of a culture as a mirror image of a concept the human mind has of the world. It can be argued that a culture moves through these stages because the human mind is structured in a certain way. This means that a culture develops according to a pattern of concepts contained within the human mind. The causal force of cultural and social development is the prearranged structure of the human mind. Hegel mentions that our self-conscious minds are driven to understand themselves. Thus, our minds seeking knowledge of themselves drive a culture to develop (Hegel, 1977, p. 51). The values of a culture develop because the human mind seeks their development. All humans have the same structure of mind, even if they have different personalities. This means that a set of people collectively as a culture seek to fully understand themselves and to fully realize the values of their culture. Human culture developed because the minds of its members are prearranged to seek out truth through an exploration of a pattern of concepts. The development of a culture is the progression of this pattern of concepts.

Marx discovered Hegel during his university days, but Marx's acceptance of Hegel's philosophy was always conflicted. In Marx's earlier writings from the 1840s, he subjects Hegel's work to a materialist critique (Marx & Engels, 1978, pp. 16–25, 53–65, 106–125). In the afterword to the second German edition of the first volume of *Capital*, Marx comments on his relationship to Hegel:

> My dialectic method is not only different from the Hegelian, but is its direct opposite. To Hegel, the life-process of the human brain, *i.e.*, the process of thinking, which, under the name of 'the Idea,' he even transforms into an independent subject, is the demiurogos [God, the creator—JPH] of the real world, and the real world is only the external, phenomenal form of "the Idea." With me, on the contrary, the ideal is nothing else than the material world reflected by the human mind, and translated into forms of thought. (Marx & Engels, 1978, p. 301)

In this passage, we see that Marx set himself apart from Hegel's idealist philosophical outlook. Marx finds that concepts are derived from sensory data instead of the prearranged structure of humans' minds. The chapter on ideology will deal with Marx's theory of ideas in greater detail.

Marx was always critical of Hegel's work and method, but he took dialectic reasoning seriously as a description of the world. As discussed, Hegel understood that the development of a mind's concepts would eventually allow a culture to fully develop. For Hegel, the history of humans is a movement from one concept to the next, all interconnected by the flaws of the previous concepts. A flawed idea allows a new concept to emerge, and the new concept tries to correct the flaws of the previous concept.

Marx took this Hegelian development of ideas and found a similar movement in the development of human societies. For Marx, a society was organized according to the structure of class relationships. These class relationships determine who can use what natural resource, building, or machine in production. In addition, these class relationships determine who receives what amount of the total product within this society. These class relationships must be seen as natural and just for society to reproduce itself. A society develops until these class relationships for organizing social life are called into question. At this point people no longer find the class relationships to be natural and just. A social crisis ensues, the old society falls apart, and a new society that addresses the problems of the old society develops.

There are some strong general similarities between Marx and Hegel's theories of history, but Marx diverges greatly from Hegel's outlook. Hegel understood that the development of a culture was driven by a particular concept, whereas Marx understood human productive ability to be the main driver of history. Hegel's thinking was the dominant philosophic system of Marx's young life. Marx subjected this system to critique and moved beyond it by the time *The Communist Manifesto* was published in 1848. Hegel's influence on Marx's theory of history is obvious even if Marx radically changed the content. Marx's theory of history is called historical materialism and will be discussed in Chapter 5.

Hegel's outlook on the world is divergent from that of the majority of contemporary social scientists. Hegel lived and worked at a time when social science was becoming distinguished from philosophy and theology. His theories do not embrace the generalized materialist outlook that is standard within the social sciences. Hegel finds that culture and technology are a reflection of ideas that are innate to the human mind (Hegel, 1991, p. 365). In contradistinction, contemporary social science, and the work of Marx, understands culture to be the product of previous cultures and technology to be the accumulation of tools and their application. Marx's pioneering work on the evolution of societies is more at home in contemporary social science than in 19th-century philosophy.

Feuerbach and the Young Hegelians

In the late 1830s and early 1840s, a series of thinkers developed Hegel's ideas in new directions and also critiqued what Hegel had said. These thinkers have been called the Young Hegelians and included David Strauss, Bruno Bauer, Karl Friedrich Köppen, and Ludwig Feuerbach. Many of these thinkers were interested in subjecting religious views to scientific scrutiny. Strauss's work is of particular importance. In 1835, Strauss published

Life of Jesus, which was a historical analysis of Jesus's life and Gospel stories. Strauss's book attempted to find historical events to connect with Biblical stories. His book's viewpoint was thus an attempt at a scientific appraisal of belief. Strauss did not try to defend the stories of the Bible as literal. This was quite shocking in the mid-19th century since it called the authority of the Bible into question. Bauer continued Strauss's work on ascertaining the veracity of Bible stories. His conclusions were even more shocking. He concluded that there was no historical basis for the events documented in the Bible. It was all a fantasy (Mehring, 1936, p. 22).

Ludwig Feuerbach persisted with the Young Hegelians' assault on religious philosophy. Just as Strauss and Bauer had argued that Bible literalism had no factual basis, Feuerbach tried to demonstrate that Hegel's own work was only divine inspiration with the divine absent. Instead of examining one's mind to understand the truth of the world, Feuerbach thought people should look to nature and other people to comprehend reality. Feuerbach loved rural life and enjoyed the seclusion it offered. Feuerbach's work was a product of observing and reflecting upon nature and what he found to be humans' true existence. He hoped that the essence of man could be discovered by understanding what natural man is. Feuerbach attempted to develop a materialist understanding of humans without the recourse to the religious aspects of Hegelian systematic philosophy.

Marx was influenced by Feuerbach's materialist outlook, but he found that Feuerbach's materialism did not take human productive ability into account and was thus not historical. Feuerbach took the world as he found it to be, a source of insight into the human condition. Marx criticized Feuerbach for neglecting the social dynamics, which made the world what it was at the moment of observation (Marx & Engels, 1978, p. 170). Marx describes the shortcomings of Feuerbach's materialism in 1845 as "Feuerbach wants sensuous objects, really distinct from the thought objects, but he does not conceive human activity itself as *objective* activity" (Marx & Engels, 1978, p. 143).

Economists

After Marx criticized Hegel and the Young Hegelians, his work significantly shifted perspective away from the philosophy of the time and toward political economy. Works like *The Poverty of Philosophy* and *The Communist Manifesto* demonstrate a concern with the problems of poverty, class antagonisms, inequality, and economic crisis rather than critiques of philosophers. Marx began a serious study of economics in the 1850s when he had to move to London after being exiled from Brussels, Germany, and France due to his political opinions. Marx read the contributions of political economists from the 18th century to his own time, including Smith, Ricardo, Malthus, and Mill. His notes and comments on this research are published as *Capital*, the *Grundrisse*, and *Theories of Surplus-Value*.

In particular, what Marx received from his economic predecessors was a consideration that the origin of economic value was through laboring as opposed to utility. Marx developed and refined the labor theory of value. It forms the general outlook of his economics and is the basis for many of his contributions. Marx's explanation of the origin of surplus value is based on the labor theory of value. This theory allows Marx to argue that surplus value extraction is exploited, unpaid labor.

In addition, economics takes material factors such as population, income, trade, and employment to be factors in the development of a society. These are materialist factors. Marx's interest in a materialist explanation of the development of human civilization is addressed by these economic thinkers. Marx was intrigued by how these materialist ideas were developed by these previous authors, but he found their outlook to be mainly an apology for capitalism. To Marx, these authors ignored the actual occurrences of capitalism, which include exploitation, crises, unemployment, and poverty. Marx subjected their theories to critique and developed his own theory of capitalism. Marx thought that his own theory of capitalism demonstrates why capitalism is prone to slumps, explains why growth does not eliminate poverty, and shows why unemployment and exploitation are necessary features of capitalism. An analysis of these economic concepts Marx developed will be discussed in greater detail in the chapter on economics.

Conclusion

This introductory chapter introduced the broad outlines of Marx's influences and his reception of them. The next chapter will provide a more detailed presentation of Marx's social scientific project and the assumptions he utilizes to construct his theories. Before we turn to an examination of Marx's materialism, here are a few questions for thought:

- What does Marx take from and add to the legacy of Enlightenment values?
- How is Marx's social theory different from social contract theory?
- What do Marx's writings tell us about the limitations of capitalism regarding human liberation, and do these limitations still exist within capitalist societies?
- How did Hegel's philosophy influence Marx and how did Marx break with Hegel's philosophy?
- Why is the development of the productive forces such an important aspect of Marx's explanation of the evolution of societies?

2

Marx's Materialism

This chapter will introduce the fundamental outlook of Marx's social analysis, which is his theory of materialism. Marx's materialist theory forms the basis for his explanations of how individuals interact within society and how societies develop and provides the ground for his critique of capitalism and his advocacy of communism. Marx's materialist conception of reality was a means for him to understand human engagement with the natural and social worlds. If we understand why Marx found a materialist conception of reality fundamentally correct, this can help us understand his conception of human history, his social theory, and his critique of capitalism.

This chapter will first consider Marx's materialism analytically. This will include an overview of the materialist basis of Marx's class theory. In light of his materialist theory, the second section will be an examination of Marx's conception of how individuals and society interact. Finally, Marx's method will be discussed.

An Overview of Marx's Theory of Materialism

The overarching theoretical assumption of Marx's social analysis is that humans are material beings and their social world should be understood as material in its actuality. To say this in another way, Marx has a **materialist** conception of the world and of human thought. In general, **materialism** is a theory that considers the entire existence of people and the universe as physical matter. In particular, a materialist theory holds that humans and their interactions are intrinsically organic, physical, and temporal. This means that all human activities and all human societies can be analyzed according to humans' organic, physical, and temporal characteristics. Marx argues that if we attempt to determine human social organization along other lines (such as according to an ideal conception of social organization or according to religious ideas), this will lead us astray from the actual causal processes of social development.

Marx's theory of materialism was in response to the idealist theory of Hegel. Hegel's idealism held that humans are essentially self-conscious beings and that if we understand the self-consciousness of humans, we can understand what people are, what human history is, and what the ultimate end of human civilization is. Idealism is not a theory of how humans process impressions from the external world, nor is it a theory of how the human brain structures consciousness. Rather, idealism is a theory that holds that all the ideas one can have of oneself or of the world are intrinsic to the structure of our minds. This means, essentially, that the world as we know it is actually an idea whose origin is our mind and not the world. Thus, a political regime, social structure, or phase of human civilization is not the product of culture or technological development. Rather, these regimes, structures, or phases are the results of our mind revealing itself to itself. The act of discovery is to discover what we already know but have not yet realized.

As was briefly discussed earlier and will be discussed at great length in what follows, materialism holds that human existence is physical matter, the interaction of this physical matter, and the development of this matter by humans over time. Also, social institutions of people's lives are the result of previous social institutions, technological advances, and environmental conditions. Why certain societies develop is not because our mind is structured to produce that society. Rather, certain societies arise due to certain material factors: the kinds of social institutions present, the level of technological development, resources available, and contact with other societies. Materialism holds that social and physical factors, not the structure of our minds untouched by history, produce societal outcomes.

This section will consider the three characteristics—physical, organic, and temporal—of Marx's materialism in turn.

Theory of Materialism Characteristic 1: Physical

First, let us consider humans and their social world as essentially physical. We will deal with the organic and temporal characteristics next. If one neglects or does not attend to this irreducible aspect of humans then one considers humans in a manner that is incongruent with reality. One cannot conceptualize humans as being without physical form and having a physical existence. In addition, we cannot think of humans as existing outside of a physical world. Not only do humans require the earth to live, but it would be incredibly abstract to think of humans not occupying space or specific physical environments: for example, forests, deserts, cities, or the sea. Marx notes the primacy of humans' physical existence: "The first premise of all human history is, of course, the existence of living human individuals. Thus the first fact to be established is the physical organization of these individuals and their consequent relation to the rest of nature" (Marx & Engels, 1978, p. 149).

This determination, while seeming mundane and obvious to contemporary readers, is actually a rebuttal and critique by Marx of the modern philosophic tradition beginning with Descartes. Descartes initiated the subjective and phenomenal turn within Western philosophy. He is famous for arguing that human self-consciousness is essentially what humans are and that other qualities of humans such as their physical form are less essential:

> I can infer correctly that my essence consists solely in the fact that I am a thinking thing. It is true that I may have (or, to anticipate, that I certainly have) a body that is very closely joined to me. But nevertheless, on the one hand I have a clear and distinct idea of myself, in so far as I am simply a thinking, non-extended thing; and on the other hand I have a distinct idea of body, in so far as this is simply an extended, non-thinking thing. And accordingly, it is certain that I am really distinct from my body, and can exist without it. (Descartes, 1984, p. 54)

This consideration of the human self-consciousness as essentially what humans are was accepted and refined by the German idealists Immanuel Kant and G. W. F. Hegel. Thus, the importance that Marx attached to stressing the physical existence of humans is in response to his intellectual predecessors.

It can be noted that Marx wanted the physical existence of humans to be understood as an essential characteristic of what humans are instead of their abstracted self-consciousness (Marx & Engels, 1978, p. 113). In addition, humans as physical objects are intrinsically interrelated to all other physical objects, in the sense that they can affect and be affected by other objects. Humans cannot be meaningfully described apart from their physical existence. Marx thought that describing humans in a way that Descartes or Hegel describes them runs the risk of misdiagnosing humans' social reality and the horizon of their political actions. Marx realized that the idea of humans as physical beings subject to physical laws means that humans are laboring beings. Humans can labor and alter the physical world according to physical laws (Marx, 1990, p. 1022).

Theory of Materialism Characteristic 2: Organic

Now, considering the organic characteristics of humans, which are determined by their biological existence, this existence must be taken into account when conceiving of humans. Marx thinks that humans, as organic biological creatures, intrinsically have needs, drives, impulses, and requirements due to their biological nature:

> *Man* is directly a *natural* being . . . *Hunger* is a natural *need;* it therefore needs a *nature* outside itself, an object outside itself, in order to satisfy itself, to be stilled. Hunger is an acknowledged need of my body for an *object* existing outside it, indispensable to its integration and to the expression of its essential being. (Marx & Engels, 1978, pp. 115–116)

This is once again obvious to contemporary readers, but in Marx's day, this was a radical break with the idealist and religious traditions of the time. Both traditions considered humans to be essentially spiritual and self-conscious beings, as opposed to worldly, needful animals.

Marx also wanted to stress that organic beings have certain abilities that are intrinsic to their biological makeup. This biological focus is developed by him throughout his life. Marx notes that humans have the biological ability to attempt to meet their biological needs and to accumulate knowledge and alter the natural world. This means that as a species, humans have a specific set of abilities (Marx & Engels, 1978, pp. 155–157). Marx was concerned that attempts to understand humans without taking their biological needs and abilities into account would result in a misdiagnosis of humans' political situation and prospects.

For example, if humans alter their natural world, this changes their needs. Humans as organic beings seek to satisfy their needs. One will have an incorrect understanding of potential social futures if one doesn't realize that humans will react to their changed circumstances. If one thinks that humans have fixed abilities or needs, as Marx found many orthodox social scientists of his day did, then society is changeless. And, even more important, any call for the change of society can be met with the rebuttal that the proposed changes are against human nature (Marx & Engels, 1978, p. 172). A changeless human nature is a powerful intellectual weapon of reactionary politics. Marx notes this tendency in defenses of private property by capitalists:

> The selfish misconception that induces you to transform into eternal laws of nature and of reason, the social forms springing from your present mode of production and form of property . . . this misconception you share with every ruling class that has preceded you. What you see clearly in the case of ancient

property, what you admit in the case of feudal property, you are of course forbidden to admit in the case of your own bourgeois form of property. (Marx & Engels, 1978, p. 487)

Another aspect of humans as biological beings is that they are a social species. This means humans exist in groups as an evolved trait, as opposed to humans consciously deciding to exist in groups. Accordingly, humans cannot be accurately analyzed by the **social contract** method because it is an assumption of this method that humans choose to enter into a society. Whereas Marx finds that humans have always existed in societies, they never have chosen to form societies where none have previously existed:

Production by an isolated individual outside society—a rare exception which may well occur when a civilized person in who the social forces are already dynamically present is cast by accident into the wilderness—is as much of an absurdity as in the development of language without individuals living *together* and talking to each other. (Marx & Engels, 1978, p. 223)

When one analyzes humans, one must realize that they have always depended on each other for the satisfaction of their needs. This cooperative nature of humans is a result of the biology of *homo sapiens sapiens*. Humans require the assistance of other humans to survive at a basic level and require the assistance of other humans to acquire the current level of knowledge through learning.

Marx again has political reasons to be concerned with humans' social nature being ignored. If humans are not social animals then they have decided to come together. Thus, impoverishment or the powerlessness people who suffer from within society is not due to people being dominated or exploited by others. It is only due to their own shortcomings. Marx, in contrast, wants to argue that if humans are social animals then they can only be denied the ability to satisfy their needs if someone else prevents them. Simply put, the impoverishment or powerlessness that people suffer from within societies is due to them having been separated from the resources that they require to meet their needs. Marx calls this separation **alienation** and **primitive accumulation** (Marx & Engels, 1978, p. 70 and p. 431). Alienation will be discussed in Chapter 3 and primitive accumulation will be discussed in Chapter 6.

Theory of Materialism Characteristic 3: Temporal

The third characteristic of Marx's materialist theory is that humans change over time. As humans acquire capacities, they are able to live in new ways and understand new phenomena. In order to understand human social development, one must take humans' temporal existence into account. An important aspect of this temporal nature is that Marx also thinks that humans have no ideal form or special natural existence. Humans are always natural; they can never be unnatural. This means that humans are not supposed to be a certain way that they once were or will eventually become (Marx & Engels, 1978, p. 148). Marx finds Feuerbach's philosophy to be indicative of this position (Marx & Engels, 1978, pp. 169–170).

In contrast to this idea, Marx finds that humans have certain needs, some of which change over time when human desires need to be fulfilled (Marx & Engels, 1978, pp. 156, 169–170). This means that Marx's materialism has a temporal element because humans alter themselves and the natural world over time (Marx & Engels, 1978, p. 476). Thus, materialism is not the same as naturalism. Naturalism is an analysis of human beings that essentially reduces them to their biological capacities and requirements. Some versions of naturalism select a certain period in humans' social development or hypothesize an idealized time and argue that humans are essentially the characteristics of this actual or idealized time, whereas materialism is an analysis of human beings as biological beings that have the ability to alter the natural world and alter their capacities. Thus, in order to provide a materialist explanation of humans, one must identify a specific historical epoch that will be explained. For example, the types of mathematical analysis that humans could perform during the 5th, 17th, and 20th centuries are distinctly different. Another example, the possibility for individuals to own private property, is distinctly different for people in Prussia and England during the late 18th century (Marx & Engels, 1978, p. 157).

Marx's temporal consideration of human beings moves beyond a critique of an idealized natural existence of humans. Rather, the capacities of humans to manipulate the natural world, learn about it, transmit these manipulations, and use them as knowledge form the ground for social development. Human history is thus the history of humans' accumulated capacities (Marx & Engels, 1978, pp. 4, 116–117). This ability of humans to learn and alter their world is a natural capacity. Humans utilize their capacities to satisfy their needs. This satisfaction of needs through learning and altering the world creates a feedback loop in which the first needs are satisfied by the creation of new needs: "the satisfaction of the first need (the action of satisfying, and the instrument of satisfaction which has been acquired) leads to new needs; and this creation of new needs is the first historical act" (Marx & Engels, 1978, p. 156).

Additionally, it can be seen that the feedback process of societal development discussed in Chapter 1 is one version of the causal process of humans' material existence. Simply put, we can understand that the three character-istics of Marx's materialism—physical, organic, and temporal—are also involved in a feedback process. This feedback process occurs because humans are a kind of animal that changes itself, the natural environment, and societies over time.

The Materialist Basis of Class

Class is a fundamental category of Marx's social analysis. A full discussion of class will be provided in Chapter 4. Here we will give an overview of the materialist basis of Marx's theory of class.

The class of a person is determined by that person's ownership of various amounts of the **productive forces**. The productive forces are composed of labor power and the means of production. The basic relationships of capitalism are demonstrated in Table 2.1.

In order to understand how the classes in Table 2.1 are determined according to material relationships, it must be stressed that the **forces of production** (labor power and the means of production) are material. This means that what determines a person's class is whether they own labor power or a sufficient amount of the means of production. A person's labor

Table 2.1   Basic Classes of Capitalism

Class	Owns their own labor power?	Owns a sufficient amount of the means of production to provide subsistence through laboring?	Owns a sufficient amount of the means of production in order not to labor?
Worker—Proletarian	Yes	No	No
Independent Producer—Petite Bourgeoisie	Yes	Yes	No
Capitalist—Bourgeoisie	Yes	Yes	Yes

Source: Adapted from Cohen, G.A. *Karl Marx's Theory of History.* C1978, 2000. Princeton University Press, 2001 expanded ed. with new intro and chapters reprinted by Princeton University Press, p. 65, Table 1.

power is their physical and organic capacity to alter the natural world. The means of production are physical accumulations of resources produced by labor or natural raw material. An example of the former are machines and of the latter, coal or water.

As we can see, classes are determined by whether people own certain productive forces and what amount of these productive forces these people own. In capitalism, people own their own labor power and not another person's labor power. If you own another person's labor power then that person is a slave or a serf. These noncapitalist classes won't be dealt with here but will be considered in Chapter 4.

Within capitalism, people can own different amounts of the means of production. The meaningful amounts that they can own are less than a sufficient amount to provide subsistence, a sufficient amount for subsistence, or a sufficient amount not to labor. Subsistence means the amount of consumption required to live at the socially determined minimum. This socially determined minimum is different for different societies and for the same society at different times (Becker & Rayo, 2010, pp. 179–184; Freeman, 2010, pp. 135–142; Marx, 1968, p. 222). It is the amount of food, clothes, shelter, transportation, information access, education, and leisure activities that are considered basic in a given society at a given time.

My own society, the United States of the early 21st century, considers many subsistence items now to be basic that at one time were considered luxuries. Take for example powered transport, telephones, televisions, and computers. All of these items were once items that only a few people consumed. Now they are considered essential for people's lives. It is also important to note that the discussion here will talk of a person's subsistence, but all comments can apply to households with dependents. Therefore, in the discussion to follow, we will simply talk of individuals, but households are implied as well.

To own a sufficient amount of the means of production to provide for one's subsistence means that you can utilize the means of production that you own to provide goods and services for sale. The proceeds from these sales you can use to purchase items to live off at the socially acceptable minimum.

For example, let's say a person owns a set of tools they use to fix cars. If this person can sell enough car repair services and then buy the socially acceptable minimum subsistence, they own a sufficient amount of the means of production to provide for their subsistence.

Now consider another person who owns a set of tools for fixing cars but cannot sell enough car repair services to buy the socially acceptable minimum subsistence. They do not own a sufficient amount of the means of production to provide for their subsistence.

Finally, consider a third person who rents their tools out or hires people to use their tools to buy the socially acceptable minimum subsistence. They do own a sufficient amount of the means of production to provide for their subsistence without laboring.

It is important to point out that people own numerous items that could allow them to provide for their own subsistence through the sale of goods and services they create. People who own stoves, washing machines, or computers could sell baked goods, washed clothes, or computing services to others. Thus, ordinary consumption goods can and do become means of production. It is important to realize that it is not relevant for Marxian class analysis that you can sell pies baked in your kitchen. It is relevant if you can sell enough pies to provide for your own subsistence. Thus, it is relevant for Marxian class analysis that a person could quit their job and make enough money to provide for their subsistence utilizing the means of production they own.

Now on to the class designations, as demonstrated in Table 2.1. We can see that all the classes of capitalism can sell their labor power if they wish; they are free to do so. This is why Marx sometimes calls workers within capitalism free laborers. This is in contradistinction to serfs, who were not free to sell their labor to anyone they wished. The feudal lord had a claim on a portion of their labor and serfs were obligated to provide this labor when the lord wished.

If a person can sell their labor power but does not own enough of the means of production to provide for their own subsistence then this person is in the **working class**. They would be called a **worker**. Members of this class are also called **proletarians** in classical Marxian terminology. These persons must sell their labor power in order to have sufficient subsistence.

If a person can sell their labor power and does own enough means of production to provide for their own subsistence then this person is in the **independent producer class**. They would be called an **independent producer**. Members of this class are also called **petite bourgeoisie** in classical Marxian terminology. They do not have to sell their labor power to obtain subsistence, but they must labor using the means of production they do own to obtain subsistence.

If a person owns their own labor and does own enough means of production to provide for their own subsistence through hiring people to use it or renting it out then this person is in the **capitalist class**. They are called **capitalists** also called **bourgeoisie**, again in classical Marxian terminology. They neither have to sell their labor power to obtain subsistence nor have to labor with the means of production they own.

As we can see, the basic class distinctions of capitalism are all determined in relation to what amount of the means of production a person has access to.

This is why Marxian class distinction is considered materialist (Wright, 1986, pp. 106–108). In addition, Marxian classes do not require people to be aware of their classes to have their class position affect their lives. A person does not have to identify as working class to be in the situation to have to sell his labor power. Nor does a person have to identify as a capitalist in order to enjoy the option of not having to labor (Cohen, 2000, pp. 73–77).

Finally, Marxian class analysis is an attempt to understand the antagonistic nature of all class societies. Indeed, Marxian class analysis would conclude that class societies are fundamentally antagonistic, because class is determined according to exploitation. **Exploitation** means that one person gains at the expense of another. If the exploitative situation were changed, the exploiter would lose out while the exploited would gain (Wright, 1985, p. 65 and p. 72). As we shall see in Chapter 6, Marx attempts to demonstrate that capitalism is based on the exploitation of workers. This exploitation has a materialist basis. Workers are exploited because they do not own enough means of production to labor with to provide for themselves and their dependents. If they could, they could escape being exploited by capitalists.

Review of Marx's Materialist Theory

In review, Marx's materialism can be described as being focused on the physical, organic, and temporal characteristics of humans and their societies. These characteristics are used by Marx to call into question the notion that capitalism is a social arrangement that is a timeless natural state of affairs for humans. If capitalism is neither natural nor timeless then it can change and it can be replaced with other kinds of social arrangements. In addition, Marx's categories of social analysis are shaped by his materialist perspective. Class is defined by Marx according to how much of the means of production are owned by people and not people's perception of their own class position.

Individuals and Society

The interrelation of individuals and society has been discussed in many contexts but not directly. This section will outline Marx's understanding of how individuals and society are interrelated.

Humans, Societies, and Information

Marx stressed on many occasions that humans are social animals and naturally exist within social groups. This is not a radical idea for anthropologists and most sociologists. As we have already pointed out with the social contract doctrine discussed in Chapter 1, dominant schools of contemporary economics and some political scientists assume that society is a combination of individuals who have chosen to coexist. When evaluating behavior and preference selection, the social contract doctrine hypothesizes that individuals are the basic unit that must be examined. In the social contract view, people in groups do not demonstrate behavior or preference selection that are different or changed by being part of a group. In addition, there do not exist macrogroup phenomena that are different in their effects from the choices of the individual members. As will be discussed further in the next section, contemporary economics and political science often find all macrophenomena can be reduced to microbehaviors and micropreference selections. This conception of human action has been described as *Homo economicus*. Heap and colleagues (1992) provide a cogent explanation:

> In theories that use the model of *Homo economicus* extensively, most obviously neoclassical economic and rational choice accounts of politics, the emphasis is upon the way in which individual agents work out the consequences of their preferences over alternative outcomes in a context in which other individuals have different and conflicting preferences over those outcomes. The elaborated theories of markets and collective choice take individual preferences as given, and consider how preferences are aggregated within specified institutional arrangements. (pp. 62–63)

In contradistinction to this notion, Marx thinks that the behavior of individuals is determined by their natural needs and their social situation. Their preferences are shaped and dependent on other people's choices. They make selections based on current information, and their preferences are subject to change and altered as other people's preferences are satisfied and new information arises. Individuals' preferences are products of these societies and, in turn, their own preference selection alters how others' and future generations' preferences will be formed. Marx famously commented on this process as:

> Men make their own history, but they do not make it as they please; they do not make it under circumstances chosen by themselves, but under circumstances directly found, given and transmitted from the past. The tradition of all the dead generations weighs like a nightmare on the brain of the living. (Marx & Engels, 1978, p. 595)

Humans build the world together as societies and enable their individual members to become more than what they started as due to their collective efforts. The development of human civilization is not simply cooperation in which all members benefit equally. Marx finds that human social organization can reproduce its norms and roles even in circumstances in which the outcomes for many of its individual members are not as advantageous as they could be. Since humans always exist in societies, we should not take nonadvantageous outcomes as always being the result of social breakdown. This idea that outcomes have to be advantageous for all members in order for a social order to be stable is an assumption indicative of the classical social contract theory. Marx thinks that societies change when a sufficient mass of their members' needs go unmet. These social changes punctuate stable periods that can be extremely long (on the scale of human social evolution).

The upshot of this is that the continuance of a society is not dependent on the satisfaction of individual preferences to the maximum degree possible. Rather, societies can exist at a level where many people's preferences are satisfied at less than a maximum degree and a few can have satisfaction levels that exceed the optimal level of satisfaction for a society. This means that societies can exist for long periods and appear stable even though exploitation and detriment to well-being is inherent in the social system.

Why exploitative societies are possible must be explained by Marx, since the social contract explanation appears false to him. An important difference between the social contract view and Marx's view of society is how they treat information. The social contract view usually assumes that the individual members of a society all have perfect information. All members know the gains and losses for all possible future states of affairs. Individuals do not have to guess other people's actions. They know how people will react in all situations. Thus, exploitation is impossible since the exploitative scenarios would be known by all and could be avoided.

The Marxian social view sees information as limited and incomplete. There are some circumstances in which people can have a better grasp of possibilities than in others. In most circumstances, people are obstructed by limited knowledge due to their inhibited access to others, inhibited access to communication, and inhibited access to education. This situation is sometimes called false consciousness by social scientists. It is possible for people to learn from one another and begin to gather information to gain an approximation of their situation (Marx & Engels, 1978, pp. 480–481, 608).

Marx finds that people do not live within conditions in which they always have perfect information. Nor does he seem to think that perfect information is possible, since people require science to explain their social world. Its underlying dynamics and regularities are not readily apparent (Marx, 1991, p. 956). Marx thinks that more or less information is possible. Two of the main causes for an increase in information are communication between people and the increased capacities of the means of production. In short, people's preferences are formed and reformed by social development, in particular technological development. They are not given or unalterable.

Microfoundations and Macrophenomena

Social scientists have been interested in not only describing the conditions of social change but also trying to understand and explain how these social changes come about. These explanations are usually twofold: micro and macro. Macroexplanations attempt to explain social changes by the fluctuations of aggregates: the presence or absence of saving, the size of certain groups, climatic changes, or the change in political orders, to name a few. Macroexplanations thus attempt to correlate aggregates with aggregates, for example, hypothesizing the cause of a saving decline due to stagnating wages.

Microexplanations attempt to explain changes in aggregates through the actions of individuals such as preference orderings, norms, or psychological behaviors, to name a few. Thus, microexplanations attempt to demonstrate that macroaggregates are the result of individual actions. It is true in that social aggregates are composed of the actions of individuals. When a person doesn't save money, it is factored into the aggregate savings rate. It is possible for different individual behaviors to result in the same macrophenomena.

For example, lowered savings may be the result of changing preferences (consumption over saving), or it could be that people's living costs leave no remainder for savings. These are two different microexplanations that result in the same macrophenomenon. Different microexplanations will yield different policy choices. For example, if saving is low because it now represents people's preferences then a policy to increase saving must consider how to change preferences toward greater saving. Alternatively, if saving is low because people's wages are too low to save, then higher wages are required to bring about a policy goal of greater saving.

Marx explained macrophenomena through correlation with other macrophenomena: epochal social change from one mode of production to another is due to the arising of new classes that supplant the old classes. Additionally, macrophenomena can be identified as the various interests of these different classes, such as the interests of capitalists in having private property law enforced. Marx does not stop at the macro level. He identifies the microbehaviors of new classes in respect to the old classes. In addition, he discusses the behaviors of different actors in respect to various determinations of behavior such as nationality, history, religion, and their class interests (Marx, 1990, pp. 739–742; Marx & Engels, 1978, pp. 612–613).

Marx does not wish to reduce all explanation to microphenomena indicative of the *homo economicus* conception. Individuals do make history but not as they please. The formation of individual preferences is subject to macroevents. In deriving an explanation of why an event has occurred, one can ultimately identify the preference sets of the responsible actors. These preference sets in turn have been created by preceding macrophenomena. Marx's analysis of why the French peasantry supported and elected Louis Napoleon in 1848 (which resulted in his *coup d'état* and establishment of himself as emperor) was based on the preferences of the French peasantry for a strong leader. This preference was formed when Napoleon Bonaparte (the uncle of the latter-day Louis Napoleon) legally consolidated French peasants' rights to use their land won during the French Revolution of the 1790s. In addition, the welfare of the peasants had been in decline since the French Revolution due to competition with capitalist landowners. Explaining the success of the eventual *coup d'état* of Louis Napoleon by a microexplanation of French peasants' preferences does not explain how those preferences were formed by the French Revolution and the dynamics of capitalist competition, both of which are macrophenomena (Marx & Engels, 1978, p. 608). Engels approximates the matter as such in a letter:

> According to the materialist conception of history, the *ultimately* determining element in history is the production and reproduction of real life. More than this, neither Marx nor I have ever asserted. Hence, if somebody twists this into saying that the economic element is the *only* determining one, he transforms that proposition into a meaningless, abstract, senseless phrase. The economic situation is the basis, but the various elements of the superstructure: political forms of the class struggle and its results, to wit: constitutions established by the victorious class after a successful battle, etc., juridical forms, and then even the reflexes of all these actual struggles in the brains of the participants, political, juristic, philosophical theories, religious views and their further development into systems of dogmas, also exercise their influence upon the course of historical struggles and in many cases preponderate in determining their *form*. There is an interaction of all these elements in which, amid all the endless host of accidents (that is, of things and events, whose inner connection is so remote or so impossible of proof that we can regard it as non-existent, as negligible) the economic movement finally asserts itself as necessary. Otherwise the application of the theory to any period of history one chose would be easier than the solution of a simple equation of the first degree. (Marx & Engels, 1978, pp. 760–761)

Can one conclude that Marx and Engels considered there not to be a simple set of microphenomena that can be utilized as the building blocks to any explanation? Yes, but with an important caveat. Marx lists human impulse or drive and the requirements of life as micropsychological behaviors

(Marx & Engels, 1978, pp. 115, 155–157). These microbehaviors are subject to historical reformation. Marx's theory of materialism has three characteristics: physical, organic, *and* temporal. The use of humans' physical and organic capacities over time allows for the alteration and expansion of the people's needs. Providing explanations for events based on the original material microbehaviors of humans is only sufficient for explaining the ultimate causal factors for the possibility of human social development. As we have already noted, Marx is very critical of people pointing at the microbehaviors of a current period and declaring these to be the natural and unalterable behaviors of humans. Human behaviors, other than the general drive to fulfill their needs, change over time.

Class Relations

Class is the major relationship Marx utilizes to understand the relationship between individuals and society. The material basis of class has been discussed previously, but now we can focus on how class relationships structure societies and how individuals are formed by class actions and interests and how people form themselves into classes.

As has already been noted, Marxian class relationships are determined by people's control over amounts of the productive forces. Ownership of different amounts of the productive forces establishes a structural determination of people's interest. People who own similar amounts of the productive forces are grouped into classes. People who own meaningfully different amounts of the productive forces are grouped into exploiters, exploited, or neither exploiter nor exploited.

Within capitalism, people own their own labor power. Thus, only different amounts of the means of production can be owned. Those who do not own enough of the means of production to employ themselves are workers. They must work for another to provide subsistence for themselves and their dependents. Those who own enough of the means of production to employ themselves are independent producers. Those who own enough of the means of production to employ others are capitalists.

Classes form dependent relationships because of exploitation. Within capitalism, capitalists are dependent on exploiting workers to maintain their class position as capitalists. Workers are dependent on being allowed to work for capitalists and are thereby exploited. If capitalists did not exploit workers, they would not receive surplus value. If capitalists do not receive surplus value from exploitation, they cannot reproduce themselves as capitalists. Exploitation occurs when workers are not paid the full value of their expended labor power. If they were paid their full value then the surplus value created by workers would be kept by the workers. If this occurred, capitalists would not receive any income through the employment of workers. In order for capitalists to be capitalists and to stay capitalists, they must exploit workers. If capitalists cannot and/or did not exploit workers, they would have to labor to provide for their subsistence. The details of exploitation and surplus-value extraction are described in Chapter 6 on Marx's economics.

Class societies reproduce themselves through exploitation. This means that for capitalism to exist, individual capitalists must continually exploit individual workers. If exploitation did not occur, this would result in a new form of society. If all people owned amounts of the means of production as private property and everyone worked for themselves, no exploitation would occur. This would be an independent producer society.

If society had no classes, this would be communism according to Marx. There would be no exploitation because all individuals in that society would own the means of production as public property. The difference between communism and an independent producer society is that within communism, no one can lose public ownership of the means of production. All individuals own the means of production as public property as long as their society stays communist, whereas in an independent producer society, people could conceivably lose portions or all of the property they own. If this were the case, they would become workers and would have to sell their labor power. Exploitation would then occur. By contrast, in communism, exploitation is not possible since people cannot lose ownership of public property.

The individual lives of people will be formed by the types of class relationships that exist in their society. Being in a class structures the material possibilities of a person's life. Within capitalism, a person's life is determined by the amount of the means of production they have control over. This includes the amount of public control that they have. For example, if we take two people in two different class positions in the same society, we can analyze how their lives will be affected by the amounts of the means of production they have control over. We will have a worker and an independent producer in this example, and the topic will be education. It will be taken for granted that people must pay for education in this example, that education is not publicly financed or publicly provided without a fee. The ease with which independent producers can receive education for themselves or their dependents is different from the ease with which workers achieve the same end. This is the case because the worker owns less of the means of production than the independent producer does. It will be easier for the independent producer to finance an education via a loan taken out on the means of production they own. Individuals' lives are shaped by class relationships because class determines a person's material possibilities. The social institution of class shapes the life prospects of individuals.

Class Interests and Class Consciousness

As we have seen, class relationships form the material possibilities of individuals' lives. Marx is very interested in how people become aware of the material possibility to live a different kind of life. This is called **class consciousness**. In particular, people become class conscious when they realize what their interests are as a class. This means that what people think their interests are may not actually be best for them. This is the case because they do not correctly understand how the achievement of those interests will affect their future material possibilities.

For example, Marx definitely thinks it is in the workers' best interest to achieve a communist society. He believes that workers will have more material possibilities within communism than within capitalism. Workers may not be aware of the possibility of communism and its forecasted potential benefits. Rather, workers may be strong advocates of policies that benefit capitalists. Perhaps they are advocates of these policies because they wish to become capitalists or they believe that what is beneficial for capitalists is beneficial for workers. If this is the case, workers have not achieved class consciousness because they do not have a proper understanding of their interests. Their procapitalist position will lessen their future material possibilities. Marx thinks this is true because procapitalist policies will increase exploitation, thereby lessening workers' incomes and limiting their access to nonwage benefits.

Various studies have demonstrated that class position does affect a person's perception of his or her class interests. People who are working class favor proworker policies and capitalists dislike proworker policies (Wright, 1985, 1986). This has also been demonstrated in surveys that utilize non–Marxist class distinctions (Gilens, 1999, pp. 52–53). This is of particular interest to social scientists because it appears that **class position** can determine people's interests and their political intentions.

Class Antagonisms

Class interests can be antagonistic. This is especially the case in Marxian class theory since class is determined according to exploitation and control over the means of production. Exploitation is the exploiter gaining at the expense of the exploited. This does not mean that a society cannot become wealthier overall. Marx notes that this can be the case (Marx & Engels, 1968, p. 222). A wealthy class society is still a class society. The interests of each of its members are, according to their class position, at odds with those of other classes.

In addition to interclass antagonisms, there are also intraclass antagonisms, which is conflict between the members of the same class (Marx & Engels, 1978, p. 481). For example, capitalists are in competition with other capitalists for a market share of their particular products. Competition motivates capitalists to take risks in order to try to outcompete other capitalists. If they are successful, they face less competition. They then have to take less risky actions to maintain their position as capitalists. Additionally, capitalists may be in antagonistic relationships with capitalists from other branches of industry and commerce. Capitalists in manufacturing may want lower food prices so they can pay lower wages whereas agriculture capitalists want higher food prices so they can have higher revenues. These conflicts can occur between various industries: energy producers versus manufactures or finance versus heavy electrical industries.

In addition, capitalists can be antagonistic with capitalists from other countries for a market share and access to raw materials. Alternatively, capitalists who own multinational companies can be in conflict with national capitalists, with the former seeking lower tariffs and the latter seeking higher tariffs or other trade protections. Competition between capitalists can result in workers being forced to accept lower wages to facilitate competition or being subject to unemployment as their employers' businesses fail.

Workers are often in competition with one another for jobs since there is usually less than full unemployment. This intraworker competition can occur within a country or between the workers of different countries. Competition between workers is usually beneficial to capitalists since it fractures the working class. Capitalists utilize workers from discriminated-against groups such as people suffering from racial bias, women, or immigrants in order to put downward pressure on wages and increase the ranks of available workers. This makes unemployment a greater threat to all workers. Workers may focus on the race, ethnicity, nationality, or gender of these workers rather than on the benefits these divisions in the working class provides for capitalists (Baran & Sweezy, 1966, p. 263; Gomberg, 2007).

Societies can thus be shaped and their politics driven by intra- and interclass conflicts. The interests an individual has are influenced by their class position. This can bring about conflict within a society and between societies.

Class Alliances

Classes can form alliances with one another. This can even be the case for classes that are exploiter and exploited (Neuman, 2009, pp. 184–218). It is more common for classes to form alliances with other classes that are not the main source of exploitation or to form alliances only with a segment of a class. Class alliances could be formed between certain parts of the working class or between independent producers and capitalists. For example, professionals may form an alliance with capitalists to receive privileged treatment in the form of higher wages or protected employment. This privileged treatment could help mediate their affinity for other people who work for wages. Alternatively, independent producers may form an alliance with capitalists since they identify as capitalists. Additionally, workers and capitalists in developing countries may form alliances in order to obtain national sovereignty (Mandel, 1994, pp. 130–142).

Marx's Methodology

In the preface to the first edition of *Capital* (published in 1867), Marx states that "the ultimate aim of this work, [is] to lay bare the economic law of motion of modern society" (Marx & Engels, 1978, p. 297). This aim can be understood as the general aim of most of Marx's work, from at least 1844 if not earlier. We can understand that Marx tried to discover the laws of motion for societies, which are the laws of societal development. Marx attempts to discover these laws of development through the utilization of abstraction and dialectics. To be specific, Marx arrives at abstracted categories through the use of dialectics. First, we will consider why abstraction is used by Marx. Second, we will examine his comments on dialectics. Third, we shall see which abstract categories are decided on by the use of dialectics. In addition, we will discuss Marx's materialism in light of his method.

Abstraction

Marx finds that abstraction must be utilized in social science:

to the successful analysis of much more composite and complex forms, there has been at least an approximation. Why? Because the body, as an organic whole, is more easy of study than are the cells of that body. In the analysis of economic forms, moreover, neither microscopes nor chemical reagents are of use. The force of abstraction must replace both. (Marx & Engels, 1978, p. 295)

Marx realizes that society cannot be analyzed as a body can, where we can identify and account for all of its parts. Society cannot be dissected after death or observed in a habitat. Rather, theories must be formulated that designate concepts that provide an abstract model of social reality. It is only through the utilization of an abstract model that social science can provide an approximation of its object of study.

Today, social science has developed statistical and other mathematical models to approximate the social world. Marx utilized the available statistical data of his own day, which is nowhere near as detailed as the data available to the current social scientist. Additionally, he lived in a time before the development of many of the statistical methods used today. These current methods take mathematical constructs as models of the actual world. Social scientists thus utilize formal models to understand empirical reality. Marx thought that an excellent place to begin would be to analyze the most advanced capitalist country of the day, which was England. England could be used as a stand-in for a formal model of capitalism. Marx could thus understand the processes of capitalist development by observing the most developed specimen:

> The physicist either observes physical phenomena where they occur in their most typical form and most free from disturbing influence, or, wherever possible, he makes experiments under conditions that assure the occurrence of the phenomenon in its normality. In this work [Capital] I have to examine the capitalist mode of production, and the conditions of production and exchange corresponding to that mode. Up to the present time, their classic ground is England. That is the reason why England is used as the chief illustration in the development of my theoretical ideas. (Marx & Engels, 1978, p. 295)

Capitalism in Marx's day was becoming the common social system of the entire world. But the varieties of capitalism that existed were almost endless. Capitalism existed in democracies, monarchies, frontier societies, ancient nations, and colonial outposts. All of these kinds of capitalism were different, but they were all linked by the accumulation forces of capital. How to discuss capitalism in general, or where to begin, with such a wealth of data? Marx chose to abstract from the myriad forms of capitalism and examine what he found to be the most developed capitalist economy, which was England. Abstraction from reality allows theories to be constructed and social forces systematized. It is the essential work of all social science.

Dialectics

Marx selects what he finds to be the best object for his analysis and gives the reasons for it. How does Marx arrive at abstract categories to develop an explanation of this best object of analysis? This is where dialectics comes into play. Dialectics is an ancient form of analysis and presentation. It has been used by many authors in various ways. Some considered dialectics to be a discussion of a topic to arrive at truth (Plato, 1968, p. 211). Others considered it to be a method for the reconstruction of the development of ideas (Hegel, 1977, p. 51; 1991, p. 60). What is common to all understandings of dialectics is that it is an attempt to understand the objects being studied either through a developmental process of inquiry and/or through the abstract presentation of the object in its analytical components. Marx utilizes dialectics as a means of inquiry and a means of presentation.

Many of Marx's works use dialectics as a means of presenting an object of analysis. This is how Marx decides on which abstract categories will be utilized in his arguments. In the *Grundrisse*, Marx gives an overview of the dialectical process of concept determination:

> It seems to be correct to begin with the real and the concrete, with the real precondition, thus to begin, in economics, with e.g. the population, which is the foundation and the subject of the entire social act of production. However, on close examination this proves false. The population is an abstraction if I leave out, for example, the classes of which it is composed. These classes in turn are an empty phrase if I am not familiar with the elements on which they rest. E.g., wage labor, capital, etc. These latter in turn presuppose exchange, division of labor, prices, etc. For example, capital is nothing without wage labor, without value, money, price, etc. Thus, if I were to begin with the population, this would be a chaotic conception of the whole, and I would then by means of further determination, move analytically toward ever more simple concepts, from the imagined concrete towards ever thinner abstraction until I had arrived at the simplest determinations. From there the journey would have to be retraced until I had finally arrived at the population again, but this time not as the chaotic conception of a whole, but as a rich totality of many determinations and relations. (Marx & Engels, 1978, p. 237)

This quotation demonstrates Marx's method of inquiry. First, the method is a process of abstracting from the whole and analyzing its simplest determinations. Second, it is a process of examining these parts and then reconstructing them into their original relationships. Finally, the object of inquiry can now be explained according to its causal relationships.

We have already discussed the most basic elements of Marx's method of social analysis: the material characteristics of human social reality. Marx arrived at these elements by observing a whole phenomenon such as production and analyzing this phenomenon into its simple determinations.

After this was done, Marx could reconstruct a given phenomenon and explain its operation and his expectations for further development. In the following chapters, we will consider various abstract categories Marx utilized.

Marx would begin with an object of inquiry, such as the commodity or the worker. He would then go on to list a series of simple determinations of that object. Marx does not present the dialectic of inquiry in his works. He presents the reconstruction of simple determinations and explains how these determinations produce a social whole. For example, in the next chapter on alienation, we will consider the "Estranged Labour" essay by Marx. He begins with a presentation of the economic world, discussing competition, property, labor, capital, and other appearances. He then focuses in on the condition of the worker in which "the worker becomes all the poorer the more wealth he produces, the more his production increases in power and range" (Marx & Engels, 1978, p. 71). Marx takes his object of inquiry to be the impoverishment of the worker while at the same time societal wealth increases. He then develops a set of simple determinations that he thinks provide the causal factors for the occurrence of poverty while the general wealth of society increases. In brief, Marx notes the separation of workers from control of the means of production causes certain objects and people to become antagonistic to the worker. The result of these antagonisms is that the workers' own labor enriches others but does not enrich the workers themselves. Marx concludes that the worker is in a condition of alienation.

Another example is Marx's analysis of class. Confronted with the market relations of individuals within capitalism, it appears as if all people are on equal footing. Each person can buy and sell as their purse and their preferences allow. But Marx wonders why this supposed equality of the marketplace results in inequalities of wealth and the detriments of unemployment, poverty, and squalor. Why do class distinctions emerge from a supposedly equality-preserving activity? First, Marx considers people from a different perspective than their market exchanges. He looks to see from where their income is derived, which for most people is the selling of their labor. When Marx looks at the selling of labor, he finds that the value at which people sell their labor is less than the value they create in production. Also, Marx finds that the surplus value that does not go to workers is absorbed by capitalists. He realizes that this exploited labor value is the basis not only for inequality of wealth and the detriments of poverty, unemployment, and squalor, it is also the lifeblood of capitalism. Marx discovers that without exploited labor value, capitalists have no incomes; if they have no incomes then they can't invest; and if they can't invest then the whole system of social reproduction can't function. Marx discovers that the simple determinant of exploitation is the keystone to the overall functioning of capitalism. His dialectal abstraction breaks down the different class outcomes of capitalism into simple parts, and then he reconstructs the system with exploited labor value as the casual mechanism of class interconnection and social reproduction.

Method and Materialism

Now that we have looked at Marx's method, we can consider two classic statements of Marx's materialism in light of it. First is a passage from *The German Ideology*:

> We must begin by stating the first premise of all human existence and therefore, of all history, the premise, namely, that men must be in a position to live in order to be able to "make history." But life involves before everything else eating and drinking, a habitation, clothing and many other things. The first historical act is thus the production of the means to satisfy these needs, the production of material life itself. And indeed this is an historical act, a fundamental condition of all history, which today, as thousands of years ago, must daily and hourly be fulfilled merely in order to sustain human life. (Marx & Engels, 1978, p. 156)

Human activity is essentially material activity, the fabrication of the natural world into items that maintain people's organic requirements. What is of importance here is that Marx begins not with the fundamental material aspects of human existence. That is the simplest determination. Rather, what is important is that Marx begins with the object of inquiry, which is history. Marx is interested in human history, but how does one begin to discuss such an object? There are numerous types of histories: social, natural, military, class, biography, and so on. In addition, there are numerous topics: immigration, national, international, ancient, regional, women, segregation, and the like. At the ground of it, people must be able to make history for it to be history for us. Thus, people must be alive in order to act in their world and create social reality. This leads Marx to the simple determination that humans as material beings and their material needs are at the basis of action and, accordingly, the ground of what becomes history. As we saw in this chapter and will see again throughout this book, Marx analyzes objects of inquiry into their simplest determinations. These simplest determinations will be the material parts and activities that form theories that are attempts at explaining the totality of human social reality.

Next we will consider part of the classic historical materialist statement from the preface of the *Introduction to the Critique of Political Economy*:

> The general result at which I arrived and which, once won, served as a guiding thread for my studies, can be briefly formulated as follows: In the social production of their life, men enter into definite relations that are indispensable and independent of their will, relations of production which correspond to a definite stage of development of their material productive forces. The sum total of these relations of production constitutes the economic structure of society, the real foundation, on which rises a legal and political superstructure and to which correspond definite forms of social consciousness. (Marx & Engels, 1978, p. 4)

In this passage, we see the material productive forces as a definitive causal force. This is a simple determination that is a result of Marx's inquiry. The starting point of his inquiry, the whole object under examination, is the social production of life. Now this object corresponds to countless social phenomena: family, work, state, community, nation, civil society, recreation, and the list could go on. Here Marx abstracts the totality of social life into **relations of production** and the material **productive forces**. Relations of production are classes and the productive forces are the means of production and labor power. These two simple determinations are in a causal relationship in which the productive forces determine the relations of production. Additionally, these relations of production can be considered the economic structure of society, another simple determination. Finally, the economic structure provides the foundation for legal and political notions, also simple determinations. What Marx has done here has been to analyze social life into the simple determinations of productive forces, production relations, economic structure, and legal and political notions. Now these objects are not only identified and analyzed, they are also constructed as a "totality of determinations and relations" and are no longer a "chaotic conception of a whole." Marx has hypothesized that the whole of social life can be abstracted into the simple determinations listed along with their determinate causal processes. Marx conjectures that political relationships are determined by the current economic structure, which is finally the product of material productive forces at a certain level of development.

When reading passages written by Marx, it is important to remember that he is always searching for underlying sources of social activity. The surface appearances of law, politics, or stated desires are always, in his thinking, determined by material objective factors that people have inherited. Marx wanted to find and explain how these inherited conditions have produced the current social world. Also, he wanted to understand which dynamics can be harnessed by current social actors to produce a social world more in alignment with their need for self-development. Marx's method of abstracting the social totality into simple determinations and reconstructing these simple determinations in a relationship that explains the social totality is Marx seeking the material objective factors that structure social phenomena.

Conclusion

This chapter has covered a wide range of topics, but the unifying theme of all of them is Marx's materialist theory. Marx's materialist outlook is the result of his inheritance of Enlightenment values and theories. Marx's social scientific project is structured around his materialist critique of social contact theory and **German Idealism**. Marx's materialism conceives of humans as physical, organic, and temporal beings. This materialist outlook sets Marx's social theory decisively at odds with the theories of his intellectual predecessors.

Marx's new materialist outlook allows him to analyze the antagonisms and the longevity of exploitative social systems without utilizing the simple considerations of ignorance, personal failure, and automatic justification that he found indicative of orthodox social science. Humans do not have perfect knowledge of their social situation. They also have not chosen the rules of the society they are born into. People are inculcated by their societies and accept the values of their societies not only because they have little choice in doing so but also because their framework of knowledge is structured by the organization of the society they belong to. The longevity of exploitative relationships is understandable if humans accept and emulate their social organization.

Humans' capacity to learn and explore the natural and social world allows people to ask, "Why is our society structured in this way?" "Are the gains and losses for certain people in our society natural and inevitable?" There appears to be a threshold at which humans will begin to question and rebel against the rules and justifications that they have learned, accepted, and perhaps even defended (Marx & Engels, 1978, pp. 4–5). Humans are not simply learning machines in Marx's conception. Rather, Marx understands that humans will seek to understand their world and can reach the conclusion, as they have in the past, that there are better ways of organizing our social interactions and the distribution of gains and losses. The impetus for Marx's investigation into the possibility of social failure and the possibility for new social organizations is the conjectured propensity for people to seek satisfaction of their needs and expand their abilities.

Before considering Marx's examination of how capitalism limits people's ability to improve their lives, here are a few questions for further reflection on this chapter's content:

- What are the advantages and disadvantages of using a materialist focus for social analysis?
- Does materialism still offer any insights for current social analysis?
- Can Marx's focus on development and change be seen as a genuine contribution to social science?
- Does Marx's understanding of individuals and society provide a useful basis for conducting social scientific research? Would it be more useful to attempt to explain all macrophenomena by the use of only microbehaviors and preferences?
- Does Marx's method actually allow him to grasp the reality of the social condition he analyzes?

3

Alienation

N ow that we have introduced the general themes of this book and
Marx's theory of materialism, we can begin to consider the individual
categories and concepts of his work. This chapter will be devoted to alienation, which is one of the terms Marx used to explain the lack of well-being
that people suffer from within capitalism. It must be noted that *alienation* is
generally a term used by Marx early in his writing career; his later works do
not contain a systematic use of the concept. Nonetheless, the content of the
concept of alienation is intrinsic to Marx's writings.

This chapter will first provide a general overview of the conception of
alienation. Second, we will consider Marx's classic statement on alienation
from the "Estranged Labour" essay. Next is a comparison of Marx's analysis
of the effects of capitalism on workers from *The Communist Manifesto* with
his classic statement on alienation. Marx doesn't use alienation as a category
of analysis in his discussion of the detrimental effects of capitalism on workers in *The Communist Manifesto*, but there are some strong similarities.
Finally, some passages from Marx's mature economic and historical materialist writings will be compared with his classic statement on alienation. In
particular, we will examine the dynamics of social change as being driven by
alienation or the related notion of exploitation. We will consider exploitation
as being a related but different concept.

Overview of Alienation

Before we get into the details, it is necessary to have a brief discussion of
what alienation is in general. First, let us define **alienation**. The common

understanding of alienation is that something is alienated from a person when they have no control over it. Thus, a person can alienate their property by selling it or abandoning it. The more philosophic understanding of alienation is when something is hostile, detrimental, or not accepting of a person or to a person. Thus, a person is alienated when another person is hostile, detrimental, or not accepting of him or her.

For example, when a person is in economic competition with another person, the success of one person can be detrimental to the other person. Alternatively, a person is alienated when an object is hostile or detrimental to the person—for example, the existence of a new machine that makes a current worker redundant. The machine is detrimental to the person's future employment prospects. Or the machine is detrimental to a person's skill set since the machine replaces the activity of skilled labor with only unskilled machine tending. The detriment people suffer from alienation also impacts them on a psychological level. When people are unable to find work, face ruthless competition, or are subject to deskilling at work, the detriment they suffer can affect them as a psychological loss of self and/or a loss of a feeling of place in their social world.

A brief note on terminology: Marx uses the terms *alienation* and *estrangement* usually in ways that are interchangeable. This chapter will consider alienation and estrangement to have the same meaning.

Next, let us consider alienation in respect to Marx's materialist theory. Marx's fundamental understanding of human existence as materialist provides the foundation for his general conception of human action. Previous to this chapter, we introduced the materialist approach of Marx's social analysis; the concept of alienation draws on all three aspects: physical, organic, and temporal. The material existence of humans means that they are composed of matter and they rely on the physical and organic world for their existence. Humans satisfy their material requirements through use of the natural world. Thus, humans need to have access to the natural world to provide for their material requirements. Humans can be separated from the resources of the natural world temporarily. They will, of course, die if they are separated for too long.

Now this very obvious point about humans' material requirements and the necessity for them to have access to the natural world forms the basis of the concept of alienation. When humans are perpetually separated from the resources of the natural world, this would result in their death. People can utilize the natural world for food and shelter. In our own time and in Marx's, people receive money through wages, which they can use to purchase natural products to meet their material requirements. If people cannot freely utilize the natural world, they need to sell their labor in order to obtain subsistence in kind or through money.

This access, which is conditional on the performance of labor for another person, is where alienation comes into play. Marx finds that when people sell their labor, the result is an increase in the wealth of society in general and an increase in wealth for the buyer of the labor, but there is a loss of wealth for the workers themselves. This means that the separation of some humans from nature produces a situation in which workers gain less from their laboring than they could if they did not have to sell their labor. This condition could be alienating in various other ways: The worker has no say over what gets made, how it is made, or the pace at which it is made; selling one's labor may result in the enrichment of the employer, which can lessen the bargaining power of the worker; and if access to nature is scarce enough to encourage people to labor for others, then unemployment is possible. Thus, when the natural world and its resources become the private property of a few people within a society, people suffer alienation. People are supposed to have access to nature as material beings, and they suffer detriment when they are separated from it.

These repercussions from the condition of having to sell one's labor can result in relationships with people or objects that are alienating. That means that having to sell one's labor can result in relationships with people or objects that are detrimental, hostile, or not accepting. Having no control over the output, pace, or planning of labor can be detrimental to people physically. People can be overworked or work in repetitive conditions. The work can be psychologically detrimental, or the work can be boring or fail to allow for self-development. Having employers become wealthy allows them to wait out a strike or move the workshop to another location. These are obvious detriments to people. Being in competition with other workers can be a detriment by driving down wages. Workers may be hostile to one another since they are in competition for jobs. In addition, people will not be accepting of others' goals and aspirations since their material well-being is dependent on another person not gaining as much as they do.

A more detailed contemporary example will help explain the concept of alienation. Suppose that in this example, Juanita is a skilled welder at a car plant. One day she finds out that her job at the plant is going to be replaced by a welding robot. Her job is replaced, but she is kept on as a machine tender, which is a person who feeds manufacturing materials into an automated assembly line. Juanita can suffer alienation from losing her skilled job due to the detriment she suffers from having a job that is now repetitive and boring. Next, Juanita's current machine tender job is replaced by further automation, but this time she is not kept on for a new position and she becomes unemployed. Juanita now suffers alienation from being unable to find work in addition to the detriment she suffers from not having sufficient income, including the psychological worry about unpaid bills and an uncertain future. Thankfully, Juanita is hired to work at a clothing store stocking shelves and operating the cash register. At this new job, Juanita does not design the clothes, plan the purchases, or get a voice in the organization of her schedule. These aspects of her job are alienating to Juanita due to the detriment she suffers from not being able to creatively participate in her work. She finds that her creative potential as a person is not being satisfied and she is thus alienated.

In review, the separation of people from nature results in some people controlling access to nature and some people lacking this control. This situation requires those without access to nature to sell their labor to others. The selling of one's labor is premised on conditions in which people can be taken advantage of by those who buy their labor. When people sell their labor to others, they become alienated. This is the case because when people sell their labor, the results are hostile or detrimental to their well-being. When others are not accepting of them due to competition for jobs, people are alienated. According to Marx, if people could participate in decisions about production and were not in competition for jobs, then people would not be alienated.

The "Estranged Labour" Essay

The "Estranged Labour" essay appears in the *Economic and Philosophic Manuscripts of 1844*. This collection of writings is sometimes called the *Paris Manuscripts* because Marx was living in Paris at the time they were written. The *Manuscripts* contain an unfinished theoretical analysis of capitalism, critiques of Hegelian philosophy, and reflections on communism. Overall, they comprise many interesting early attempts by Marx to develop a systematic appraisal of social dynamics.

Introduction of the Concept of Alienation in the "Estranged Labour" Essay

Marx begins the "Estranged Labour" essay with a statement of the object of inquiry, the increasing impoverishment of workers while society's wealth increases:

> that the wretchedness of the worker is in inverse proportion to the power and magnitude of his production; that the necessary result of competition is the accumulation of capital in a few hands, and thus the restoration of monopoly

in a more terrible form; that finally the distinction between capitalist and land-rentier, like that between the tiller of the soil and the factory-worker, disappears and that the whole of society must fall apart into the two classes—the property-*owners* and the propertyless *workers.* (Marx & Engels, 1978, p. 70)

What are the objects that Marx wishes to explain? Marx wishes to understand (1) why the dynamics of a capitalist economy causes the worker to become impoverished while the productive capacity of society grows, (2) why the dynamics of the economy cause a change in social classes, and (3) why there are antagonisms between classes. Based on the quoted passage, we can see that Marx wants to analyze the current political-economic state in an attempt to find determinate simples, as his later reflections of method would describe. The determinate simple that Marx develops to explain all of these relationships and effects of capitalist production is the concept of alienation. For a discussion of Marx's method, see Chapter 2.

Before Marx arrives at a description of the effects of alienation, he further examines the situation of the worker in which poverty is a result of wealth creation:

> This fact expresses merely that the object which labour produces—labour's product—confronts it as *something alien,* as a *power independent* of the producer. The product of labour is labour which has been congealed in an object, which has become material: it is the *objectification* of labour. Labour's realization is its objectification. In the condition dealt with by political economy this realization of labour appears as *loss of reality* for the workers; objectification as *loss of the object* and *object–bondage;* appropriation as *estrangement,* as *alienation.* (Marx & Engels, 1978, pp. 71–72)

Workers are thus alienated by capitalist production. We have not yet reached Marx's description of alienation's various effects, but we have a description of what alienation is: The worker's product is alien; the product is a power independent of the worker and a loss of reality for the worker. Objectification is not alienation; rather, the objectification of alienated labor is different than labor alone. Why is this the case?

First, let us consider labor as objectification alone. Labor creates useful objects and effects, from the simplest movement to an elaborate feat of engineering. Labor becomes objectified in the object of its labor through the act of laboring. When a person chops wood, they take an object that is not useful for the task of building a fire, such as a large log, and turn it into an object useful for building a fire, chopped wood. What makes a useless item into a useful item is labor. A person's activity of laboring shapes the natural world into a new object: "The worker can create nothing without *nature,* without the *sensuous external world*. It is the material on which his labor is manifested, in which it is active, from which and by means of which it produces" (Marx & Engels, 1978, p. 72).

This is even the case for the simple movement of items. Chopped wood is useless on a wood storage lot for those who need wood to burn. The transferring of the chopped wood from the lot to a location where it can be burned is the creation of a useful object: chopped wood ready to burn where it can be burned usefully. Labor becomes objectified in the process of laboring. The objectification of labor is not a detriment to people. It is a benefit since it creates useful objects.

If labor makes objects useful, then what is different about alienating labor? As was mentioned in a previous quote, alienating labor is a loss of reality. If people are unable to use the objects they create then this is a loss of their capacity to provide for their material requirements. When people cannot utilize the useful objects they have created, they are unable to meet the requirements of their material existence. People are separated from the means to produce their material existence. Marx provides a fuller description of this loss of reality:

> The *alienation* of the worker in his product means not only that his labor becomes an object, an *external* existence, but that it exists *outside him*, independently, as something alien to him, and that it becomes a power of its own confronting him; it means that the life which he has conferred on the object confronts him as something hostile and alien. (Marx & Engels, 1978, p. 72)

Alienated labor creates items that are detrimental to the worker. Even if these items are useful to someone, they are not useful to the worker. This can be the case if we understand that a useful item satisfies a need or a want. The wood a person has chopped is useful to them if it satisfies their need for a fire. If the wood chopper creates useful items but cannot enjoy their use, they then become items that are useless to their creator.

This doesn't answer why the object is hostile and detrimental to the worker. In order to understand this, we need to answer the questions: How can items created by people cease to be under their control? Why are the items no longer part of their creators' reality? The answer is that the people do not own the objects they create. The objects that workers create are owned by capitalists. The worker makes useful items that are useful to the capitalist but not to the worker. This is why Marx states:

> The *alien* being, to whom labour and the produce of labour belongs, in whose service labour is done and for whose benefit the produce of labour is provided, can only be *man* himself. If the product of labour does not belong to the

worker, if it confronts him as an alien power, this can only be because it belongs to some *other man than the worker*. If the worker's activity is a torment to him, to another it must be *delight* and his life's joy. Not the gods, not nature, but only man himself can be this alien power over man. (Marx & Engels, 1978, p. 78)

Alienated labor is not the production of items that are harmful in their material qualities, such as poison gas, or even items that are harmful when consumed in large quantities, such as food or water. It is not the material qualities of an item that are detrimental. Rather, it is the social situation that makes an item detrimental. The control over what is being produced and decisions over who is able to use the produced products are the sources of alienation. The capitalist and the worker are both humans who have the same material needs and the same vulnerabilities. They are not different species with different biological requirements. The objects the worker creates are useful to the capitalist and not the worker because the capitalist can satisfy their needs and wants with these objects, whereas the worker cannot. Ownership of the means of production by capitalists results in a situation in which people have to sell their labor to survive. Marx considers the situation to be similar to *voluntarium imperfectum* (choice under dire necessity): "His labour is therefore not voluntary, but coerced; it is *forced labour*" (Marx & Engels, 1978, p. 74). People are forced to labor under undesirable conditions. These conditions exist because people have been separated from nature. Within the conditions of choice under dire necessity, people's labor is alienating to them. It is a detriment.

Overview of the Four Aspects of Alienation

Marx provides more than just a general explanation of alienation as due to capitalist ownership of the means of production. He also describes alienation as having four aspects: (1) people are alienated from the products of their labor; (2) people are alienated from the activity of labor; (3) people are alienated from their species being; and (4) people are alienated from other people (Marx & Engels, 1978, pp. 73–77). We will consider each in turn.

The First and Second Aspects of Alienation

The first and second aspects of alienation, which are alienation from the products of labor and alienation from the activity of labor, have already been discussed indirectly. Since alienation is hostility, detriment, or nonacceptance, we can see that when people labor under capitalist conditions, they are alienated by their products of labor and their activity of labor by enriching capitalists at the expense of themselves: "labour for the worker appears in the fact that it is not his own, but someone else's, that it does not belong to him, that in it he belongs, not to himself, but to another" (Marx & Engels, 1978, p. 74). The products of labor do not produce benefits that are as useful to the actual laborer as they could be. People labor to satisfy their needs and wants. The worker's act of laboring results in the needs and wants of capitalists being satisfied. Under different social conditions, such as the absence of private property, Marx conjectured that the worker would enjoy greater benefits. For example, Marx thought that when private property was converted into public property and was democratically controlled, unemployment and poverty would be eliminated, education would be free at the point of service (no tuition), and people would be able to freely use the means of production to satisfy their creative potential (Marx & Engels, 1978, pp. 486, 490, 529).

When workers produce goods and services, capitalists earn profits that exceed what individual workers receive in wages. This allows the capitalist to have greater political power than individual workers. The wealth that a capitalist controls enables them to hold out during strikes, move their workshops, and support political candidates. Thus, the product of labor is alienating to workers since it is used by capitalists to prevent improvements in the lives of workers.

Since workers are unable to make decisions about what is made or the pace of production, their activity of laboring is detrimental to them in the workplace. When workers are not in control of the production process, they may be forced to work long hours, work in dangerous conditions, perform work that is unimaginative, perform work that is repetitious, or work at speeds that injure them. Thus, the activity of labor is alienating to workers since it can be physically and psychologically harmful to them.

The Third Aspect of Alienation

The third aspect, the alienation of people from their **species being,** requires some explanation. *Species being* is a term used by Marx mostly in his writings before 1845, a terminology Marx takes from Feuerbach. Marx's use of the term basically disappears after that. The idea of species being, that humans are animals that can fabricate their world, is an idea intrinsic to Marx's materialist conception of humans that he utilizes throughout his writing career. Humans have the biological ability as a species to learn about their environment and to alter it. This includes themselves. Humans can conceptualize themselves as something that can be changed. Humans have the capacity to think of themselves and their social lives as being different from what they currently are and can attempt to become that:

> Man is a species being, not only because in practice and in theory he adopts the species as his object (his own as well as those of other things), but—and this is only another way of expressing it—but also because he treats himself as the actual, living species; because he treats himself as a *universal* and therefore a free being. (Marx & Engels, 1978, p. 75)

Marx's terminology *universal* can be defined as an open range of development for human abilities. Humans are universal, meaning there is not a foreseeable endpoint for their capacity to develop their abilities. Other animals are not as universal as humans because they cannot develop their abilities to the same degree. Marx appears to think that there is no limit to the development of humans' abilities (Marx & Engels, 1978, p. 75).

Humans are material beings that utilize their physical and organic capacities to manipulate the physical and organic world to construct their lives. As was discussed, humans must have access to nature to exist. Separation of humans from nature will not only jeopardize the maintenance of their lives, it will also prevent the development of their abilities. Alienation of humans from their species being thus prevents the expansion of life's activities from occurring:

> In estranging from man (1) nature, and (2) himself, his own active function, his life-activity, estranged labour estranges the *species* from man. It turns for him the *life of the species* into a means of individual life. First it estranges the life of the species and individual life, and secondly it makes individual life in its abstract form the purpose of the life of the species, likewise in its abstract and estranged form. (Marx & Engels, 1978, p. 75)

Estranged labor is labor that is separated from the means of production, which allows humans to utilize their capacities. When humans are separated from the means of production, this means that another person has ownership over the means of production. In order to gain access to the means of production, the nonowners must sell their labor to the owner. Workers are able to support their basic biological requirements, but they are unable to expand their capacities. This is why the estrangement of people from their species life (their ability to develop their abilities) results in the individual life of a person (i.e., their mere biological existence) becoming the purpose of the species. This is opposed to the seemingly true purpose of the species, which is to be universal and free beings: organisms that can develop and become something new.

Revisiting an old example can help elucidate the concept of alienated species being. In this example, Juanita is still working at the clothing store. As was noted previously, Juanita was alienated, and she suffered detriment by not being able to creatively participate in her work—for instance, Juanita has no input on the design of clothes and the organization of work tasks. This means that Juanita is alienated from her species being. Being able to organize one's labor so that one's dreams and aspirations can be actively developed through one's work is the satisfaction of species being. When one can't organize one's labor in this way then one is alienated from their species being.

The Fourth Aspect of Alienation

The fourth and final aspect of alienated labor is the alienation of individual people from other people (Marx & Engels, 1978, p. 77). Individual humans are separated from each other when they do not have control over the means of production; the result is alienation from one another. Humans who are in this condition are workers because they must sell their labor to survive. Why does separation from the means of production lead to alienation from other people? The following passage can shed some light on this question: "Hence within the relationship of estranged labour each man views the other in accordance with the standard and the position in which he finds himself as a worker" (Marx & Engels, 1978, p. 77).

This passage leads us to the following considerations: (1) people are alienated in their lives because they are in alienated relationships with other people and (2) the social position a person occupies that results in alienated lives and alienated relationships is that of the worker. Why is a person's relationship with others the cause of alienation in his own life? A person's relationship is the cause of alienation because people are workers. Being a worker means one is separated from the means of production and must sell one's labor to survive. We have already gone over how selling one's labor implies lack of sufficient ownership of the means of production and how this results in alienation. The relationship workers have with other people results in alienation either with capitalists or with other workers. The relationships workers have with capitalists are detrimental: The labor of a worker enriches the capitalist but does not enrich the worker. The relationships workers have with each other are detrimental because workers are in competition with other workers.

Certain conditions must obtain in order for the relationship between workers to be detrimental due to competition. First, there need to be more workers than job openings to keep wages low (Marx & Engels, 1978, p. 214).

Second, it must be difficult for workers to leave the working class. This means that it must be difficult for workers to become independent producers or capitalists. Both of these conditions must be obtained in order for there to be competition between workers for scarce jobs. If only one of them obtains, workers will find either enough jobs or enough ways out of the working class to keep competitive pressures low. Interestingly, if there is little or no competition between workers, capitalists will have a difficult time enriching themselves at the expense of workers. With the absence of meaningful competition, workers' wages will rise as capitalists seek scarce workers. This will result in capitalists gaining less from hiring labor, all else held equal.

Additionally, capitalists may have to offer terms so advantageous to workers when there is no meaningful competition between workers that it may result in capitalists putting themselves out of business. Marx shows in his later work that capitalists exist through exploiting the labor power of workers. If workers were paid the full value of their expended labor power, there would be no surplus value available for capitalists to live on. If there were no competition between workers, the surplus value that is appropriated by capitalists would be reduced to zero. At this point, how would capitalists hire workers? Only by offering co-ownership in the means of production the capitalist owns. Capitalists wouldn't even be able to rent the means of production to workers because there would be no competition for the rental. Capitalists would have to sell the means of production to have anyone work on it. This would result in capitalists being reduced to independent producers and workers also becoming independent producers.

Solutions to the Problem of Alienation

This example is fanciful since it assumes labor to be scarce and the means of production to be plentiful in proportion to the available workers. This is not the case in the actual world, where labor is plentiful and capital is scarce, resulting in competition between workers with detrimental results. This means that in the short to medium term, workers are detrimental to other workers as long as the means of production are either scarce or held as private property. Thus, in order to end the alienation of workers, one must make either the means of production plentiful or labor scarce. Alternatively, one must make private property public property in order to prevent people from using its scarcity to exploit workers. The first of these solutions is trade unionism and the second is communism. Marx is an advocate of the latter but thinks the former can assist in the obtainment of the latter. Before we look at Marx's advocacy of the abolition of private property in the "Estranged Labour" essay, let's consider the trade union solution first.

In the "Estranged Labour" essay, Marx does not advocate the trade unionism solution, only the communist solution. It will be useful to consider the benefits and limits of unions in the limitation and prevention of detriment to workers by mediating competition between workers. The greater pay and benefits that unionized workers receive over nonunionized workers have been documented (Mishel et al., 2009, pp. 198–209). For our current purposes, we will only consider trade unionism as a theoretical proxy for making workers scarce. The fictitious example demonstrated that a scarce labor force would result in the diminishing ability of capitalists to exploit workers. Unions do not reduce the number of workers, but they reduce the competition between workers through collective bargaining. Workers negotiate as a single unit, thus making it difficult for capitalists to bid down the price of labor. This lessens the degree of alienation since it helps mediate the effects of not owning the means of production. Workers have better access to the fruits of the means of production because they have reduced competition between workers.

Trade unionism has its limitations. In particular, unions coexist with capitalists. If capitalism is dependent on the exploitation of workers, this means that unions limit but do not eliminate exploitation. If they did, there would be no capitalists to extract surplus value and no workers to have the surplus value extracted from. Thus, the full possible range of achievable human abilities is not obtained even within a unionized capitalism. If exploitation is possible then separation from the means of production still obtains and alienation is the result, even if it is minimized. Additionally, unions do not prevent capitalists from finding new workers to compete with unionized workers (Foster, McChesney, & Jonna, 2011b, p. 12). This makes unions subject to the pressure of lower wages. Theoretically, communism avoids these problems by eliminating the source of alienation: separation of workers from the means of production.

The second solution to alienation, and the one endorsed by Marx in the "Estranged Labour" essay, is the abolition of private property through the achievement of communism. We can show why Marx thought that the end of private property will result in an end to alienation. First, we need to examine the different types of property that are pertinent to the topic. The types are common, personal, private, and public.

Common property is when all people have equal access to a given property without consent of others. Common property was typical throughout the feudal period and is an important means of subsistence for many people today. An example of common property would be a forest people could utilize as they pleased without asking the permission of other people who hold it in common. Thus, a person could take wood, fruit, game, and water without limit and without permission from a forest held as common property. The world's oceans are held in common.

Personal property is the objects a person consumes to provide for their needs. This includes items such as shelter, clothing, food, personal transportation, tools for preparing food and clothing, and personal effects. Personal property is under the exclusive control of a person or persons. People must obtain permission from the owners of the personal property to use it.

Private property is a means of production that is under the exclusive control of an individual or group of individuals, but not all individuals. People must obtain permission from the owners of private property to use it.

Public property is a means of production that is under the exclusive control of a political entity, such as a community, town, city, county, province, state, or nation. People must obtain permission from the owners of the public property to use it. Some public property is not a means of production, such as public parks and other recreational facilities.

As we can see, these categories can overlap in certain ways. There could be public-private property where the public owns a portion and a private person owns another portion of a means of production. There is an important distinction between personal property and private property. If a person owns a stove and bakes bread to feed themselves, this stove is personal property. If a person owns a stove and bakes bread for sale, this stove is private property. If an object is utilized as a means of production (i.e., to produce commodities for distribution) and is not publicly owned, then this object is private property. If an object is utilized as a means of production and is publicly held, then this object is public property. If an object is utilized as a means of personal reproduction and is not publicly owned, then this object is personal property. If an object is utilized as a means of production or as a means of personal reproduction and is not publicly owned, privately owned, or personally owned, then this object is common property. For example, a forest is public property if the public can restrict its use. A forest is private or personal property if a person or persons can restrict its use. A forest is common property if no one can restrict its use.

Now that the types of property have been introduced, Marx's proposed communist solution to the problem of alienation can be discussed. The type of property that Marx finds should replace private property he calls "truly human, social property" (Marx & Engels, 1978, p. 80). It is somewhat unclear what kind of property social property is. Marx's comments in *The Communist Manifesto* and elsewhere lead one to conclude that social property is public property (Marx & Engels, 1978, pp. 486, 490, 527–532). The conversion of a sizable portion of private property into public property is usually considered one of the necessary conditions for the existence of communism.

This is why the conversion of a sizable portion of private property into public property is called the communist solution to alienation.

Why does the conversion of private property into public property lead to an end of alienation? This seemingly is the case because it leads to an end of people being separated from the means of production. People are in detrimental situations when they cannot fully develop their capacities because they do not have sufficient access to the means of production. In addition, those who sell their labor do so under conditions of *voluntarium imperfectum*. They are thereby in jeopardy of losing their subsistence if their job performance or job discipline is not according to the wishes of capitalists.

Marx found that public property ownership of the means of production would rectify these problems. Public property would prevent loss of access to the means of production. People will always have access to the means of production since they own the means of production as citizens or residents. People may lose an individual job, but they will always have a claim over the publicly owned means of production. People will not only use the means of production to produce goods for consumption, they will also have decision-making power over what is made and how the productive forces will be developed. This means that people can participate in deciding how the productive forces could be used to develop their own and other people's capacities.

Now that we have analyzed the classic statement by Marx on alienation, we will consider if some of Marx's later criticisms of capitalism are reminiscent of his theory of alienation.

The Concept of Alienation in *The Communist Manifesto*

Marx does not use the concept of alienation as a consistent means of analyzing social conflict and social change. As has been noted, alienation is what Marx called the detrimental effects of people being separated from the forces of production. Additionally, class distinctions for Marx are determined, mainly according to who has control over what and how much of the productive forces. Thus, the necessary first condition for alienation to occur, separation from the productive forces, is demonstrated by the existence of classes—or, within capitalism, separation from the means of production, since all classes own their own labor power within capitalism (at least legally). Since class is one of the main categories, Marx uses it to analyze society during and after writing the *1844 Manuscripts*, with class being a precondition for alienation. So can we find aspects of alienation in Marx's post–"Estranged Labour" essay writings using the category of class even if the terms *alienation* and *estrangement* are not systematically used? The simple answer is yes, the four aspects of alienation do occur in some form in Marx's later writings. This section will consider how these aspects appear in *The Communist Manifesto.*

We will consider Marx and Engels's analysis of the detriments caused by class antagonisms according to the following criteria: (1) the creation of the classes of capitalism and the separation of people from the means of production, (2) the resulting detriment caused by this separation, and (3) the solution to the detriments caused by the separation, which is abolition of private property.

Marx and Engels consider the modern period to be one in which new class antagonisms have developed, and these antagonisms determine the long-term political trajectory:

> Our epoch, the epoch of the bourgeoisie, possesses, however, this distinctive feature: it has simplified the class antagonisms: Society as a whole is more and more splitting up into two great hostile camps, into two great classes directly facing each other: Bourgeoisie and Proletariat. (Marx & Engels, 1978, p. 474)

As was discussed, the appearance of alienation follows from the separation of some people from the means of production, and this alienation first appears as the alienated relationship between people (the fourth aspect of alienation). Capitalist class structure has these two causal parts: the separation of some people from the means of production (the creation of classes) and the resulting determent that is caused by this separation (class antagonisms).

At the time *The Communist Manifesto* was written, Marx and Engels found that the control of the means of production by capitalists was extensive and the detriments that were suffered by workers were profound. We will look at a few passages that can be grouped according to the four aspects of alienation. We will start with a passage that can be considered indicative of the first aspect:

> But does wage-labour create any property for the labourer? Not a bit. It creates capital, *i.e.*, that kind of property, which exploits wage-labour, and which cannot increase except upon condition of begetting a new supply of wage-labour for fresh exploitation. Property, in its present form, is based on the antagonism of capital and wage-labour. (Marx & Engels, 1978, p. 485)

To refresh our memories, the first aspect of alienated labor is alienation from the product of labor. This passage is strongly reminiscent of Marx's passages from the "Estranged Labour" essay. Once again, the product of a worker's labor is to the benefit of capitalists and the detriment of workers. This relationship of benefit and detriment is how exploitation is defined.

The following passage demonstrates detriments suffered by workers according to the second and fourth aspects of alienation:

> In proportion as the bourgeoisie, i.e., capital, is developed, in the same propor-tion is the proletariat, the modern working class, developed—a class of labour-ers, who live only so long as they find work, and who find work only so long as their labour increases capital. These labourers, who must sell themselves piece-meal, are a commodity, like every other article of commerce, and are con-sequently exposed to all the vicissitudes of competition, to all the fluctuations of the market. Owing to the extensive use of machinery and to division of labour, the work of the proletarian has lost all individual character, and conse-quently, all charm for the workman. (Marx & Engels, 1978, pp. 478–479)

Here we see that the second aspect of alienated labor, alienation from the activity of production, is observed by Marx and Engels within capitalist production. The activity of laboring has become routine and without autonomy. The worker has little to no control over how or in what way their labor activity is used. Additionally, the four aspects also appear; work-ers compete with one another to sustain their material requirements. In addition, capitalists competing with other capitalists drive down wages to try to maintain their position as capitalists. This creates hostility between workers, hostility toward capitalists by workers, and hostility between capitalists who must gain at the expense of others to materially survive and maintain their class position.

The third aspect of alienated labor, alienation from one's species being, is represented in *The Communist Manifesto* also. As already noted, "species being" is not used by Marx or Engels in any systematic way after the mid-1840s. By the time the *Manifesto* was written and published, in 1847 to 1848, its use in their work had basically disappeared. The ideas represented by Marx's use of the term *species being* in the "Estranged Labour" essay are retained. Species being is the capacity for humans to use the natural world to satisfy their needs and to develop new needs. Marx and Engels find this human capacity is prevented from being utilized by workers due to the existence of private property. They also find that the use of this capacity to improve people's abilities can only be achieved through the abolition of private property:

> The average price of wage-labour is the minimum wage, i.e., that quantum of the means of subsistence, which is absolutely requisite to keep the labourer in bare existence as a labourer. What therefore, the wage-labourer appropri-ates by means of his labour, merely suffices to prolong and reproduce a bare

existence. We [communists] by no means intend to abolish this personal appropriation of the products of labour, an appropriation that is made for the maintenance and reproduction of human life, and that leaves no surplus wherewith to command the labour of others. All that we want to do away with, is the miserable character of this appropriation, under which that labourer lives merely to increase capital, and is allowed to live only in so far as the interest of the ruling class requires it. (Marx & Engels, 1978, p. 485)

Humans' capacity to meet their needs and to develop new ones is subordinated to the demands of capitalist control of the means of production. As noted by Marx and Engels in the quoted passage, the solution to the detriments caused by capitalism is to eliminate the root cause of the detriments, which is private property. Private property will be converted into public property to be managed by the working class after they come to political power (Marx & Engels, 1978, p. 490). The result of this conversion of private property into public property is that eventually classes disappear and people are able to utilize their capacity for self-development (Marx & Engels, 1978, pp. 490–491).

The causal analysis utilized by Marx in the "Estranged Labour" essay is used again by Marx and Engels in *The Communist Manifesto* but with different terminology. The origin of detriments and intraclass and interclass antagonisms is due to the separation of some people from the means of production and thereby the creation of classes. Classes by their very existence are premised on exploitation in which the dominant class group that controls strategic amounts of the productive forces benefits at the expense of a subordinate class. The solution to this antagonistic situation is to eliminate private ownership of the means of production. This diagnosis of the problems of capitalism is the same, in content, as the diagnosis in the "Estranged Labour" essay.

As a side note, Marx and Engels think that human needs can only be met through the consumption of the products of society. This means that personal property must exist in some form for people to exist. This can be understood as the case if we consider the requirements of food or shelter. People need the food they will consume to exist as personal property. It must be exclusively under their control for consumption of it to satisfy a need. If one's food could be taken away at any point then it would not be able to satisfy a need. The same could be said of shelter. If people's shelter could always be taken away, it could not be used as personal property. This necessity of personal property can be seen for a variety of personal items: papers, personal effects, transport, and so forth. People must have personal property to live. This fact is acknowledged by Marx and Engels (Marx & Engels, 1978, pp. 485–486).

The conversion of private property into public property only prevents people from losing control of the means of production so that class antagonisms will not reemerge. The elimination of private property is not the elimination of personal property. Marx intended that people within communism would collectively control the means of production. Once they purchased or were given useful items, these items would be personal property for them to consume as they pleased.

The detriments suffered within capitalism are caused by class antagonisms and are corrected by the conversion of private property into public property. This is the solution offered by Marx throughout his writing career. As we shall see, Marx expands the range of what is considered a detriment. He also deepens his analysis of the relationship between the separation of some people from the means of production and the reproduction of capitalism. One can find further elaborations by Marx of detriments suffered by people in the works between *The Communist Manifesto* and his economic writings of the 1860s (in particular see Marx & Engels, 1978, pp. 292–293).

Alienation in Marx's Later Works

A common understanding of Marx's analysis of alienation is that Marx thought that once people were separated from nature, themselves, and others, there would be continually decreasing well-being for workers. Many of the passages from "Estranged Labour" and *The Communist Manifesto* describe this (Marx & Engels, 1978, pp. 70, 479). These passages take the position that as the general wealth increases, the well-being of workers decreases. Such comments appear to be contrary to people's experience in industrialized countries, since wages have grown, dangerous working conditions have been mediated for some workers, life expectancy has increased, and new conveniences are enjoyed by large segments of the population.

Well-being can be difficult to define, but a simple approximation can be made with three components: (1) social conditions, (2) working conditions, and (3) wages. Using these components to provide a consideration of well-being also matches Marx's concerns, since he finds people's separation from the means of production to affect people's means of subsistence, their activity at work, their ability to participate in the development of their society, and their relationships with other people.

The first component of social condition takes the macrosocial situation of workers into account. Are they able to control the natural, economic, cultural, and political activities of their country? Marx thinks that all people must have a meaningful engagement in the natural, economic, cultural, and political activities to fully develop. This is why he advocated universal suffrage, universal education, and public ownership of the means of production (Marx & Engels, 1978, pp. 489–491). In addition, Marx is concerned about the environmental conditions of people and thinks that environmental degradation is a problem (Marx, 1990, p. 638; 1991, p. 949). This natural component also can include the health and longevity of the person, which is deeply affected by one's environment.

The second component of working conditions takes the conditions of work and the conditions of management into account. Marx thinks that people can improve their well-being only if they have decent working conditions and are able to manage their own work environment. Marx considers both of these factors as aspects of the division of labor in which the activity of labor is divided into skill-less and creative parts. In addition, the organization of the labor process is divided into those who labor and those who design products and organize the production. The third and final component is the wages people receive for their work.

All three of these components are factored into understanding a person's well-being. Accordingly, we can say that when a person does not achieve gains in any of these component areas, their social and working conditions are detrimental and they are alienated. Marx's comments from the "Estranged Labour" essay and *The Communist Manifesto* are somewhat indeterminate. They generally can be taken as finding that the well-being of workers in all three component parts decreases as the overall wealth of society increases.

Many commentators have thought that Marx conjectured that the decline in well-being for workers would be continuous within capitalism (Galbraith, 1958, p. 56). That the well-being of workers in all three component parts has continually declined since the 1840s for all workers in the advanced industrialized capitalist countries is undoubtedly incorrect. The condition of workers in advanced countries has greatly improved since the mid-19th century, even if their wage growth has slowed or stagnated since the 1970s (Mishel et al., 2009). This general increase in well-being brings Marx's analysis of the detriment caused to workers by the conditions of capitalism into question.

Unknown to some critics, Marx altered his theory of the detriment caused to workers' well-being in his later works. Ernest Mandel provides a thorough treatment of this issue, but we can only briefly address it here (Mandel, 1971, pp. 140–153). In particular, Marx found that wages of workers could rise and the working conditions of workers could be improved through workplace regulation and the reduction of hours (Marx, 1990, pp. 610–635; Marx & Engels, 1968, pp. 221–226; Marx & Engels, 1978, p. 517). In 1865, Marx published *Wages, Price and Profit*, in which his comments are indicative of his later ideas on wage levels and well-being in capitalism. Marx finds that the wages of workers can be variable according to the physical requirements of workers and social standards of a society (Marx & Engels, 1968, p. 222). Wages can increase or decrease. Nonetheless, Marx always found that there was a tendency for capitalist accumulation to drive down wages (Marx & Engels, 1978, pp. 211–217, 422–428). Capitalists wish to control wages to increase profits and to cut costs, or both. This enables capitalists to outcompete other capitalists and increase their own chances at survival. Workers can limit this tendency through political action. Workers can petition for limitations of the workday, minimum wages, and age requirements for workers. Thus, there is not an inevitable trajectory of declining wages within capitalism if political intervention is considered. Even though workers within capitalism can improve their well-being, Marx, in his later writings, still is an advocate of the overthrow of capitalism:

> At the same time, and quite apart from the general servitude involved in the wages system, the working class ought not to exaggerate to themselves the ultimate working of these everyday struggles. They ought not to forget that they are fighting with effects, but not with the causes of those effects; that they are retarding the downward movement, but not changing its direction; that they are applying palliative, not curing the malady. They ought, therefore, not be exclusively absorbed in these unavoidable guerilla fights incessantly spring-ing up from the never-ceasing encroachments of capital or changes of the market. They ought to understand that, with all the miseries it imposes upon them, the present system simultaneously engenders the *material conditions* and the *social forms* necessary for an economical reconstruction of society. Instead of the *conservative* motto, "*A fair day's wage for a fair day's work?*" they ought to inscribe on their banner the *revolutionary* watchword, "*Abolition of the wages system!*" (Marx & Engels, 1968, p. 226)

We should return to the list of the well-being components to refresh our memories on why Marx thinks reform is not politically viable. Capitalism can deliver on increased wages, reduced working hours, improved working conditions, universal suffrage, and improved health. It can even maintain full employment even if such outcomes are unfashionable in current main-stream economic thinking. It has been able to improve or maintain environ-mental conditions, but capitalism's ability to do this has been extensively questioned by contemporary Marxist scholars, as will be discussed in Chapters 9 and 10. Capitalism has been unable to deliver on widespread and compulsory workplace democracy and general democratic control over the economy, including investment decisions. This means simply that capi-talism has not abolished private property in the means of production and converted it into public property. This would of course end capitalism. Those who used to be capitalists would no longer gain the same benefits from their investment income, which is substantial for some. Even if capitalists were bought out by the state and given public bonds as payment for their nationalized capital, their ownership of large wealth holdings would no longer allow them to dominate others through the control of production. Marx did not appear to favor such a measure; he seemed to favor confiscation of the means of production without compensation (see Marx & Engels, 1978, p. 510).

Marx definitely thinks that democratic control of the means of production owned as public property would improve people's well-being, since it is separation of people from control of the means of production that is detrimental to their lives. In other words, separation from the means of production causes alienation. Being able to control the means of production would allow people to voice their opinion on what they and others will make, how they will make it, and what the conditions of their work will be. Workers would also no longer be in competition for access to the means of production since everyone would own the means of production as public property. This would reduce the alienation of labor in the four different aspects including species being.

Conclusion

This chapter has shown that ideas similar to the category of alienation and his early analysis of capitalism's detrimental effects are still utilized by Marx in his later work. The cause of alienation is the lack of control of the means of production. This is a condition that still affects people. This should not surprise readers, since capitalism can only exist if the vast majority of people do not own sufficient amounts of the means of production. Before this book moves on to examine Marx's theory of class, here are a few questions for thought:

- What is the relationship between Marx's materialist outlook and his theory of alienation?
- Are people, according to Marx's definition, currently alienated within capitalist societies?
- Can we understand alienation to be a social or a psychological condition, or both?
- Can we understand both workers and capitalists to be alienated?
- Even if alienation still exists, do the gains from economic growth and technological advancement since Marx's lifetime outweigh the detriments of alienation?

4

Class

In the previous chapters, we have utilized Marx's understanding of class relations and have already discussed the material basis for his definition of class. In particular we have seen that class for Marx is related to amounts of ownership of different productive forces. Classes have objectively divergent interests that cause the economic detriment of exploitation to occur. This exploitation would be impossible if classes were eliminated. This is why Marx advocates a classless society as a desirable solution to these divergent interests and resulting detriments.

This chapter will contain an analytical reconstruction of Marx's class theory. This section will include a structural presentation of classes, a presentation of the objectivity of classes and the objectivity of class interests and class antagonisms, a presentation of class formation and class consciousness as subjective phenomena, and a presentation of class alliances. The second section will be an analysis of Marx's classic treatments of class and class relations in *The Communist Manifesto*. The final section will be an overview of the material presented with some considerations for new elaborations of materialist class structures.

A Reconstruction of Marx's Class Theory

Marx uses the category of class throughout his writings. But a definitive elaboration of classes is absent in his work. The third volume of *Capital* contains an unfinished beginning of Marx's attempt at elaborating a concept of class, but it is not conceptually more sophisticated than his other statements (Marx, 1991, p. 1025). Since class is a socially determinate and objective manifestation of humans' material interests, Marx finds it to be an excellent category for conducting social analysis that frames long-term social dynamics. This section will build on what I have found to be useful and sophisticated notions about materialist class structures based on Marx's writings and contemporary class writers. The presentation of Marx's class analysis I think is true to his statements about class because it utilizes the existence of ownership of various productive forces as the main structural feature that determines class. This allows one to clearly construct the main antagonistic classes of the epochal modes of production analyzed by Marx.

As will be shown when we consider the various works by Marx, he mentions many class locations that don't simply fall into the structure developed in what follows. Some locations are in between the main antagonistic classes, and their objective class interests are not as clear as those of the main classes. In addition, some classes listed by Marx, in particular the lumpen proletariat or slum proletariat, have class alliances attributed to them that are not consistent with the structural theory laid out. This doesn't mean their objective class interests can't be determined. It means that Marx's analysis concerning them is somewhat incomplete. Marx provides such an analysis for other classes such as the poor peasantry, where the reasons for their particular class alliances are analyzed and their objective class interests are also determined.

Some in-between classes could be described as the middle class or middle classes in contemporary terminology. It is very unclear in common discourse what designates the middle class or middle classes. The manual–office divide, or the blue collar–white collar divide, is unhelpful since some white-collar office workers receive low wages, have little autonomy over their work, and have little prospect of mobility up the job ladder or into higher income brackets. In addition, some manual workers may have high wages, work autonomy, and job and income mobility, making them similar to many professional white-collar workers. The current vagueness regarding the middle class in common usage also doesn't attempt to objectively determine the class interests of the various middle-class groups, particularly in light of Marx's hypothesized necessity of class antagonisms as intrinsic to capitalism. This objective determination of class interests and class antagonisms is a centerpiece of Marx's theory of class. A theory of contemporary class structure according to income groups does little to develop an understanding of class interests. The well-paid manufacturing or public worker of today could be the poorly paid service worker of tomorrow. That people who received profit income from manufacturing today and will receive profit income from services tomorrow may tell us something about long-term objectivity of class interests. Marx's theory of class allows such determinations to be developed.

Marx analyzes class locations that could be called middle classes, such as the petite bourgeoisie, bourgeoisie intellectuals, army officers, priests, and bureaucrats, to name a few. His analysis attempts to explain their current class alliances and sometimes considers their objective class interests. This analysis by Marx attempts to explain why the class interests of these middle groups are variable in the short and medium term and why their class interests are aligned with proletarian interests in the long run. These considerations will be developed in the final section in the hope of demonstrating that Marx's writings may provide the basis for current analysis of middle classes.

Overall, this section will provide a reconstructed outline of Marx's class theory, which attempts to preserve its materialist structure while not glossing over or attempting to correct its shortcomings. A contemporary author who goes beyond Marx while retaining the materialist structure of class location is Wright (1985). His work and G. A. Cohen's (2000) has been an influence on the presentation that follows, but I have purposely left out Wright's advancements in order to preserve Marx's original presentation. I will mention some of his insights when they are helpful and don't disturb Marx's own analysis. Wright has attempted to analyze middle-class locations according to a Marxian framework. Many of the problems discussed in the previous paragraphs were considered by him. Marx's class theory is a product of his century, and some of its shortcomings are due to its antiquated social observations. This doesn't mean Marx hasn't provided some fascinating insights into social structures.

A Structural Materialist Theory of Class

To begin, Marxian class theory is structured around who owns what productive force and the amount of the productive forces they own. To refresh our memory of the definition of the productive forces: the productive forces are composed of the means of production and labor power. Labor power is the capacity of people to produce objects and activities of value that can be used and exchanged. Labor power includes the capacities of humans, including physical and intellectual capacities. The means of production are the tools, machines, raw materials, spaces, and buildings used in production (Cohen, 2000, p. 32). The combination of labor power and the means of production produces items and services that are useful to people. The use of the productive forces fulfills human needs and allows for new needs to be fulfilled that were impossible to fulfill in the past.

Classes are determined according to who owns which productive force and in what amount. The main classes of Marx's theory and their class location according to ownership of the productive forces are listed in Table 4.1.

Table 4.1   Marxian Classes

Class	Owns all of their own labor power?	Owns some but not all of their own labor power?	Owns all of another person's labor power?	Owns some but not all of another person's labor power?	Owns a sufficient amount of the means of production to provide subsistence for oneself through laboring?	Owns a sufficient amount of the means of production in order not to labor?
Slave	No	No	No	No	No	No
Slave Owner	Yes	No	Yes	No	Yes	Yes
Serf	No	Yes	No	No	Yes	No
Lord	Yes	No	No	Yes	Yes	Yes
Worker—Proletarian	Yes	No	No	No	No	No
Independent Producer—Petite Bourgeoisie	Yes	No	No	No	Yes	No
Capitalist—Bourgeoisie	Yes	No	No	No	Yes	Yes

Source: Adapted from Cohen, G.A. *Karl Marx's Theory of History.* C1978, 2000. Princeton University Press, 2001 expanded ed. with new intro and chapters reprinted by Princeton University Press, p. 65, Table 1.

As can be seen from Table 4.1, the classes that are considered by Marx are derived from the three modes of production that he thinks have comprised human class civilizations so far: slave societies, feudal societies, and capitalism. Before these modes of production, there was a classless society. Communism, which Marx thinks will arise after capitalism, will also be a classless society. Only slave societies and feudal societies entail ownership of another person's labor power. In fedualism the **lord** own some of the serfs labor power. In **slave** societies a slave owner owns all of a slaves labor power. Capitalism eliminated the formal ownership of labor power. As is known, slavery still exists within capitalism but is illegal.

Marx's theory of class is structural because people's **class position** is determined by the ownership relations of their society and not their own awareness of their class position. Societies have classes according to differential ownership of different productive forces and not due to people's awareness of these classes. Individuals' potentials for action are determined by their class position even if they are unaware of their class position. For example, workers must sell their labor to gain their subsistence. The necessity of selling one's labor is not dependent on one being aware that this necessity is determined by one's class position.

People may seek to leave the working class with increased vigor when they understand the intrinsic antagonisms of capitalism and the necessary exploitation of workers. In addition, awareness of one's class position (class consciousness) seems to be necessary for concerted class action. This means that people must be aware of their class position and their objective class interests to take action, which would allow them to improve their situation regarding their access to the means of production. Thus, awareness of class position is a precondition for revolutionary class action (Marx & Engels, 1978, pp. 481, 518).

Marx's theory of class is materialist because its positions are determined around the fundamental requirement of human life, which is access to the resources of the material world. This access to the material world is determined according to differentials of ownership. Differentials of ownership structure classes. Classes in turn determine how people access the productive forces to provide subsistence for themselves and their dependents, how they can reproduce their current class position, and how their current class position can be changed. This means that classes structured according to ownership of the means of production provide an insight into current social dynamics and future social changes. People must conform to their class position to provide for their subsistence and maintain their class position. Additionally, people must take their potentialities for action into account as determined by their class position when attempting to expand the satisfaction of their needs.

The Objectivity of Class: Interests and Antagonisms

In order to understand the potentials any society has for preservation and change, in particular preservation of its given class structure, we must consider the objective interest of the various class positions. To understand class interests, we need to address the following questions: What are class interests and why are class interests objective?

All people have needs that must be satisfied. All people need food and shelter, but they also need access to information and control over their social world to ensure their lives turn out the way they wish. Thus, even if one isn't a power seeker, one still needs the power to control one's life. The class position of a person will determine whether or not that person's needs will be satisfied. For example, workers, because they are not in control of the means of production, do not have a secure satisfaction of their needs. On the other hand, capitalists, due to their control of the means of production, have a very secure chance their needs will be met.

Different classes have different possibilities that their needs will be met. This means that classes have different interests in increasing or maintaining the potential for the satisfaction of their needs. Workers have an interest in increasing the potential for the satisfaction of their needs, while capitalists have an interest in maintaining or increasing the potential for the satisfaction of their needs. For example, workers have an interest in gaining greater control over the means of production in order to have a more secure satisfaction of their needs, whereas capitalists have an interest in preserving their control over the means of production in order to maintain their current potential for the satisfaction of their needs. In short, different classes have different interests because they have different levels of control over the productive forces.

The objectivity of class interests is based on Marx's material theory of social reality. All people require access to the means of production to meet their needs. If people wish to do anything in the world, they need the material resources to do it. Even if people do nothing with their time except spend it in idleness, this presupposes they already provided for their mere needs of food, clothing, and shelter, or they would be physically wasting away. Even in the extreme case of a person who supplies all of their mere needs by scavenging through refuse, they still must meet these needs to live and to scavenge. These needs are objective in the sense that people cannot decide to not satisfy them and still live. In a more extended sense, people must satisfy the whole range of their socially current basic needs to engage in the life of their society. People cannot decide to engage in the life of their society without the necessary education and communication needs being met. They will be unable to access the activities and institutions of their society and will be unable to understand them.

We can see that the needs of people are objective and, in turn, their class interests are objective in the same way but indexed according to class. For example, since workers do not own any usable amount of the means of production, their capacity to satisfy their needs could be increased if they had more secure access to the means of production. This means that workers have an objective interest in gaining secure access to the means of production. No matter what they do in life, they require access to the means of production, since this access satisfies their needs. It is always in workers' interest to gain more secure access to the means of production, whether they are aware of it or not. Indeed, many people are concerned with matters of art and beauty, but to enjoy objects of beauty, one must have the time available to appreciate them. This means that no matter what one seeks in life, one has an objective interest to increase one's capacity to access the means of production. As Wright puts the matter concerning the objectivity of class interests: "Whatever else the concept of 'interest' might mean, it surely includes the access to resources necessary to accomplish various kinds of goals or objectives. People certainly have an 'objective interest' in increasing their capacity to act" (Wright, 1985, p. 28).

Marx thus finds that workers have objective class interests in changing their society into a communist one, since they will have more secure access to the means of production by converting it to public property. As residents of a communist country, they will be unable to be separated from publicly owned property. Fascinatingly, no matter the personal opinions of workers, even those who are anticommunist, they have an objective interest in the establishment of communism because it will increase their capacity to meet their needs.

Capitalists have objective class interests also. Individual capitalists have secure access to the means of production and thus a relatively stable satisfaction of their needs. They have an objective interest to maintain their control over the means of production if they wish to stay within the capitalist class. Of course, capitalists have high incomes and can consume more and higher-quality items that satisfy their basic needs and consume items not required for life in their society but which are highly desirable.

Wolff and Zacharias (2007) estimate that the mean income of capitalists in the United States in 2000 was $825,826.00 (in 2005 dollars), and 84.3% of their income was from nonhome wealth—that is, income derived from investments and not from work (p. 33). Capitalists comprised 2% of all households during the year 2000 (Wolff & Zacharias, 2007, p. 30). Capitalists are able to receive such high incomes because they own a sizable amount of the means of production. This means that the high nonwork incomes of those people who are capitalist are so high because they are part of the capitalist class.

If capitalists wish to continue to receive these amounts of nonwork income, they must stay capitalists and accordingly preserve the capitalist mode of production. Their interests are objective in the sense that they must preserve their class position in order to enjoy the gains from owning the amounts of means of production that locate them with the capitalist class position. If individual capitalists do not attempt to preserve their status as capitalists, they could lose these gains. Simply put, capitalists must accept the exploitation of workers to stay capitalists. This is beyond their choosing. A person cannot choose to have unearned income of this amount and not be a capitalist. It is possible that individual capitalists may no longer wish to be capitalists and may choose not to accept the objective interests of their capitalist class position. They could instead choose to accept the class interests of another class; but they must still divest themselves of their ownership of the means of production to no longer be in the capitalist class.

The Subjectivity of Class: Class Formation and Class Consciousness

People have objective interests as humans and as members of a class. People have these interests even if they are not aware of them. People must be aware of their interests to plan to achieve them. This awareness of one's interests is the subjectivity of class and is a decisive factor in the development of class consciousness and the formation of classes into political groups. It is important to stress again that people are not part of a class because they are aware of being in that class or identify with the goals of a certain class. Considering each of these in turn, workers are in the working class because they must sell their labor power to gain their subsistence. They must do this whether they are aware of it as designating their class position or not. Some people may think they are part of a class and be mistaken in their approximation. A higher-income worker may think they are in the capitalist class because they have a high income, but since their income is derived from selling their labor power, they are in the working class. We will consider questions about income and class position in the section on class alliances. A worker may identify with capitalists or a capitalist with workers, and each may be advocates of class interests different from their own. This does not change their class position. A worker may advocate for laws that make it easier to exploit workers and may actually lose out because of these new laws, but this does not make him a capitalist, only an advocate of capitalist class interests.

One of the major subjective elements of class is **class consciousness**. Class consciousness is when a person becomes aware of what class they are in. Additionally, class consciousness is becoming aware not only of the objective interests of one's class but the revolutionary and counterrevolutionary interests of one's class (Mandel, 1994, pp. 84–91; Marx & Engels, 1978, pp. 480–483). Class consciousness is thus an educative process in which people learn what their objective interests are and learn about possible ways to achieve these interests. Marx and Engels note that workers gain class consciousness through political struggles. They believe that workers will learn about the limits of reform and that only a transition to a socialist society will allow their objective interests to be securely met.

Class formation is the conscious grouping of people into political organizations that seek to achieve the interests of their class. Marx thinks that some objective factors facilitate class formation, such as concentration of members of the same class in a given area and the development of communication technology (Marx & Engels, 1978, pp. 481, 608). Marx finds that people will realize they are in a class, become aware of their objective interests, and form political groups around these class interests when they are among others of the same class. Marx thought that workers live in such conditions because they cluster in cities and in workplaces with others who have the same objective interests. This allows workers to realize that the dynamics of capitalism create and reproduce the conditions that keep workers propertyless. Communication aids in awareness and class formation because workers from across countries, across continents, and across the world can realize that they not only have the same interests but they can also organize their political actions.

Class consciousness and class formation are not necessary. Countries with similar class compositions can have very different levels of class consciousness and class formation. Countries such as the United States and Sweden have a similar working class size of about 40% of the labor force (Wright, 1985, p. 195), yet they have very different levels of class consciousness and class formation (Wright, 1985, pp. 260–261). This is not surprising given the antisocialist history of the United States and the prosocialist history of Sweden.

The Limits of Social Change: Class Alliances and Ideology

Classes' objective interests are structurally determined, but they must be aware of and act on these interests for social change to occur. This means that dominant classes can seemingly prevent revolutionary social change from occurring by preventing the formation of class consciousness through strong class alliances, weak class alliances, and cross-class identification. Strong class alliances allow a part of a subordinate class to become a member of the ruling class. An example of a strong class alliance is when segments of the working class or the independent producer class are allowed entry into the capitalist class. This is most obviously the case with managerial workers or professional workers who are made partners of capitalist firms.

Weak class alliances are when the satisfaction of basic needs for a certain part of the subordinate classes are improved. An example of a weak class alliance is when the wages and benefits of the working classes rise with productivity increases. This increase in wages and improvement in living standards mediates revolutionary class sentiment. Also, weak class alliances can be structured according to race or nationality. The exclusion of some workers from living standards increases can be based on race. This was the case when Black workers were banned from federal financed housing (Rothstein, 2013).

Cross-class identification is when a dominant or privileged class identifies with the interests of a subordinate class or when a subordinate class identifies with the interests of a dominant or privileged class. An example of a privileged class identifying with the interest of a subordinate class is given by Marx and Engels in *The Communist Manifesto* when bourgeoisie ideologists accept the revolutionary class interests of proletarians (1978, p. 481). But a more common cross-class identification is when the working class identifies with the interests of capitalists and attempts to emulate their standard of living. This emulation was not explored by Marx but was extensively analyzed by Thorstein Veblen (1994). Class alliances and cross-class identification inhibit the formation of revolutionary class consciousness (or prevent the maintenance of capitalist class consciousness in the instance of bourgeoisie ideologists). This is done by fracturing subordinate classes into distinctive groups in the case of a strong class alliance, mediating the need for revolutionary action by raising living standards, or fracturing a subordinate class into privileged and disparaged groups in the case of a weak class alliance, or distracting workers with impossible hopes of becoming capitalists themselves in the case of cross-class identification.

Additionally, ideology can play a role in the mediation of revolutionary tendencies. As we have already discussed, people have to be conscious of themselves as part of a class and their objective interests to take revolutionary action. Accordingly, a sizable number of individuals of a class or several classes need to have class consciousness, and those people need to be in communication with one another to forge a revolutionary class movement. A revolutionary class movement can be prevented if class consciousness can be prevented. This is where ideology can come into play. Class consciousness is the awareness that class antagonisms are intrinsic to society. If people understand their society as not having intrinsic class antagonisms then there is no reason to advocate for a change in class relationships.

Marx discusses weak class alliances and ideology as limits to revolutionary action since they were the common mechanisms used in his lifetime. He also considers cross-class identification to help explain why dominant members of the ruling class or privileged members of wage-laboring classes would form alliances with workers. The later sections of this chapter will consider his analysis of these mechanisms. We will briefly consider strong class alliances first in order to provide a sufficient overview of the benefits and limits of each mechanism.

Strong class alliances are when individuals from the subordinate classes are directly made part of the ruling class. An individual being made directly part of the ruling class is a costly procedure and seemingly is only desirable where new productive forces have been seized. An example of this would be the granting of feudal titles to individuals of lands that were just seized, such as the conquest of the Americas from the 15th century onward, the seizure of Muslim lands during the Crusades, or the Norman invasion of England. In short, the direct admittance of individuals into the ruling class is a rare occurrence, especially within capitalism. In addition, its cost when there is no net addition to the total stock of means of production is contrary to the interests of current capitalists.

There is an obvious limit to strong class alliances due to stretching ownership of the means of production too thin. Thus, weak class alliances are a much more common mechanism for the limitation of revolutionary class action because they are not a direct thinning of dominant class control of the means of production. Weak class alliances are simply increased satisfaction of subordinate class needs, which do not alter dominant class control over the productive forces. This increased satisfaction can be for either a part or the entirety of subordinated classes. These methods are costly to capitalists since they require increased wages, which in turn lessen their share of surplus value. Their applicability depends on how affordable they are.

Increased basic need satisfaction for the entirety or an influential component of the working class through direct development of the productive forces allows for cheaper satisfaction of basic needs (Galbraith, 1958, 1967). The development of the welfare state during the first three quarters of the 20th century is the definitive demonstration of weak class alliances in effect (Esping-Andersen, 1990). In the United States, Black people were excluded from such gains until affirmative action and state employment provided a means to increased need satisfaction (Reich, 1981, p. 8), even though their income and wealth levels are still drastically below what is earned and held by Whites (Mishel et al., 2009, pp. 177, 271).

The general idea of such weak alliances is that revolutionary action can be precluded or limited by decreasing the gains to be achieved through revolutionary action. Subordinated classes will see class compromise as desirable since they are gaining from the current social system. The applicability of such weak alliances is dependent on the success of capitalism to provide growing incomes to the subordinated classes. This process is periodically upset by capitalist crisis, which Marx finds to be an inevitable recurring feature of capitalism (Marx & Engels, 1978, pp. 450, 478).

Another mechanism for the limitation of revolutionary class action is ideology. This limitation mechanism forms a major component of Marx's analysis of class in *The 18th Brumaire of Louis Bonaparte*. A larger presentation of ideology will be made in Chapter 7. For now, we can provide an analytical overview of ideology as a mechanism to limit revolutionary action. Ideology can be understood as ideas that prevent people from realizing their objective class interests. They could be rather direct, such as criticism of communism or class analysis, or indirect, such as the byproducts of mainstream social science that preclude the social dynamics of revolutionary politics. In addition, the presence of other ideas and theories that provide an explanation of social dynamics and do not conjecture that capitalism is unable to meet people's needs, such as religion, nationalism, free enterprise fanaticism, or racism, can be used to limit revolutionary class action (Marx & Engels, 1978, pp. 54, 519).

Finally, cross-class identification is when members of the dominant class or privileged members of the subordinate class identify with subordinate class interests or possibly vice versa. This could be the case if a capitalist, a highly paid professional, or a potentially highly paid professional sides with a subordinated class. Marx thinks such alliances are possible and, in particular, thinks that some bourgeois ideologists (such as social scientists, teachers, journalists) will side with the interests of workers (Marx & Engels, 1978, p. 481).

A possible case, which is not analyzed by Marx, is the occurrence of people who identify with dominant class interests because they wish to become part of the dominant class. This desire to leave a subordinate class position is completely understandable given the precarious economic condition of many workers. Workers seeking self-employment or becoming capitalists is a rational course of action given the objective interests of the working class. Marx would find that it is a course of action that will not work for all of the working class, since it is impossible that all workers will become independent producers or capitalists.

In review, Marx's theory of class takes into account objective structural arrangements in order to derive a set of objective interests. These objective interests are not innately known to people. Individuals can become aware of their objective interests through political action, communication, and education. When workers become aware of their interests and the commonality of their interests with others of their class position, they become class conscious. Class consciousness in not an automatic process and can be prevented from being attained through class alliances or ideology.

The Communist Manifesto

Marx's use of the category of class extends throughout his entire career. A few documents by him provide an extensive overview of his understanding of class. In this section, we will look at Marx and Engels's comments from *The Communist Manifesto*. We will use the analytical reconstruction of

Marx's class theory developed earlier to ask questions about what are the classes listed by Marx and Engels in the *Manifesto*? Do all of these classes listed correspond to the structural definition of class? What are the interests of the classes listed and are these interests objective? What is the level of class consciousness of the classes listed? What class alliances are noted? What ideological limitations are listed?

What Classes Are Listed by Marx and Engels in the *Manifesto*?

We will only consider the classes that exist in capitalism that are mentioned by Marx and Engels in the *Manifesto*. The classes are

1. Bourgeoisie/capitalists: includes landlords (Marx & Engels, 1978, p. 479)

2. Proletarians/workers

3. Petite bourgeoisie/independent producers/lower middle classes: includes small tradespeople, shopkeepers, artisans, handicraftsmen, small manufactures, and peasants (Marx & Engels, 1978, pp. 479, 481–482)

4. Bourgeois ideologists (Marx & Engels, 1978, p. 481)

5. Lumpen proletariat: called the "dangerous class" and the "social scum" in the *Manifesto* (Marx & Engels, 1978, p. 482)

This list has been grouped by attempting to follow the distinctions provided by Marx and Engels. Page numbers for Marx and Engels (1978) are provided for the smaller classes. Additionally, a few classes have been left out due to their redundancy or vagueness of their position, in particular the pawnbroker and retired tradesmen. Pawnbrokers are listed as members of the capitalist class and retired tradesmen are listed as independent producers (Marx & Engels, 1978, p. 479). Why pawnbrokers should be listed as capitalists is unclear. It is noted they exploit workers like capitalists, but also listed as exploiters are shopkeepers. Pawnbrokers and shopkeepers could exploit workers as independent producers or as capitalists. For example, both could extract surplus value from workers with loans. A shop and a pawn brokerage could both be run by an independent producer or a capitalist. There is nothing about pawnbrokers that merits their explicit inclusion as capitalists or as independent producers. Their class position is easily encapsulated in the other stated classes. Retired tradesmen could be either independent producers or capitalists depending on whether they employed people. Marx does not provide any substantial analysis of the class position of retired people. This being the case, retired tradesmen can be analyzed according to the class position of independent producers or capitalists.

Do These Listed Classes Conform to the Structural Definition of Class?

Capitalists and workers. Marx and Engels note in the beginning of the *Manifesto* that within capitalism, the two great hostile classes are bourgeoisie and proletarians (Marx & Engels, 1978, p. 474). The clearest definition of capitalists and workers is provided in a footnote by Engels from 1888:

> By bourgeoisie is meant the class of modern capitalists, owners of the means of social production and employers of wage-labour. By proletariat, the class of modern wage-labourers who having no means of production of their own, are reduced to selling their labour-power in order to live. (Marx & Engels, 1978, p. 473n5)

Using Table 4.1 as a starting point, we can see that the questions used to compile the table are basically commensurate with the definitions added by Engels in 1888. The workers' definition conforms to this analytical table quite exactly with the mention of not owning enough of the means of production to provide for oneself. Being free to sell one's labor power is not directly stated, but it is implied in Engels's definition. The definition of capitalists also conforms to the questions of the table as owning sufficient amounts of the means of production. The definitive definition of not having to labor is not provided by Engels. This question about not having to labor due to owning a sufficient amount of the means of production is a development of later class analysis and is a means to distinguish capitalists from independent producers. Marx and Engels distinguish between capitalists and independent producers in passages of the *Manifesto*, since they find the class interests of independent producers as being distinct from the class interests of capitalists (Marx & Engels, 1978, p. 482). These definitions of worker and capitalist are structural definitions that determine class according to individuals' ownership of the productive forces. We can see that the analytical Table 4.1 is a reconstruction of such definitions.

Independent producers. The majority of the lower middle class or independent producers are people who labor for themselves and may be able to hire small numbers of other people. The unclear class position is the small manufacturers, which will be considered separately. The remaining classes listed by Marx and Engels—small tradespeople, shopkeepers, artisans, handicraftsmen, and peasants—can reasonably be considered as independent producers and thus fit into Table 4.1. Marx and Engels note that these independent producer classes control "diminutive" amounts of capital (Marx & Engels, 1978, p. 480). This would conform to the Table 4.1

question of whether these individuals own enough means of production to work for themselves. Since Marx and Engels set these classes apart from workers and capitalists, this can be understood to provide the textual basis to determine the independent producer class position of Table 4.1.

The small manufacturers are listed together with the clearly defined independent producers. This class is ambiguous, since a small manufacturing firm may be a single person or perhaps dozens of people. What determines a small manufacturing firm when large firms employ thousands or tens of thousands of people is unclear, since Marx and Engels give no clear determination of small and large capitalists. In addition, a manufacturing firm is not as definitive in regard to size as is a shopkeeper or an artisan. Small manufactures are described, along with the clearly determined independent producers, as owning diminutive amounts of the means of production. We can take Marx and Engels's lead and put them into the independent producers' class position.

Marx and Engels call these classes the "lower middle class" or the "lower strata of the middle class" (Marx & Engels, 1978, pp. 479, 482). How are we to consider these as middle classes? Marx and Engels are using a very old definition of the middle class as residing between the aristocracy and serfs and workers. The old estate definition considers the middle class to be part of the Third Estate of the pre–French Revolution estate system. The Third Estate also includes serfs and workers. The First Estate is the Church and the Second Estate is the aristocracy. The estate system is more of a cast structure than a class system, especial according to Marx's structural definitions. People from all three estates could own property, and the Church could own property. The middle class is used to define the emergence of the new class in society, which had become very influential with the rise of capitalism. This new class is of course the capitalists. The term *middle class* signifies a position of social stratification, which is part estate position and part class position. Simply, the middle class is between the First and Second Estates and the remainder of the Third Estate.

Marx utilizes this term to discuss the lower strata of the middle class, which can best be defined according to their structural class position as independent producers. If they do hire workers, they must also labor. This distinguishes them from capitalists who do not have to labor and can live off their investment income.

In respect to contemporary usage of the term *middle class,* independent producers only partially encompass the current class position determined to be middle class, since the vast majority of people that are considered middle class are wage laborers, such as office workers, managers, and professionals. As we shall see with bourgeoisie ideologists, this complicates matters for the Marx and Engels structural definition of class.

Bourgeois ideologists. Marx and Engels mention bourgeois ideologists during their discussion of class alliances. We will give a fuller consideration of class alliances between capitalists and workers in what follows. For the time being, we should concentrate on what supposedly makes bourgeois ideologists separate from capitalists and workers. First, what is a bourgeois ideologist? We have discussed ideology briefly in previous chapters, but our discussion defines ideology as a set of ideas and beliefs that explain, sanction, and justify the current social structure of positions, outcomes, and authority. Ideologists are people who produce and disseminate these ideas, beliefs, information, and theories at least part of the time they labor. Professions that correspond at minimum to this definition are social scientists, psychologists, teachers, journalists, scholars, lawyers, clerics, bureaucrats, and writers. Other groups such as natural scientists, physicians, engineers, and technicians can occasionally be included. Chapter 7 has a longer treatment of Marx's understanding of ideology.

The former group is composed of people who disseminate information where social, legal, and cultural information is being produced and disseminated. The latter group are not necessarily producing social, legal, and cultural information; rather, they produce natural scientific and technical information. Information that is structured as natural scientific and technical can be utilized for social, legal, and cultural ends. In addition, natural scientists, engineers, and technicians could attempt to use their training to influence cultural, social, and legal matters. For example, an engineer could conclude that only a certain type of power plant can be used in a certain country, thus affecting the social outcomes in the country. Whether the engineer was biased in her assessment, conscientiously or not, affects what ideas, beliefs, information, and theories are considered legitimate. The production of natural scientific or technical knowledge can have bias contained within it. More directly, information could be selectively disseminated to further a particular interest.

Today the majority, if not all, of these professions that can be classified as bourgeois ideologists are wage-labor jobs or independent-producer jobs. That is, the practitioners of these positions must sell their labor or the products and services of their labor to gain subsistence. This means that each of the ideologist professions could be easily classified as either in the worker or independent producer class positions.

But Marx and Engels set them as a separate class position from workers and independent producers. This means that the delineation of bourgeois ideologists does not conform to the structural definition of class as laid out by Marx and Engels. When we consider class interests and class alliances, it will become clear that bourgeois ideologists can be considered class allies of the working class if they identify with working-class interests. They could be class allies of capitalists if they receive high wages and identify with the class interests of capitalists, or they could identify with the interests of workers even though they receive high wages. Marx thinks that some bourgeois ideologists will do so because they know the truth of capitalist social dynamics. We will look into this further when we consider objective interests below.

Lumpen proletariat. The *lumpen proletariat* is the term used in *The 18th Brumaire of Louis Bonaparte* and in *Capital* to describe the class that Marx and Engels call the dangerous class and social scum in the *Manifesto*. They describe the lumpen proletariat as such:

> The "dangerous class," the social scum, that passively rotting mass thrown off by the lowest layers of old society, may, here and there, be swept into the movement by a proletarian revolution; its conditions of life, however, prepare it far more for the part of a bribed tool of reactionary intrigue. (Marx & Engels, 1978, p. 482)

The description provided for the lumpen proletariat is somewhat unclear. Commonly, the **lumpen proletariat** is defined as the chronically unemployed, the homeless, and career criminals (Marx, 1990, p. 797). These groups are not coextensive, such as the chronically unemployed may be homeless, some homeless people are employed, and not all career criminals are not employed in legal occupations or homeless. In these groups, the class location of the chronically unemployed and the homeless, according to the structural questions of Table 4.1, would be classified as workers since they own their own labor power but do not own enough of the means of production to provide for their own subsistence at a socially acceptable level. Some homeless people may labor enough to provide for their own subsistence but are unable to afford the socially acceptable level of housing. In addition, some chronically unemployed and some homeless people could own amounts of the means of production to provide for some of their socially acceptable subsistence but not all. For example, a chronically unemployed homeless person may own a vehicle that they use to haul items for a fee. They do not earn enough fees to provide for their own subsistence at a socially acceptable level, which would be to afford rent payments. They may earn just enough to eat and put gasoline in their vehicle.

Based on this analysis, why aren't the chronically unemployed and the homeless workers? Workers who are temporally unemployed have the same structural class position as currently employed workers. Homeless people who must sell their labor also have the same class position as workers. So why the separated designation by Marx and Engels? The description, which they provide in the *Manifesto*, considers the physical conditions of the lumpen proletariat as determining them as being ready to participate in class alliances with reactionary forces—that is, with capitalists.

The lumpen proletariat are disconnected from the majority of the working classes; thus, they are not able to realize their objective interests and their objective class position. They are not in workplaces with other workers and perhaps live outside of worker communities. Thus, they are not regularly in contact with workers. Additionally, because they are without a dependable means of obtaining socially acceptable levels of subsistence, their own short-term interests are met by being paid to work as a repressive force for capitalist interests. The lumpen proletariat is a pool of unemployed or underemployed people that can be used as strikebreakers or for counterrevolutionary action.

Objectively, the lumpen proletariat is in the class position of workers. Marx and Engels's description of the lumpen proletariat as a different class from workers is somewhat extreme. Rather, they are members of the working class that have not subjectively formed themselves into the working class. Marx and Engels's analysis of class is not objectively consistent, but it is consistent regarding subjective class formation. Marx and Engels's analysis is consistent with the reality of the time when the lumpen proletariat was utilized for counterrevolutionary action. But even though this classification is empirically true, it is theoretically lacking. Simply, the lumpen proletariat are members of the working class who are antagonistic with other members of the working class. Thus, they have not realized they are part of the working class and have the same objective class interests. These aspects of the lumpen proletariat will be considered further next.

What Are the Interests of the Classes Listed and Are These Interests Objective?

Capitalists and workers. The *Manifesto* and the work of Marx and Engels in general understand that the interests of one class are contrary to the class interests of another class. This antagonism may not be as simple as they present it. But, according to the processes of capitalism and the various ownership arrangements that determine structural class positions, the objective interests of workers and capitalists regarding management and ownership of the means of production are antagonistic in the long term. Short- and medium-term class alliances aside (to be discussed next), structurally, workers and capitalists gain when the other loses.

Marx and Engels develop an account of the antagonistic objective interests of workers and capitalists in the *Manifesto*. A systematic account of these antagonistic interests is developed by Marx in *Capital*, but the basic idea that capitalists' interests are met by exploiting workers and workers' interests are met by converting the means of production into public property are clear in the *Manifesto* (Marx & Engels, 1978, pp. 478–479, 484).

These interests are objective because the needs of individual capitalists and workers can only be satisfied if they maintain or alter their class position. In order for capitalists to maintain a high level of need satisfaction, they must exploit workers to do so. This means that objectively, capitalists' needs are satisfied according to their current class position. If an individual capitalist is outcompeted by other capitalists or if workers succeed in turning the means of production into public property then this individual capitalist will not be able to consume at a high level.

Workers' interests are also objective because their class position determines how their needs will be met. Workers' basic needs may be met within capitalism. The only way to alleviate the exploitation and alienation that workers suffer from within capitalism is to abolish private property. Workers benefit from public ownership of the means of production because of their class position, and they suffer from lack of public ownership because of their class position. The interests of capitalists and workers concerning ownership of the means of production are objective because it affects their need satisfaction. This is true even if they are not consciously aware of the benefits and detriments caused by capitalist class relations.

Independent producers. Marx and Engels find that the dynamics of capitalism are detrimental to independent producers. They are in competition with capitalists who eventually can outdo them (Marx & Engels, 1978, pp. 479–480). The result of this competition is a loss of ownership of sufficient amounts of the means of production, and independent producers become part of the working class. For this reason, their objective interests are ultimately the same as workers' interests (Marx & Engels, 1978, p. 482).

The long-term horizon for the satisfaction of independent producers' needs is the same as that for workers' needs because over the long term, independent producers will be forced into the working class. This does not mean that current independent producers recognize their objective long-term interests. Marx and Engels find that the short- to medium-term interests of independent producers are an attempt to maintain their current position: "They are therefore not revolutionary, but conservative. Nay more, they are reactionary, for they try to roll back the wheel of history" (Marx & Engels, 1978, p. 482).

These two very different sets of class interests are objective considering the time index mentioned. Since we have already discussed worker interests, we will consider the unique class interests of independent producers.

Short- to medium-term independent producers can attempt to prevent the encroachment of capitalists through what Marx and Engels call "Petty-Bourgeois Socialism" (Marx & Engels, 1978, pp. 493–494). This type of socialism realizes that the dynamics of capitalism are dangerous to the independent producers. Instead of intending to convert the means of production into public property, petty-bourgeois socialists wish to protect small ownership units through laws preventing the formation of large holdings. Marx and Engels find such a policy to be futile since the long-run dynamics of capitalism would outdo such ownership units. Once again, independent producers will be subject to the forces of capitalist accumulation whether they are aware of them or not.

Bourgeois ideologists. As was noted, bourgeois ideologists objectively occupy the structural class positions of either workers or independent producers, but their work of producing and disseminating information places them in a unique position of being a class ally of the working class. This consideration by Marx and Engels determines the tendencies for class formation of bourgeois ideologists but does not strictly consider their objective interests. Let us take a look at Marx and Engels's comment: "now a portion of the bourgeoisie goes over to the proletariat, and in particular, a portion of the bourgeois ideologists, who have raised themselves to the level of comprehending theoretically the historical movement as a whole" (Marx & Engels, 1978, p. 481).

Those bourgeois ideologists who join with the proletarians will be the ones who understand that the tendencies of capitalism make it strongly possible, if not inevitable, that workers will bring about a communist revolution. This theory of history, called historical materialism, will be discussed at length in the next chapter, but for now, how does historical inevitability determine objective interests? Marx and Engels don't comment on bourgeois ideologists being turned into workers, as is the case for independent producers who are not bourgeois ideologists. It is unclear what the level of need satisfaction is for bourgeois ideologists. We can infer that since they do not en masse join the revolutionary movement but only a portion does, they receive a high level of need satisfaction. According to Wolff and Zacharias (2007), in the year 2000 the mean yearly earnings in 2005 dollars for managers was $69,021.00 and professionals was $66,313.00, compared to the mean yearly earning of nonskilled workers, $42,749.00 (p. 32). Approximately the difference in mean earning between professionals and nonskilled workers was $24,000.00 a year. This is a larger difference in mean earning. Professionals' salaries are 55% more than the mean of nonskilled workers' salaries. There would be obvious differences in consumption levels between professionals and nonskilled workers. It seems that the short- to medium-term interests of bourgeois ideologists, using income as a proxy for objective interests, are decidedly aligned with capitalists. If bourgeois ideologists would take a pay cut with the institutionalization of communism, then their long-term interests are decidedly with capitalists also.

Why then would a portion of bourgeoisie ideologists then side with the working class according to their objective class interests? The simplest answer is to realize that the income amounts listed here are means, or averages; not all bourgeois ideologists make the amounts listed. Some ideologists may seek material improvement and security and are accordingly advocates of communism. Additionally, the bourgeoisie ideologists that are advocates of communism may want greater control over their society and their workplace and a less alienating society, which communist theory forecasts—which is to say they may want a more democratic society with greater social unity.

Lumpen proletariat. The lumpen proletariat's objective interests in the long run coincide with those of the working class since structurally they are workers. The lumpen proletariat lives in conditions that do not promote the consciousness of their class position. Thus, they do not form themselves into a class. The dire condition of the lumpen proletariat as chronically unemployed and/or homeless makes the satisfaction of their short-term interests absolutely important. This is why Marx and Engels (1978) said that "its conditions of life, however, prepare it far more for the part of a bribed tool of reactionary intrigue" (p. 482). Being without regular satisfactory employment and disconnected from the working class, the short-term interests of the lumpen proletariat are to serve the reactionary interests of capitalists. This is the case since only the capitalists, in Marx and Engels's analysis, can afford to hire the lumpen proletariat as violent enforcers.

What Is the Level of Class Consciousness of the Various Classes?

Workers. The most obvious and extended discussion of class consciousness is of workers in *The Communist Manifesto.* Marx and Engels outline the various stage of consciousness the working class has gone through since it emerged as a class. The first stage is when workers form units of resistance from single individuals to ultimately whole regions of workers. Marx and Engels outline that workers see the instruments of production as their antagonists at this first stage instead of their actual antagonists, the capitalists (Marx & Engels, 1978, p. 480). At this first stage, workers are not formed into a class because the physical conditions, which allow them to form as a class, are absent: concentration of large numbers of workers in small areas and means of communication. Lacking awareness of their class position and their objective interests results in workers seeing each other as competitors and not as allies (Marx & Engels, 1978, p. 480). This intraclass antagonism is even present at higher stages of development.

The next stage of consciousness is caused by the development of industry. The formation of industry towns and centers to bring workers together fulfills one physical condition for consciousness generation, concentration of workers: "But with the development of industry the proletariat not only increase in number: it becomes concentrated in greater masses, its strength grows, and it feels its strength more" (Marx & Engels, 1978, p. 480). At this stage, trade unions are formed and consistent action against capitalists becomes planned. Workers thus begin to realize their class position and their objective class interests. These interests are not long-term interests concerning a transition to communism. Rather, they are interested in rising wages.

The third stage, and the stage of consciousness that workers were currently in according to Marx and Engels at the time the *Manifesto* was written, is one in which the means of communication allow for increased development of trade union strength (Marx & Engels, 1978, p. 281). At this stage, workers are on the verge of realizing their class position and, accordingly, their objective class interests. Once again, competition between workers upsets this class formation (Marx & Engels, 1978, p. 281).

The Communist Manifesto can be understood as an attempt by the Communist League to further the awareness of the working class to realize their long-term objective class interests, which is the transition to communism (Marx & Engels, 1978, p. 484). The section of the *Manifesto* titled "Proletarians and Communists" is an attempt to demonstrate that (1) the long-term objective interest of workers is the transition to communism; (2) capitalism is not a natural social condition of human beings, including such social formations as the modern family and the role of women within capitalism; and (3) workers nationally and internationally are part of the same class. The first and second notions will be considered in later chapters on communism and ideology. The last idea, internationalism, should be commented on. It is a distinctive feature of Marxian socialism/communism to stress the fact that workers across the globe have the same long-term interests. As was noted, intraclass competition between workers prevents workers from realizing their class position. If one group of workers sees another group of workers, whether domestic, immigrants, or of another nation, as its enemy, this lessens worker political power and distracts workers from their true capitalist antagonists.

Marx and Engels even note that what makes the Communist League different from other worker parties is its acknowledgment of workers being an international class (Marx & Engels, 1978, p. 484). This is an important point, since the greatest asset workers have is their sheer numbers. Wright estimates the working class as 40% to 59% of the U.S. workforce in 1985, and Wolff and Zacharias (2007) put the estimate at 40% to 48% in 2000, depending on classification and working class interest identification (p. 30; Wright, 1985, pp. 195, 260). Samir Amin estimates the raw numbers of the international working class at half the world population, about 3 billion persons (Amin, 2004, p. 38). These contemporary estimates demonstrate the potential Marx and Engels realized. Theoretically, materialist class analysis renders an overwhelming understanding of the international political power of workers.

Capitalists. Even though the *Manifesto* is an attempt to inform workers of their objective interests and thereby help them become aware of their situation, there are some notable comments on the class consciousness of capitalists. The awareness of capitalists of the objective reality of the social situation, class conflict due to unequal ownership of the means of production, is not stated by Marx and Engels in the *Manifesto*. Rather, there is listed a series of conceptions of the world that Marx and Engels list as the dominant capitalist understanding of the world. These will be considered in greater detail in Chapter 7, but here we will consider only two, the naturalness of capitalism and the conservative socialist movement. Both of these notions can be understood as two types of class consciousness held by capitalists. Thus, capitalists, according to Marx and Engels's analysis, do not think that capitalism produces intractable antagonisms due to its class structure. This means that capitalists find that harmonious class relations are possible within capitalism. The two forms of capitalist class consciousness considered are commensurate with this conclusion.

The first of the two forms of class consciousness held by capitalists is the notion that capitalism is a timeless and/or natural state for human social forms. This means that capitalism is the true state of social existence for humans. Any past societies that were not capitalist, such as feudalism, can be understood not as developmental stages in human social evolution, as Marx understood them, but rather as tyrannical detours from humans' true nature. This vision of humans as naturally existing in capitalist relationships has been noted in previous chapters in the discussion of social contract doctrine. The naturalness of capitalism is part of this social contract vision. Either humans own private property naturally (Locke) or they decide that private property is the best state of affairs (Hobbes and Hume).

Either version considers capitalism as natural as human bodies or the result of an uncoerced decision (Marx & Engels, 1978, p. 487).

The upshot of this view of human societies is that any attempt at altering humans' true social nature will result in problems and eventually failure. This view is of course common today with the widespread holding of the idea that communism is contrary to human nature. Many contemporary socialist authors have attempted to dispel this idea (Gomberg, 2007; Schweickart, 1996, 2002). Marx's theory of historical materialism attempts to demonstrate that class relationships are the result of human technological development and accordingly change over time. This means that human need satisfaction and technological development determine class relationships and that any given class relationship is neither natural nor timeless. These issues will be considered in greater detail in Chapters 5 and 7.

The second form of class consciousness, conservative socialism, acknowledges that capitalism can result in detrimental outcomes for certain people but that these detriments can be rectified (Marx & Engels, 1978, p. 496). This reformist class consciousness seeks to make capitalism work better by locating inefficiencies and market failures in its current operation. Marx and Engels's discussion notes such actions as trade duties and prison reform, but we could easily include public education, sanitation, health and safety regulations, public housing, transfer payments, and unemployment insurance (Marx & Engels, 1978, pp. 496–497). Marx and Engels recognize that bourgeois socialism is a real political movement that seeks to improve people's lives by addressing the shortcomings of capitalism. As was noted, they do not recognize that these reforms can be a major mechanism to postpone revolutionary action. Marx and Engels find that the structural tendencies of capitalism will produce economic crisis and detrimental outcomes for the working class. The result of these detriments is revolutionary action. This means that a reformist measure, which is basically a welfare state, can never change the outcomes of capitalism.

As will be shown in later chapters, Marx analyzes the operation of capitalism to be based on exploitation. One can't have capitalism without exploitation. Thus, the welfare state only slows down the transition to socialism by lessening the impact of exploitation on people's lives. The welfare state does not eliminate exploitation; only communism does. In short, the class consciousness of capitalists, of both forms, is an incorrect grasping of the dynamics of the social world according to Marx and Engels.

Independent producers. It was discussed that the long-term objective interests of independent producers are the same as those of workers, since in the long run most independent producers will be outcompeted by capitalists.

Being outcompeted will result in these independent producers falling into the working class. They do not understand their long-term goals because their consciousness of social reality is incorrect. As previously noted, independent producers wish to preserve their class position in society. This, according to Marx and Engels, is impossible since capitalist economic development tends toward the concentration and the centralization of capital. This is a tendency for small groups of capitalists to own large shares of the means of production (Marx, 1991, p. 349).

Bourgeois ideologists. Bourgeois ideologists have a unique place in Marx and Engels's class analysis, since they objectively conform to the class position of workers, but they are obviously class allies of capitalists due to their privileged income levels. Their consciousness of the social structure is based upon their objective interests if they can count on maintaining a higher income than workers do. The portion of bourgeois ideologists that sides with the working class politically does so because they "have raised themselves to the level of comprehending theoretically the historical movement as a whole" (Marx & Engels, 1978, p. 481). This means that this portion of bourgeois ideologists correctly grasps the tendencies of social development; their class consciousness is a correct approximation of social reality. That some bourgeois ideologists have a correct understanding of their social world does not answer the question of why they have this correct understanding, in particular, since in general the objective class interests of bourgeois ideologists are in alignment with those of capitalists, at least in the short to medium term. This is especially the case if we consider income alone. Other factors, such as an interest in such traditional communist goals as workplace democracy or democratic control over investment or moral considerations, are unclear in the *Manifesto*. In the end, a more nuanced appraisal of the material interests of different sections of bourgeois ideologists—or, in today's parlance, different sections of the middle class—would help shed light on this question. This has been done by Wright (1985, 1986) but won't be discussed further here since it extends beyond Marx's original analysis.

In review, bourgeois ideologists as a whole have an awareness of their situation that is basically correct: They are paid high wages by capitalists, and thus their interests are in alignment with those of capitalists. It is unclear why a certain portion of bourgeois ideologists sides with the working class. It is also unclear why some of them have an understanding that correctly approximates the tendencies of their social world.

Lumpen proletariat. As discussed previously, the lumpen proletariat are objectively located in the working class position, but they have not formed themselves into a class that understands its class position and its interests due to their lack of correct class consciousness. To review, the lumpen proletariat have an incorrect grasp of their social world because they are physically separated from the working class, being chronically unemployed or homeless. Their class consciousness accordingly does not have the causal factor of interaction with members of the working class. The concentration of the working class brought about their own development of class consciousness. Thus, it seems that the lumpen proletariat's separation is the cause of their lack of correct class consciousness, at least of their long-term interests. In the short and medium term, the lumpen proletariat, due to their dire economic position, meet their needs by acting as a counterrevolutionary force for capitalists or through criminal activity. The lumpen proletariat's reactionary actions make sense given their objective needs.

What Class Alliances and Cross-Class Identifications Are Noted?

Capitalists and workers. Marx and Engels of course see the main class conflict dynamic of capitalism to be between capitalists and workers. More extensive contemporary analysis has attempted to identify the formation of weak class alliances and cross-class identification of workers with capitalist goals, at the expense of workers in other countries or at the expense of some workers being reduced to second-class status, such as racial minorities or women (Baran & Sweezy, 1966; Marcuse, 1964; Wright, 1985). Marx and Engels find that there is only conflict between workers and capitalists other than this instance: Previous to capitalism, workers and capitalists were allies due to cross-class identification with the common goal of overthrowing feudalism (Marx & Engels, 1978, p. 481). Capitalists desiring to have the freedom to own the means of production and workers desiring to have the freedom to sell their labor brought them into an alliance against a common enemy, the aristocracy, whose political rights under feudalism allowed them to seize property and command labor.

Conservative socialism can be understood as a weak class alliance in which capitalists promote workers to identify with the goals of capitalism. It makes the basic need satisfaction more assured in order to prevent the development of revolutionary consciousness of workers.

Independent producers. On the one hand, independent producers' objective interests are contrary to the interests of capitalists. Any legislation that preserves their small business prevents the growth of capitalists' ownership of capital. Marx and Engels do not note any cross-class identification with capitalists by independent producers. A desire to identify with or emulate successful capitalists is not noted. On the other hand, independent producers are noted for allying with workers due to the long-term prospects of them being reduced to workers:

> If by chance they are revolutionary, they are so only in view of their impending transfer into the proletariat, they thus defend not their present, but their future interests, they desert their own standpoint to place themselves at that of the proletariat. (Marx & Engels, 1978, p. 482)

It is interesting to point out, and to reinforce the centrality of objective class interests in Marx and Engels's analysis of class formation, that independent producers may have cross-class identification because it is in their own interest.

Bourgeois ideologists. The alliance between the portion of bourgeois ideologists and workers is due to cross-class identification. As has been pointed out many times, it's unclear how siding with workers serves the interest of this portion of bourgeois ideologists.

Lumpen proletariat. The lumpen proletariat are clearly in alliance with capitalists in the short term due to their dire economic circumstances. They have formed a weak class alliance, where their allegiance to the goals of capitalists is due to the pay that they receive as their reactionary force.

It is interesting to note that the alliances between classes mentioned by Marx and Engels that occur are overwhelmingly, other than the lumpen proletariat, due to cross-class identification, and all of these are due to common interests except the ambiguous position of the bourgeois ideologists. The lumpen proletariat have a weak class alliance with the capitalists due to their dire poverty. In addition, and contrary to Marx and Engels's analysis, contemporary class alliances between workers and capitalists are composed of weak alliances due to the welfare state and workers' cross-class identification with capitalist interests due to the materially rational desirability of increased income and wealth.

What Ideological Limitations Are Listed?

As was discussed in the analytic sections, individuals can act against their class interest either because they gain by acting against them, such as the lumpen proletariat's reactionary activity, or they can be limited by certain ideologies, which prevent them from understanding their objective class interests and their objective class position. Ideological limitations are a kind of incorrect comprehension of reality. They thereby prevent correct class consciousness from developing. These ideological limitations can take the form of not having a conception of one's class position, thinking one is part of another class position than one is, identifying with another class or the goals of that class even if it is detrimental to one's own interests, and identifying with other notions about one's social formation that do not address one's interests fully or are even detrimental to one's interests, such as nationalism, racism, free enterprise enthusiasm, or supernatural ideas about social formation.

Workers. Two ideological limitations are listed in the *Manifesto* that can prevent workers from achieving revolutionary class consciousness: other-worker bias and nationalism (Marx & Engels, 1978, pp. 481, 484, 488). Other-worker bias is when workers do not identify with other workers as members of the same class. This nonidentification can be due to competition between workers or workers finding another group of workers, based on skill, type of work, race, or gender, as being opposed to or outside of their interests and concerns. Other-worker bias limits workers from forming class organizations, which represent their common objective interests. Nationalism as an ideological limitation prevents workers from identifying workers from other countries as having the same objective class interests. This includes immigrants within a worker's own country.

Capitalists. Many ideological limitations are listed for capitalists in the *Manifesto*. They could be held by any class even if some, like the notion of private property, are exclusively to the benefit of capitalists. We previously discussed the ideological notion that capitalism is a timeless natural state of affairs. We will consider here the idea of freedom as Marx and Engels conceive of capitalists as holding it. In the chapter on communism, we will consider Marx's critique of private property.

The notion of freedom comes up in the *Manifesto* when Marx and Engels are defending the key goal of communism: the conversion of private property into public property. One of the most important critiques of this communist goal is that the elimination of private property will abolish all freedom (Marx & Engels, 1978, pp. 485–486). Marx and Engels do not find freedom to be a simply defined matter. In particular, they think that capitalist ideology reduces the definition of freedom to mean only freedom to own private property. There could be other types of freedom, such as freedom of thought, speech, or movement, or other notions such as to be free from harm or disease, and even other constructions such as freedom to seek an education or the freedom to form a family. There are many ways of understanding freedom, but in the *Manifesto*, Marx and Engels accuse capitalist ideologists of playing a game of sleight of hand in which freedom only means freedom to control private property.

The capitalist notion of freedom is an ideological limitation regarding the development of correct class consciousness since, if it is true, it obviously makes communism seem undesirable. If the capitalist notion of freedom is true, it essentially means that communism is a society in which freedom does not exist. Marx and Engels's rebuttal to this notion is that communism is not the elimination of people's control over property, it is only the elimination of the exclusive control of private property that capitalists currently hold. Private property is replaced by public property, which means that any person can utilize this public property (Marx & Engels, 1978, pp. 485–486).

Independent producers. The noted ideological limitation for independent producers is their desire to turn back or halt the development of society to make sure their class position is preserved. Marx and Engels think this conception of history is contrary to the dynamics of capitalist economic development.

Bourgeois ideologists. There are no explicitly noted ideological limitations for bourgeois ideologists. The vast bulk of bourgeois ideologists, in particular social scientists and philosophers, produce and disseminate justifications for capitalism. The notion that freedom is being able to own private property is one of their productions. It can thus be concluded that most bourgeois ideologists always hold some kind of ideological limitation to be true—except, of course, the ones that are supporters of the communists, who have correctly comprehended the social dynamics of capitalism according to Marx.

Lumpen proletariat. There are no explicitly noted ideological limitations for the lumpen proletariat in the *Manifesto*. Marx and Engels note that they can be swept into counterrevolutionary action. In addition, it has been noted that the causal factors that help form class consciousness are not present for them. It is of course possible that the lumpen proletariat can hold ideologically limiting notions, as is discussed in *The 18th Brumaire of Louis Bonaparte*, but Marx and Engels do not address the issue in the *Manifesto*.

Conclusion

One of the most interesting aspects of Marx's structural class analysis is that it is defined by people's material requirements. Marx's class analysis is descriptive of class position, but it is also a prescriptive theory of what people should do to improve their lives. Marx's analysis is less of a method to categorize and study current awareness of class, as is typical in mainstream sociological literature. Rather, Marx provides a means to supposedly see through the current phenomena of ideology and understand what is truly in a particular class's best interest. This is a fascinating analysis but will probably offend many readers who prize their independence and their ability to make rational decisions for themselves. Can people make the right decisions for action in their political world if they have incorrect information? Marx documents many classes that have an incorrect understanding of capitalism. Do such incorrect understandings still exist today? These can be important questions if Marx is right that the common understanding of capitalism as natural and best is incorrect.

Class according to Marx is structured around differential ownership of the forces of production. This means that those who own a sizable amount of these forces will be able to exploit those who do not own sizable amounts. Class structures, according to Marx, are intrinsically antagonistic. These antagonisms will eventually become apparent. This means that Marx's theory of class analysis identifies possible ways a society will face social crisis and revolution. Even though Marx thought that communism will follow capitalism, his theory of class analysis also discusses possible means to limit social crises and perhaps postpone revolutionary attempts indefinitely through the use of class alliances and ideological limitations.

Marx's theory of class thus outlines some possible research areas relating to the level of class consciousness in light of the degree of class alliances and the pervasiveness of ideological limitations. This research would be particularly interesting when the level of basic need satisfaction is considered. Wright (1985) has performed some research in this area, as has Zweig (2000).

The great limitation of Marx's class analysis is the undertheorization of the middle class. According to Marx's theory, class position determines objective class interests. This means that the majority of the current middle class should have the class position of workers and thus have the same objective class interests. This conclusion appears contrary to the procapitalist attitudes of the middle class. As has been noted, Wright (1985, 1986) has developed a means of determining the middle class by new class position categories.

Marx's own work can encompass the phenomena of the working class through the notion of class allies. Using Marx's theory, the middle class can be understood as a segment of the working class, which is in a weak class alliance with capitalists. The alliance is based on higher wages and benefits and nicer working conditions. Thus, the procapitalist attitudes of the working class could be possibly explained by the existence of a particular weak class alliance between capitalists and professionals, skilled workers, and some semiskilled workers such as some office workers. This weak class alliance can be eroded by falling wages and declining benefits. Zweig discusses some of the erosion of the greater benefits of the middle class (2000, pp. 20–28).

Marx's theory of class is a central category of his social analysis. Before we show how class relates to his theory of history, a few questions for thought:

- How can people have objective class interests that are contrary to their political position? For example, how can an anticommunist worker have an objective interest in the establishment of communism?
- Are current sociological conceptions of an underclass comparable to Marx's understanding of the lumpen proletariat?
- In light of current analysis that utilizes income to determine class position, what are the benefits and detriments of Marx's structural approach to class?
- Is capitalism still a class-stratified society in which the antagonisms can only temporarily be mediated?
- Are the middle classes capitalists or workers? Are their long-term objective class interests the same as those of workers or capitalists?

5

Historical Materialism

W hat has come to be known as historical materialism is a theory developed by Marx and Engels that attempts to understand why and how societies change based on material causes. In particular, Marx was interested in how humans' ability to learn about and alter their natural environment can cause societies to change. In Marxian language, historical materialism is a theory of how modes of production come into existence and disappear due to the development of the productive forces. The theory of historical materialism is not simply an analysis of the dynamics of social change with no consideration of the consciousness of the actors. On the contrary, it appears that Marx's theory of historical materialism attempts to explain not only the physical possibility for new societies to develop but also how development of the productive forces brings a change in people's consciousness. Thus, historical materialism utilizes Marx's analysis of alienation, exploitation, and class to understand how people are motivated to change their societies.

Phrased in more modern language, Marx hypothesized that there are feedback loops of causation between macrostructures and microstructures, which causes a change in the social structure of societies. As briefly discussed in Chapter 2, Marx attempts to identify microbehaviors as the ground for social change, since individual people bring about these changes. The important caveat made in Chapter 2 was that microbehaviors are not natural or fixed. They change according to certain macrostructures and macrophenomena. The appearance of macrophenomena such as increased long-term unemployment, technological change, environmental decay, and declining wages can in turn cause individuals to view the potential for social change in a new light.

These same macrophenomena were brought about by a set of microbehaviors that caused the current problems or let the problems grow into their current form. The newly influenced microbehavior that seeks social change will seek to institute new macrostructures that try to rectify the problems of unemployment, wages, and pollution. As can be seen, there is a feedback loop between microbehaviors and macrophenomena, which causes society to change. Historical materialism is Marx's attempt to understand what the relevant micro- and macrostructures are that cause societal development.

This chapter will present Marx's theory of historical materialism in the following steps. First, the famous statement by Marx on historical materialism from the Preface to *A Critique of Political Economy* will be analyzed. This statement is the most commonly utilized passage when historical materialism is discussed. The passage is rather brief and in many ways leaves out Marx's reflections on microbehaviors. Marx and Engels's statements on historical materialism from *The German Ideology* will help clear up and perhaps fill in the absence of microbehaviors in the Preface statement. *The German Ideology* also has a wider consideration of historical change, in particular an analysis of how class positions emerged. Finally, consciousness development due to social change will be considered and the statements on this topic in the Preface will be discussed along with passages from *The German Ideology, The Communist Manifesto*, and *The 18th Brumaire of Louis Bonaparte*.

The Preface to *A Critique of Political Economy*

Much of the terminology used to discuss the conjectures and conclusions of classical historical materialism are taken from the Preface to *A Critique of Political Economy*. The usually cited section has been reprinted in its entirety below. Before we begin to analyze the section, I will review the relevant terminology.

Productive forces. Productive forces are composed of the means of production and labor power. Labor power is the expenditure of human physical and mental activity for the creation of goods and services. Labor power makes physical items such as food or steel, and it also makes items that have no enduring physical form such as singing or treatment by a nurse. The **means of production** are the tools, raw materials, spaces, machines, and buildings used to create goods and services.

Relations of production. Relations of production or production relations are relationships people have between themselves and the productive forces.

As was discussed in the last chapter, production relations determine class position. For example, people are in a capitalist class position because they own enough of the means of production to gain subsistence through the interest, profits, and rents that accrue to them as owners. Not all relations of production are class relations. Some relations of production are classless, such as the relations between people and the means of production within communism. Essentially these production relations are classless because everyone owns the means of production as public property.

Mode of production. A mode of production is determined by the dominant class position within a given time period. Thus, capitalism is a mode of production when capitalists are the dominant class. Of course, various class positions can exist simultaneously within a mode of production when various classes are vying for power. For example, during the end period of feudalism, lords and capitalists were in conflict for the dominant class position. Feudalism in general is defined as a mode of production in which feudal lords are in the dominant class position.

Terminology that has been little used in this work will be discussed below. These terms are *foundation* or *base, superstructure, fetters,* and *fettering.* The meanings of these terms have been widely discussed, and they form an important part of many Marxist debates.

The Preface statement on historical materialism was written by Marx after years of studying political economy and was published in 1859 when he was writing draft versions of his magnum opus *Capital.* The usually analyzed section is reprinted in its entirety here:

> The general result at which I arrived and which, once won, served as a guiding thread for my studies, can be briefly formulated as follows: In the social production of their life, men enter into definite relations that are indispensable and independent of their will, relations of production which correspond to a definite stage of development of their material productive forces. The sum total of these relations of production constitutes the economic structure of society, the real foundation, on which rises a legal and political superstructure and to which correspond definite forms of social consciousness. The mode of production of material life conditions the social, political and intellectual life process in general. It is not the consciousness of men that determines their being, but, on the contrary, their social being that determines their consciousness. At a certain stage of their development, the material productive forces of society come in conflict with the existing relations of production, or—what is but a legal expression for the same thing—with the property relations within which they have been at work hitherto. From forms of development of the productive forces these relations turn into their fetters. Then begins an epoch of social

revolution. With the change of the economic foundation the entire immense superstructure is more or less rapidly transformed. In considering such transformations a distinction should always be made between the material transformation of the economic conditions of production, which can be determined with the precision of natural science, and the legal, political, religious, aesthetic or philosophic—in short, ideological forms in which men become conscious of this conflict and fight it out. Just as our opinion of an individual is not based on what he thinks of himself, so can we not judge of such a period of transformation by its own consciousness; on the contrary, this consciousness must be explained rather from the contradictions of material life, from the existing conflict between the social productive forces and the relations of production. No social order ever perishes before all the productive forces for which there is room in it have developed; and new higher relations of production never appear before the material conditions of their existence have matured in the womb of the old society itself. Therefore mankind always sets itself only such tasks as it can solve; since, looking at the matter more closely, it will always be found that the task itself arises only when the material conditions for its solution already exist or are at least in the process of formation. In broad outlines Asiatic, ancient, feudal, and modern bourgeois modes of production can be designated as progressive epochs in the economic formation of society. The bourgeois relations of production are the last antagonistic form of the social process of production—antagonistic not in the sense of individual antagonism, but of one arising from the social conditions of life of the individuals; at the same time the productive forces developing in the womb of bourgeois society create the material conditions for the solution of that antagonism. The social formation brings, therefore, the prehistory of human society to a close. (Marx & Engels, 1978, pp. 4–5)

When social scientists and philosophers discuss classical or orthodox historical materialism, they usually have in mind the above passage. In addition to its statements on the causes of social change, there are considerations about the causes of consciousness, the nature of ideology, and the inevitability of social evolution. The statement will be analyzed in its entirety and, where appropriate, other works by Marx and Engels will be considered to provide as complete an understanding as possible of historical materialism.

To begin, a general outline of the Preface argument of historical materialism is given below, leaving out some of the more difficult and complex statements:

1. The development of human societies is determined ultimately by the development of the productive forces. For example, class societies are possible because the level of productive forces development allows for a class of nonlaborers to subsist on the surplus product produced by a class of laborers.

2. Certain types of societies correspond to certain ranges of productive force development. This term *types of societies* is synonymous with the term "modes of production." For example, a capitalist mode of production corresponds to a certain level of productive force development in which less productive forces development or more productive forces development corresponds to modes of production other than capitalism.

3. The relations of production can either assist or fetter (fettering means to hinder) the development of the productive forces. Whether the relations of production assist or fetter the development of the productive forces depends on the level productive forces development has reached.

4. Certain relations of production assist the development of the productive forces, managing how the productive forces development will meet the particular needs of the populace of a given society. Need satisfaction, as we shall see, is not discussed in the Preface but is an important part of Marx and Engels's exposition of historical materialism in *The German Ideology.*

5. The meeting of the needs of a society's population thus encourages further development of the productive forces since the populace feel that their lives are being supported and enhanced by the current relations of production. In other words, people find that the current system that distributes gains and losses is beneficial.

6. People's needs go unmet because the given dominant relations of production are unable to meet those needs. This is when the relations of production begin to fetter the development of the productive forces.

7. When this fettering occurs, people's consciousness of their society changes from acceptance to criticism and, if bad enough, to contempt. At this point, Marx finds that social revolution is possible.

8. Through a revolution, the relations of production are changed. The new relations of production are assumed to meet the needs that previously went unmet. The dynamic of a populace accepting a given social system due to need satisfaction reasserts itself and the new mode of production becomes accepted.

Now that the Preface theory of historical materialism has been outlined, an examination of the various causal factors should be considered.

Productive Forces Development as the Ultimate Cause of Social Development

First to be considered is the conjecture that the development of human societies is determined ultimately by the development of the productive forces. This point is implicitly argued in the Preface. Marx is mainly concerned with social crisis and the potential for revolution, so the material basis of all human social development is glossed over. The first sentence after the colon in the Preface does note that there is correspondence between relations of production and the forces of production, but this is getting too far ahead to properly understand the theory of historical materialism. In order to fill in the gap, a look at an earlier exposition of historical materialism will help. Marx notes in the Preface that this earlier exposition by him and Engels on historical materialism was never published (Marx & Engels, 1978, p. 5). This earlier exposition was *The German Ideology*, whose first section on Feuerbach contains some detailed analysis of human history and material development.

In *The German Ideology*, Marx and Engels describe the material basis of social development as follows:

> [T]he first premise of all human existence and, therefore, of all history, the premise, namely, that men must be in a position to live in order to be able to "make history." But life involves before everything else eating and drinking, a habitation, clothing and many other things. The first historical act is thus the production of the means to satisfy these needs, the production of material life itself. (Marx & Engels, 1978, pp. 155–156)

> Men can be distinguished from animals by consciousness, by religion or anything else you like. They themselves begin to distinguish themselves from animals as soon as they begin to *produce* their means of subsistence, a step which is conditioned by their physical organization. By producing their means of subsistence men are indirectly producing the actual material life. (Marx & Engels, 1978, p. 150)

In *The German Ideology*, Marx and Engels argue that human history is the history of productive development. Humans must actively gain their subsistence. They must expend some amount of effort in order to live: searching for food, planning where to search, seeking and constructing shelters. All animals perform such activities. The important distinction is that humans can produce their subsistence by learning about their environment and changing their environment. Humans can accumulate knowledge about how to gain subsistence. This means that as humans developed, there was the tendency for later generations to know more than preceding generations about how to gain subsistence. Since human labor is one part of the productive forces, gains in knowledge are a development of the productive forces.

For example, early human societies developed from hunter-gatherers to settled agrarians over a period of several thousand years. The earliest domestication of plants (wheat, pea, and olives) occurred in Southwest Asia by 8500 B.C. (Diamond, 1997, p. 100). The period from the emergence of

modern humans 130,000 years ago and the establishment of the first settle-
ment of agrarian communities spans a period of time during which humans
migrated to all continents except Antarctica (Barraclough & Overy, 1999,
p. 32). During this span of time, humans learned about how to grow food
and eventually shifted from hunter-gatherers to settled farmers (Diamond,
1997, pp. 104–113). Humans acquired the knowledge of how to farm over
thousands of years and eventually shifted to gaining their subsistence mainly
through agriculture. Human society changed due to an increase in knowledge.
This is a development of the productive forces.

In addition, humans can accumulate and develop the other part of the
productive forces, the means of production. Humans evolved from other
tool users, meaning they have always been tool users (Barraclough & Overy,
1999, p. 30). The tools humans "inherited" from their evolutionary predecessors were used to make further tools, including buildings, and to alter
their environments. Humans have altered environments by transplanting
crops, clearing forests, damming rivers, draining swamps, making roads,
building settlements, and creating irrigation canals. These built environments
accumulate over time.

For example, the irrigation canals built generations ago can be expanded
to cover more acres of cropland. Buildings where tools are created can be
where these tools are used to create new ones. Hammers bring about new
and better hammers. Iron is used to make better iron. Towns are places
where future cities are planned. The development of the productive forces is
the accumulation of the means of production.

As the productive forces develop, humans are able to produce a surplus
of output. Mainly this surplus output is food. This allows for the growth of
population. As will be discussed in greater detail in what follows, the growth
of population allows for new types of societies. For now, it is important to
point out that the development of the productive forces is also simply more
people (Marx & Engels, 1978, p. 150). More people means that more can
be done. More swamps drained. More roads built. This is the case even holding the level of knowledge and technological development constant.

After humans satisfy their natural needs and after they have developed the
productive forces to make this satisfaction more secure, humans begin to
develop new needs (Marx & Engels, 1978, p. 156). The development of the
productive forces causes the development of new needs. For example, when
they have secure food and housing, humans may seek to develop other
abilities such as varied cooking styles, architectural flourishes, increased
interest in decorative clothing, more contemplation of their place in the cos-
mos, or increased time spent in the creation of art. Marx and Engels don't
readily distinguish between a want and a need. Many people may find their

enjoyment of art, contemplation of conscience, or the study of plants to be more important to them than anything else. This means that people may need many activities and items to make their lives fulfilling.

The development of the productive forces makes new needs possible, and humans are driven, according to Marx and Engels, to fulfill their needs. This desire for new need fulfillment is an important component to understanding the theory of historical materialism. As will be shown, the correspondence between relations of production and productive forces are best understood when need satisfaction has a role to play. Accordingly, the issues of fettering and social revolution are best understood when need satisfaction or lack thereof is considered. In addition, making the causal connection between microbehaviors and macrophenomena is accomplished when the fulfillment or frustration of needs comes into play. What causes individuals to aggregate their activity and cause social change? Social change is caused by wide-scale interest in macrochanges to allow for micro-level increases in need satisfaction.

The Division of Labor and the Emergence of Classes

The first sentence of the Preface section states that definite relations of production correspond to a definite stage of productive forces development. Marx and Engels think that the productive forces have a tendency to increase over time. In addition, Marx finds that since the development of settled agriculture, human societies have developed in a direction in which class societies have become prevalent, but not all class societies are the same. In addition, production relations, or certain types of classes, *correspond* to a certain level of productive forces development. Accordingly, a given level of productive forces development cannot have multiple types of corresponding class societies. Rather, a range of productive forces correspond either to a distinct set of relations of production or to a transitional period of two sets of relations of production. Analytically, a relationship can be established between increases in productive forces development and the development of certain sets of production relations.

Before correspondence between relations of production and forces is discussed in greater detail, the origin of relations of production must be addressed. Relations of production are mainly class distinctions. There are relations of production that are not based on class, such as primitive egalitarian societies. Marxian classes are related to differential ownership of the productive forces. A class always exists in relation to another different class. In order for a slave to exist, there must be a slave owner. In order for a capitalist to exist, there must be a worker.

How does differential ownership of the productive forces become possible? There are two necessary causes for the emergence of differential property in Marx's view: the separation of some people from control of the means of production and the **division of labor**. Mainly, Marx and Engels find that people become separated from the means of production by force. People became forced into subordinate class positions in early human societies through slavery by conquest (Marx & Engels, 1978, p. 151). Later in human history during the development of capitalism, serfs were forced off the land and made to work in factories (Marx & Engels, 1978, p. 431). These are instances of what Marx calls primitive accumulation. Marx does not find that differential ownership in the means of production occurs through thrift, natural ability, or reward for risk. Nor does Marx conceive of immigration as a possible cause. This would be the case when people emigrate to a new nation and must sell their labor to survive. This example does not consider why they must emigrate in the first place. Why must they move to sell their labor? Why don't they have access to the means of production in their own country? These are tertiary issues when the main cause of separation of people from the means of production is force.

How does the division of labor make classes possible and how is the division of labor related to force in the creation of classes? These questions will be answered in order, but first we need to review what the division of labor is. Simply, the division of labor is when people specialize in particular trades and when the mental and manual labors of a society are performed by different people.

The first kind of division of labor can be demonstrated with an example of people becoming specialists. We can imagine a simple hypothetical situation in which a group of people perform several tasks to reproduce their society. These tasks are child care, food production, and shelter maintenance. Of course, even the most technologically basic human society will have more tasks than this, but we'll keep this example simple. We'll say that all people of this society perform all of these tasks, and some people may do different tasks at different times, but they all perform some of these tasks sometime. These labor tasks would become divided if some people specialized in a single task, such as some people specializing as food producers, others taking care of children, and others as shelter maintainers.

As we see, the division of labor is the separation of the tasks a society performs to reproduce itself into tasks that people can specialize in. Why is this done? The division of labor is specialization in a particular task, and this specialization allows for greater output (Marx & Engels, 1978, p. 150). The division of labor is a development of the productive forces. This division of labor allows for greater output and accordingly greater satisfaction of people's needs. People becoming specialized at child care or food production become better carers and better producers. They produce a better outcome, better-cared-for children, and more food.

The second kind of division of labor is when mental and manual labor become divided. For Marx, the most important aspects of the division between mental and manual labor are the activities of creation, planning, and management. All labor tasks involve creation, planning, and management. Take child care, for example. A child-care person not only physically cares for a child, feeding, cleaning, teaching, and nurturing them. The carer also creates what the child will be taught and through what means. The carer decides on what combination of formal methods and experiences the child will be exposed to in order to facilitate the subjects to be learned. Carers plan when these lessons and events will take place. They also manage their time and make changes to their schedule.

All these mental labor subtasks of child caring can be divided between people. One person can create the child-care curriculum, plan its execution, and manage its implementation and make decisions about changes. Another person or persons can carry out the creations, plans, and orders of the former person.

The division of labor is an important concept in the history of economic and sociological theory. In the *Republic*, written in the early 4th century B.C., Plato discusses how the division of labor is part of the origin of settled existence. Adam Smith notes in the *Wealth of Nations*, published in 1776, that the division of labor allows for productivity increases. By the time Marx wrote about the division of labor, this idea was firmly established within the social sciences. After Marx, the sociologist Émile Durkheim discussed the importance of the division of labor and its possible biological basis in *The Division of Labor in Society*, written in 1893.

Marx and Engels in *The German Ideology* find that the division of labor corresponds to definite types of ownership. This means that the divisions of labor and classes correspond (Marx & Engels, 1978, p. 151). If ownership of the forces of production is differential ownership, then classes exist. Differential ownership of productive forces results in the owner being an authority over how the forces are used. This authority over the use of the productive forces corresponds in a rather rough way to control any labor task. The owner may not have the ability to create, plan, manage, or physically produce. Nonetheless, the owner is able to decide on what will be created and how much will be created and can decide on who will make it and what changes will be made that arise during production.

Ownership is control over labor tasks. This is a kind of division of labor that is all encompassing and mediates all other subtasks of a labor activity.

The owner of a given set of productive forces can decide when something will be produced. All other laborers engaged in this task must await their commands in order to commence. Their physical activities and their mental activities are dependent on an owner's decisions. Thus, a person who creates a product is subject to the decisions of the owner of the productive forces. The same applies to the physical laborers whose tasks can be divided or additional ones added according to the decisions of the owner. Or their tasks can be sped up or their workload reduced.

This inability to control the product of one's labor and the labor task is alienation. As can be seen, the possibility of alienation is the result not only of a division of labor but also of the existence of classes. Why must the division of labor correspond to classes? Why would people allow for some to make decisions for them when, according to Marx's theory of human nature, people find great satisfaction in having control over the productive forces so they can expand their abilities? In *The German Ideology*, Marx and Engels note that there is a gradual process of the emergence of class, which has its origin with hierarchical relationship within the family:

> The first form of ownership is tribal ownership. It corresponds to the undeveloped stage of production, at which a people lives by hunting and fishing, by the rearing of beasts, or in the highest stage, agriculture. In the latter case it presupposes a great mass of uncultivated stretches of land. The division of labour is at this stage still very elementary and is confined to a further extension of the natural division of labour existing in the family. The social structure is, therefore, limited to an extension of the family; patriarchal family chieftain, below them the members of the tribe, finally slaves. The slavery latent in the family only develops gradually with the increase of population, the growth of wants, and with the extension of external relations, both of war and of barter. (Marx & Engels, 1978, p. 151)

The family has a latent form of slavery, which forms the basis of the existence of actual slavery. What this means for the connection between the division of labor and classes is that the possibility of the division of labor allows for not only further divisions of labor but also the emergence of classes.

The division of labor at its most basic level is only possible if some people can produce enough of a given product, food most importantly, to allow other people to devote their time to other tasks. For example, a person can specialize in child care if the production of food by others in their society allows them to no longer engage in the activity of producing food. This means that food producers produce a surplus of food beyond their own subsistence needs. This same idea applies to the emergence of classes. If there exists a situation in which some people are held in bondage, as slaves, there must be others who can keep them in bondage. If there is not a sufficient amount of surplus to allow some people to watch slaves, or at least spend time capturing escaped slaves, then the existence of slavery is impossible. The emergence of classes depends on the possibility of a division of labor. Exploitation in which one person benefits at the expense of another can only exist when the laborer produces a surplus.

Types of Correspondence

Now that we have discussed how the development of the productive forces allows for the division of labor, which in turn allows for the emergence of classes, we can turn to considerations of correspondence between the productive forces and the relations of production. As has been shown, Marx finds that, first, a certain range of the productive forces development corresponds to particular sets of production relations. Second, class relations require surplus production. In short, the emergence of a surplus allows for classes to emerge and the ongoing development of the productive forces brings about the development of society from one set of production relations to another.

Marx, in the Preface statement on historical materialism, notes that the sets of production relations that have occurred can be grouped into four modes of production: Asiatic, ancient, feudal, and modern bourgeois (Marx & Engels, 1978, p. 5). In *The German Ideology*, Marx and Engels discuss the following types of ownership: tribal, ancient communal, and state ownership, feudal, or estate property (Marx & Engels, 1978, pp. 151–152). They also provide a history of the rise of capitalism within the feudal period, which can be taken as one of Marx and Engels's statements on capitalism as a separate mode of production (Marx & Engels, 1978, pp. 176–186). In addition, in *The Communist Manifesto*, Marx and Engels identify ancient slave societies, the feudal period of the Middle Ages, and modern bourgeois society (Marx & Engels, 1978, p. 474). In a footnote to the English edition of 1888, Engels notes that before slave societies existed, there were primitive communist societies in which there were no classes (Marx & Engels, 1978, p. 473, footnote 6).

From these various sources, it has become standard to consider the following modes of production in historical order: primitive communism, slave societies, feudalism, and capitalism. The Asiatic mode of production existed in China and India at the same time as slave societies, feudalism, and capitalism existed in the West. Asiatic production is studied as an alternate case since capitalism arose historically out of Western European feudalism. We will consider the development of primitive communism to slave societies to feudalism to capitalism and the outlier case of the Asiatic mode of production in future sections. For now, we will briefly comment on correspondence.

Ranges of development of the productive forces correspond to a particular set of production relations. Marx finds that there are signification similarities between instances of particular sets of production relations to classify them within a single mode of production. For example, feudalism existed from the fall of the Roman Empire until the 19th century in various European countries (Russian serfs were finally emancipated in 1861) according to Marx's analysis. Of course, some countries such as England lost many of the vestiges of feudalism much sooner and became capitalist societies.

Holding these particular historical cases aside, there is a similarity between different types of feudalism because their production relations are the same. Since the production relations of class societies are class relationships, one can look at two different periods and compare the class relationships. If they are the same then they are the same kind of mode of production. For example, feudalism is distinguished from different class societies because of the particular class relationships that exist. In particular, lords own part of the labor power of serfs, unlike in slavery, where slave owners own all the labor power of slaves, and within capitalism, where capitalists own none of the labor power of workers. Within feudalism, lords are able to decide how a serf's time is used for a particular part of the year or, in later feudalism, serfs would owe their lords a certain amount of money. What distinguishes this command over a person's time or the issuing of a payment due is that serfs cannot refuse to provide the time or the money. Workers within capitalism can refuse to labor or refuse a contract in which payments will be due in the future. This is not the case for serfs. If a person can be ordered to perform labor or to submit a payment without their consent, they are subject to the class relationships of feudalism.

Differing levels of productive forces development can correspond to the same kind of class relationships/production relations. If different ranges of productive forces development can correspond to the same kind of production relations, why do production relations change? This question is of the utmost importance to Marx since it helps him argue that capitalism will one day be replaced with communism. Why production relations change is a question about fettering, which is where our discussion will now turn.

Assisting and Fettering Productive Forces Development

Particular ranges of productive forces development correspond to certain sets of production relations. This is why Marx finds that he can group the development of human society into various stages. Why do production relations change? Marx's answer is that certain sets of production relations assist the development of the productive forces, whereas at other times they hinder the development of the productive forces. Marx's term for hindering the development of the productive forces is **fettering**. The verb *to fetter* means to restrain, hinder, or impede. To be fettered also means to be restrained, shackled, or hindered. We can simply equate fettering with the terms used to define it. Therefore, we can say that the fettering of productive forces' development is the same as restraining or hindering productive forces' development.

To begin, how can production relations affect the development of the productive forces? Since production relations are class relations in societies with classes, is there something about classes that can assist or fetter the development of the productive forces? Since Marx's theory of class demonstrates relations of exploitation, inequality, and domination, do any of these relationships help establish how relations of production can assist or fetter the development of the productive forces? As will be shown in the chapter on economics, the existence of exploitation in the production process explains the existence of surplus production. Dominant classes are able to control this surplus production because they have an unequal ownership of the productive forces. Exploitation is thus possible because of domination and inequality. Important in this dynamic is that continued exploitation is required for dominant classes to maintain their level of consumption, or their bare subsistence, without having to labor. Thus, exploiting classes have an incentive to keep exploiting others if they wish to live without laboring.

If exploiting classes have a preference to consume without laboring then they have an incentive to maintain an exploitative relationship with the subordinate classes. A preference to consume without laboring only explains why exploitation can continue; all else held equal, it does not explain how an exploitative relationship can bring about development of the productive forces. Two obvious preferences arise that would utilize exploitation as a means for development of the productive forces: (1) a preference for increasing consumption and (2) a preference to maintain one's exploitative position while there is sustained competition from other exploiters.

The first preference, for increasing consumption, could obviously be satisfied by increasing the rate or the gross amount of exploitation. Marx has a quantitative analysis for these occurrences within capitalism, which will be discussed later. For now, a simple example will suffice. If an exploiter, such as a slave owner, wishes to increase their consumption, they could make their slaves work longer, make them more productive, or obtain more slaves. All of these activities would produce more output that the slave owner could directly consume, trade, or sell. Productive forces development has occurred in particular when productivity has increased and/or the amount of people that can be used for production has increased. Working people longer without reinvesting their output for productivity increases or scale of production increases does not in itself increase the productive forces. Thus, a preference for more consumption may result in productive forces development but does not have to.

The second preference, to maintain one's exploitative position in the face of competition from other exploiters, is an important motivation that Marx assumes is a driving force of capitalism. As was discussed in the chapter on class, capitalists can be antagonistic toward other members of their class since they are in competition for market share. If people have a preference to stay capitalists, they will try to increase the exploitation of their workforce. This can be done by the same measure as above: by having their employees work longer or be more productive or by having a larger workforce. Interestingly, even though capitalists have high incomes, this income does not represent the total revenue they achieve through exploitation. Wolff and Zacharias (2007) put the mean income for capitalists in the year 2000 at $825,826, in 2005 dollars (p. 33). The gains from exploitation are reinvested in new equipment, plants, stores, and a larger workforce. Thus, the preference to maintain one's position as an exploiter would result in development of the productive forces.

Competition between capitalists as a driver of technical change is a fundamental assumption in Marx's political economy. As will be discussed in the chapter on economics, Marx uses competition-driven technical change as a means to explain unemployment and economic crises.

From the above examples, it can be understood that dominant classes have an impetus to develop the productive forces. What about the subordinate classes? As will be shown, subordinate classes are pivotal in Marx's theory of social genesis. Their role in facilitating the development of the means of production can be complex. On one hand, subordinate classes must comply with the desires of the dominant classes to survive, avoid punishment, or stay employed. They thus have good reason to go along with the increased drive for exploitation to maintain their means of subsistence or their safety. What about increased consumption? If subordinate classes can capture part of the increase in output, which is the result of development of the productive forces, they have every reason to facilitate development. Indeed, many subordinate classes seek productive improvements because they value craftsmanship or wish to make their society better. Numerous workers at all skill levels devote themselves to work that will improve people's lives through productivity increases and general increases in the quality of life, with no hope for riches as the result of their actions. Of course, this is the hope of many people who also become wealthy through their developments. People don't seek to improve their world only if it will make them wealthy.

Thus, the exploited classes can participate in the direction the exploiting classes decide for the development of the productive forces, since there can be the hope that these developments will assist themselves and others. Indeed, Marx comments in *Value, Prices and Profit* that wages have two components: a physical component and a social component (Marx & Engels, 1968, p. 222). The physical component is the bare subsistence a person needs to reproduce their labor power and provide for their household. This can be a very low amount, since bare subsistence is only minimal caloric requirements, minimal shelter, and other bare necessities. This means that the physical-component wage should allow the absolute minimum of food to be consumed along with shelter, which can be overcrowded, in disrepair, or nonstandard such as a tent community.

The social component of wages is what is above the natural component, and it has no limit other than that which would result in capitalists gaining no surplus value. Marx calls this flexible component of the wage social because it is set by the current standards of a given society. The social component of wages can range anywhere from being identical with the physical component of the wage to including consumption of items we may currently find fantastical. Such wages must provide all people with the means to purchase their own home, tertiary education for their children, an early retirement, long vacations, and so on.

The upshot of Marx's comment on wages is that the perceived needs of the exploited classes are variable and can be historically indexed as sufficient or not. If wages are perceived as insufficient by the exploited, this means that the current management of productive forces development by the exploiting classes has entered into a crisis. The current relations of production are *fettering* the development of the productive forces. As will be argued, fettering is related to the meeting of people's historically developed needs. Before this point is explained, a general look at fettering is needed first.

The fettering of the productive forces by relations of production is an intrinsic historical materialist concept. It is listed by Marx as the cause of revolution and the reason a society moves from one mode of production to another. In the Preface, it is listed as a macrophenomenon, "from forms of development of the productive forces these relations turn into their fetters" (Marx & Engels, 1978, pp. 4–5). There is no consideration of what kind of macrophenomenon it is and how it affects microbehaviors.

John Roemer (1988) takes fettering to be decline in efficiency (p. 110). A given set of the relations of production is efficient at developing the forces of production when they correspond to a particular range of these forces' development trajectory. The same set of production relations is inefficient at developing the productive forces for a succeeding range of these forces' development. Roemer's interpretation of fettering is cogent, but it does not address why fettering causes individuals to attempt a revolutionary transformation of their society. This same criticism leads Roemer (1988) to consider wider ranges of why people revolt while only considering fettering as declining efficiency (pp. 113–123).

Understanding what Marx thinks are the kinds of macrophenomena that would cause people to attempt a revolutionary transformation or what should cause people to do so can provide a better explanation of fettering. Marx's analysis of why people should and will revolt against capitalism is because capitalism can never provide a secure and dependable basis for their subsistence and the continued development of their abilities. Marx finds that within capitalism, employment is variable, wages fluctuate and tend to move down, people are prevented from participating in the governance of their society, and people are unable to develop their abilities due to private ownership of the means of production (Marx & Engels, 1968, p. 226; Marx & Engels, 1978, pp. 422–428, 486, 490).

How are these factors related to the occurrence of fettering? How is fettering related to the satisfaction of the preferences of the exploiting classes and the exploited classes? The second question will help answer the first one. If fettering is declining efficiency then this would apparently affect all classes of society. This would be the case only if their current distributional shares are kept proportional. If fettering can be managed by the exploiting class so it retains a greater share, then the brunt of declining efficiency would fall on the exploited class. If revolutionary action is taken by the exploited when fettering occurs, this means the effects of fettering are suffered by the exploited. If this was not the case, then Marx would discuss the transformation of society from one mode of production to another based on the leadership of the exploiters or the combined efforts of exploiters and the exploited. Transitions based on co-operation are not discussed by Marx. This leaves open the explanation of how fettering affects the microbehavior of the exploited. This requires an examination of what Marx considers people to be motivated by.

It appears that Marx finds that people are motivated by two types of preferences: (1) more of what they need to have and (2) a qualitative expansion of their abilities, actions, and social relationships. Marx notes that within capitalism, workers are motivated to get a greater share of what is produced by society (Marx & Engels, 1968, p. 225). This motivation is shared by capitalists also since they require accumulation in order to fight off competition from other capitalists (Marx, 1990, p. 742; Marx & Engels, 1978, p. 480). Workers form themselves into unions and attempt to raise wages, improve working conditions, and shorten the working day (Marx, 1990, p. 611; Marx & Engels, 1978, pp. 365, 480).

As noted, human history is the history of humans seeking to satisfy their needs and finding ways to make it easier or more efficient to satisfy their needs (Marx & Engels, 1978, p. 156). What is very interesting in Marx's analysis is that when humans develop the productive forces, they make the satisfaction of new needs possible: "the satisfaction of the first need (the action of satisfying, and the instrument of satisfaction which has been acquired) leads to new needs" (Marx & Engels, 1978, p. 156). In turn, humans seek to fulfill these new needs. Marx attempts to explain the tendency for human societies to change and develop based on this tendency for humans to seek the fulfillment of their needs by creating new ways to fulfill these needs. These new ways to fulfill the old needs allow for new sets of needs to arise, which will bring about humans seeking new ways to fulfill these needs.

The new needs that people develop can be types of increased consumption for new foods, clothes, housing, amenities, and ways of spending their leisure. This increased consumption could also be combinations of more goods and services: fine foods and clothes, housing with increased details, elaborate decoration, expensive materials, amenities that require more sophisticated construction and maintenance, leisure activities with more services and a greater variance of spectacles, and general higher quality of goods and services.

New needs could also be qualitatively different and may not require increased consumption. Rather, these new needs may be taken up with new activities and relationships. Marx thinks that communism will allow for new types of organizations, which will in turn let people develop new abilities (Marx & Engels, 1978, pp. 197, 491). In addition, Marx found that communism would allow people to overcome the division of labor and accordingly engage in activities that they could never do within capitalism (Marx & Engels, 1978, p. 160). Marx even goes so far as to consider communism to be the condition in which human freedom can fully develop (Marx & Engels, 1978, p. 441).

Marx's consideration of the qualitative expansion of activities, abilities, and social relationships within communism thus gives us an idea of what kinds of new needs people develop as the productive forces expand. This can help us understand why revolution is the result of the fettering of the productive forces.

Even if fettering is solely a decline in efficiency in which exploited classes bear the brunt of the decline, a consideration of how fettered productive forces affect the exploited classes has to be made. Exploited classes prefer to get more of what they need and seek to qualitatively expand their abilities. For either of these preferences to be satisfied, exploited classes require greater control over the distribution of the total product, control over investment, control over the provisioning of education, control over the rationing of skilled positions, and control of the distribution of work and leisure.

On the one hand, all of these kinds of control are held by people with sufficient wealth, at least where they have a controlling interest. They can afford to educate themselves and their children. They can purchase the means to become properly credentialed and compete against other aspiring candidates. They can influence or directly control decisions about investment, and they have the means to pursue more work or leisure.

On the other hand, the exploited classes must obtain more in money wages, in social wages, or in political achievements (legislation, etc.) to effectively control these activities. At the least, an improvement in control over distribution of total product by the exploited classes must come at the expense of the exploiting class's share. At the most, the exploited having increased control over their life trajectory requires a limitation and perhaps a curtailment of the exploiters' control over the means of production.

This means that when the productive forces are fettered, the current needs and the newly arisen or potential needs of the exploited class will not be sufficiently satisfied. If the exploited want to satisfy their needs, they must utilize revolution as a means to gain greater control over how total product is distributed and decisions regarding investment, social provision, distribution of position, and leisure and work amounts.

To review, from a microbehavioral perspective, the fettering of the productive forces is in relation to the satisfaction of the needs of the exploited classes. A productive force is fettered when it cannot satisfy the needs of the exploited. If the needs of the exploited could be met, there would be no need for revolution. Considering the problem as one of class alliances, the exploited can enter into a weak alliance with the exploiting classes by the continual meeting of the needs of the exploited. If the exploiting classes can meet the needs of the exploited while at the same time satisfying their preference for an exploiter's standard of living, there is little reason for them not to meet these improvements. If they do not, they suffer the possibility of revolution.

Based on the citations given regarding communism as a society in which the realm of freedom can be realized, Marx finds that the conditions for a qualitative expansion of abilities, activities, and social relationships are possible with the productive potential of capitalism of his own day. Whether this was true or not, current authors have argued that this point has been reached in our own time (Mandel, 1992, pp. 205–210). The important point is that if these needs cannot be met within capitalism then the development of the productive forces is fettered by capitalist relations of production. In order for the productive forces to develop in the direction of allowing people greater control over the trajectory of their lives, new postcapitalist relations of production are required. This, in short, means that the satisfaction of the new needs of a qualitative expansion of abilities, activities, and social relationship cannot occur within capitalism: "the capitalist mode of production, by its very nature, excludes all rational improvement beyond a certain point" (Marx, 1990, p. 612).

From Primitive Communism to Capitalism

The development of society from primitive communism to slave society to feudalism and then to capitalism occurs because of the development of the productive forces. Marx gives an overview in several of his writings of his understanding of the development of human society. The majority of his work is on the transition from feudalism to capitalism. He discusses the other transitions, too.

Primitive communism is the original mode of production of humans. This is when land or a herd of animals is held in common and individual property does not exist (Marx, 1965, pp. 67–70). In this early form of existence, humans are born into communities in which they are automatically possessors of the land and resources they require to live (Marx, 1965, pp. 90–91). Primitive communism is a situation in which alienation of individuals from the means of production is impossible. People are always owners of the means of production and there is no activity that can separate them from the means of production.

Society transitions from primitive communism to a slave society due to the inability of primitive communist relations of production to meet the needs of the society's members (Marx, 1965, pp. 93–94). As primitive communist societies attempt to maintain their way of life, the holding of land in common, they are confronted with a common side effect of the development of the productive forces: an increase in population. Further development of the productive forces is thus fettered. Primitive communist relations of production are unable to meet the need of individual land for each person. The solution is annexation of the neighbors' lands. These people, if they are not killed outright, are either exiled or turned into slaves. They cannot be included as full members of the invader's group since the whole reason the invasion takes place is to obtain more land.

A classless society attempting to preserve its classless nature thus becomes a class society through the pressures of population growth and invasion. It is interesting that classlessness results in classes. Would this be an obvious and smooth transition for a community? Is it hard for people who have never experienced class relations to become the forceful, dominant class? Marx and Engels mention that slavery is latent in the family (Marx & Engels, 1978, p. 151). Perhaps the move from classlessness to class has psychological components that are facilitated by the material causes.

Slave societies are the result of productive forces development, but the transition from slavery to feudalism is due to a decline of particular productive forces. In particular, Marx and Engels identify the collapse of the Roman Empire as the cause of feudalism:

> In contrast to Greece and Rome, feudal development at the outset, therefore, extends over a much wider territory, prepared by the Roman conquest and the spread of agriculture at first associated with them. The last centuries of the declining Roman Empire and its conquest by the barbarians destroyed a number of productive forces; agriculture had declined, industry had decayed for want of a market, trade had died out or been violently suspended, the rural and urban population had decreased. (Marx & Engels, 1978, pp. 152–153)

The transition from slavery to feudalism appears to be a transition that does not conform to the linear relationship between productive forces development and successive sets of production relations. Slavery's production relations are unable to develop the productive forces, and slave societies entered into a crisis phase. Slave societies fall apart because they become too large to control and are thus vulnerable to rebellion. In other words, slavery relations of production are unable to maintain development of the productive forces. Thus, an increase in productive forces development results in the transition from slavery to feudalism (Laibman, 2007, p. 29). The result of this transition is a destruction of the productive forces. Over the long history of human societies, the direction of productive forces development is to increase, but the transition from slave societies demonstrates that there can be periods of stagnation and decrease.

Feudalism is a mode of production that is centered around the manor, where warriors have subjugated peasantry through force, the result being the creation of the class relations of lords and serfs. Marx and Engels are very interested in the development of feudalism because it is the birthplace of capitalism. They provide various histories of the transition from feudalism to capitalism. Within feudalism, capitalist relations of production arose, and eventually capitalists became dominant actors who displaced the dominance of feudal lords and became the dominant class themselves (Marx & Engels, 1978, p. 475).

The Asiatic Mode of Production

The Asiatic mode of production is listed by Marx in his Preface statement on historical materialism. It is not a mode he analyzes consistently throughout his writing career. He comments on the Asiatic mode in the *Grundrisse*. These comments have been collected into a smaller volume edited by Eric J. Hobsbawm titled *Pre-Capitalist Economic Formations* (1965). In general, the Asiatic mode of production is a misnamed collection of social forms mainly outside of the historical boundaries of Europe, extending beyond East Asia and including the precolonial societies of the Americas (Marx, 1965, p. 70). What separates the so-called Asiatic mode of production from the European pattern of transition of slavery, feudalism, and capitalism is that there are no private holdings in the Asiatic mode, only communal state property: "In the Asiatic form (or at least predominantly so) there is no property, but only individual possession; the community is properly speaking the real proprietor—hence property only as *communal property* in land" (Marx, 1965, p. 79).

The Asiatic mode of production is Marx's attempt to understand why capitalism arose in Europe and not in the rest of the world. The fractured nature of power and production within feudalism promoted the development of the productive forces outside of the control of the state. The rise of capitalism is marked by an increase in trade, with individual merchants (protocapitalists) in control over the surplus achieved through trade. This surplus eventually provides the impetus for the development of capitalism (Mandel, 1962, pp. 110–116).

In areas of the world where the Asiatic mode existed, in particular India and China, the control of the means of production by the state and the use of the surplus to maintain a bureaucracy, cultural refinements, and scientific development prevent the accumulation of capital and the rise of an independent capitalist class (Laibman, 2007, p. 41). Thus, the Asiatic countries and European countries had equivalent levels of industrialization even in the year 1800 (Shaikh, 2007, p. 60). In addition, according to the historical work done by Angus Maddison, China and India were each individually wealthier than the entirety of Europe in 1700 (Maddison, 2010). Thus, these countries did not develop capitalist relations of production because they were poor. Rather, Asiatic relations of production promoted the continued development of the Asiatic mode of production without a crisis of fettered development. This successful continuation prevented the development of capitalists and proletarians.

> The Asiatic form necessarily survives longest and most stubbornly. This is due to the fundamental principle on which it is based, that is, that the individual does not become independent of the community: that the circle of production is self-sustaining, unity of agriculture and craft manufacture, etc. (Marx, 1965, p. 83)

Base/Foundation and Superstructure

The distinction between the **foundation** and the **superstructure** of a society is a point of debate in the theory of historical materialism. Up to this point, the presentation of historical materialism in this chapter has relied only on a consideration of the productive forces being an ultimate cause of the development of human societies and a feedback loop of causation occurring between production relations and the productive forces. One can thus understand, in simplified form, the causal chain as such: (1) The productive forces make certain production relations possible; (2) the newly created production relations promote productive forces development; and (3) this promotion occurs until the relations fetter productive forces development. In addition, to repeat, fettering is when the needs of a society's populace cannot be satisfied while maintaining the current relations of production.

What about how people perceive and think about their social world? Does this affect the development of society? Certainly, people would be aware they act on their preferences to satisfy their needs, but do people really think about their society and its potential for change in terms of needs and the development of the productive forces? We can readily say no, they do not, but Marx thinks that ultimately people's lives are structured by their ability to take advantage of productive forces development. Can this be true? Are people's actions in actuality not what they think of them but a dynamic concerning class struggle over control of the means of production?

In order to answer these questions, we need to identify what the **base** and the superstructure are. In the quoted Preface section, the term *foundation* is used, but this can for all practical purposes be considered identical to the term *base*. *Base* will be the term used here since it is common in discussions about base/foundation and superstructure.

Looking at the Preface, one can consider that the relations of production are the base, whereas the superstructure is made up of legal and political institutions. This means the productive forces are neither the base nor the superstructure. This interpretation is somewhat controversial and readers should be aware of it. I find G. A. Cohen's argument for these distinctions to be convincing and will follow his lead here (Cohen, 2000, pp. 28–37).

Marx notes in the Preface that the superstructure of a society corresponds to the base of society. This means that certain legal and political institutions correspond to particular relations of production. For example, feudal legal and political institutions correspond to feudal relations of production. It was legal within feudalism for people to be held in bondage as serfs. If we follow Marx's lead, this means serfdom is legal because it conforms to the relations of production. In short, the relations occur first and then they are sanctified as lawful: "The mode of production of material life conditions the social, political and intellectual life process in general" (Marx & Engels, 1978, p. 4). In addition, in the Preface passage, Marx states that the "legal, political, religious, aesthetic or [the] philosophic" are "ideological forms in which men become conscious of this conflict and fight it out" (Marx & Engels, 1978, p. 5), the conflict being the revolution brought about by the fettering of the productive forces. Finally, Marx finds that consciousness in itself does not explain the social crisis and revolution brought about by fettering; rather, "this consciousness must be explained rather from the contradictions of material life, from the existing conflict between the social productive forces and the relations of production" (Marx & Engels, 1978, p. 5).

One can begin to answer some of the questions asked at the beginning of this section with this overview of base and superstructure. First, the forms of consciousness that the institutions of the superstructure are composed of are caused by the current mode of production. This means that the legal, moral, and political ideas of a time are shaped and are, in general, in conformity with the interest of the dominant class. As Marx and Engels state in *The German Ideology*, "The ideas of the ruling class are in every epoch the ruling ideas: i.e., the class which is the ruling *material* force of society, is at the same time its ruling *intellectual* force" (Marx & Engels, 1978, p. 172). The ideas of property and freedom are capitalist ideas of property and freedom and are neither natural nor timeless concepts (Marx & Engels, 1978, pp. 485–487). Private property is understood as timeless and natural because it is the form of property held by the ruling class of capitalists. In addition, defining freedom as based on the holding of private property is not what freedom is naturally or eternally. Instead, this is the definition of freedom within capitalism because it supports and defends the type of property controlled by the ruling class of capitalists.

For example, when the exploited classes and their allies protest for higher wages or more social provisioning, their claims will always be evaluated within the structures of capitalist forms of consciousness. A demand for higher wages will be met with the conjecture of whether it is fair for the current remuneration shares to be disrupted. Capitalism, by definition, pays people what they have agreed to be paid, since all workers contract for free. So if workers demand a higher wage, this appears to be calling for the wage contract to be ignored. Marx responds to this is his theory of exploitation and unemployment, which will be considered in the economics chapter. It is important to stress that Marx's analysis of such capitalist rebuttals to workers' demands always questions whether their assumptions are really obvious or natural. Is it natural or obvious to settle distribution issues as they are dealt with within capitalism? Marx's implicit answer: only within capitalism, because capitalists can control the outcome. In other modes of production, the wage contract is not obvious or natural.

Second, the reason people have a battle of ideas is the social crisis of fettered relations of production. The forms of consciousness are a response to the fettering of the productive forces by the current relations of production. It is not caused, according to Marx, by people coming up with problems with the ideas of a society and then starting a social crisis. The social crisis is caused by fettering, and this brings about the ideological battle. As Marx states in the Preface, "It is not the consciousness of men that determines their being, but, on the contrary, their social being that determines their consciousness" (Marx & Engels, 1978, p. 4). As was discussed in the chapter on Marx's materialism, this is not a revolutionary idea today, but it was revolutionary in Marx's day. It was part of his response to Hegelian idealism.

Third, how people represent the social crisis of fettered relations of production is not an explanation of the crisis. Rather, the crisis is explained by why the current relations of production cannot develop the productive forces in ways that meet the needs of the revolutionary classes. The second point is not controversial, but this claim by Marx is very controversial. Essentially, it finds that people will respond to a crisis according to the ideas and categories of dominant social analysis. In reality, these responses are based on a false understanding of social reality that will incorrectly identify the problem.

This apparently does not mean that social science cannot approximate the actual dynamics of a society. Rather, Marx finds that social analysis can identify the actual dynamics if social scientific practitioners are not attempting to be apologists and defenders of the interests of a particular class. Marx's position is that ideological mystification does occur, but it can be dispelled by correct social scientific methods and reasoning. This is obviously a controversial position since it condemns the majority of social scientific research while still championing social science as a means of explanation. Responses to this conjecture range from people finding Marx to be right to finding Marx's analysis of mainstream social science to be wrong to finding Marx's own analysis wrong to seeing Marx as right but his methods as wrong and, most interestingly, to believing that all social science is so mystified that it has no chance at identifying and explaining social dynamics. Marx himself definitely thinks that carefully done and nonapologetic social science can accurately explain social reality.

Fourth, the reasons people cite as the cause of their action during a revolutionary transformation are not necessarily the actual causes of their actions. In the Preface, Marx states,

> Just as our opinion of an individual is not based on what he thinks of himself, so can we not judge of such a period of transformation by its own consciousness; on the contrary, this consciousness must be explained rather from the contradictions of material life, from the existing conflict between the social productive forces and the relations of production. (Marx & Engels, 1978, p. 5)

People have particular needs but it can be unclear to them what these needs really are, what the actual causes are, and what is the correct solution.

Two examples from Marx's writing can help demonstrate this point. First, within capitalism, workers suffer from separation from the means of production, resulting in alienation. This includes low wages and lack of control over production and investment of society's resources. Workers, when they feel their lack of power and their material deprivation, may think these conditions are caused by the machines they work on. This is called a Luddite response, named after the workers who destroyed their machines in response to their deprivation (Marx & Engels, 1978, p. 480). The use of machines doesn't cause people to be deprived or unemployed. Rather, all employment, wages, and the quality of employment are subject to social policy. According to Marx, there is no natural level of wages, employment, or workplace quality. All of these matters can be decided by a society at large.

Workers may blame other workers, domestic or foreign, for their alienation. This can be the case since workers are in competition with other workers for employment. Marx finds that workers learn through their struggles that other workers are their allies and not the cause of their problems (Marx & Engels, 1978, p. 481). Blaming workers of other races or nationalities for the ills the working class suffers has, unfortunately, always been a common problem for solidarity. This is the reason Marx was an advocate of internationalism, which is the movement to seek commonality of political purpose among all working people of the world. This is why Marx and Engels found that workers have no country since their interests lie not only with their own fellow citizens but with all workers (Marx & Engels, 1978, p. 488).

A second example: When Marx analyzed the revolution of 1848 in France, he wanted to identify why the peasants would support the ascendency of Louis Napoleon instead of the workers. He found this curious since the interests of peasants, in his estimation, would best be met by the victory of the working class. In addition, he found that the peasants who were suffering from excessive debt and land holdings that were too small to be profitable lent their support for a person whose policies would mainly benefit the capitalists, who were the holders of peasant debt. Marx concluded that the peasants supported Louis Napoleon Bonaparte over the workers because they thought their problems were not caused by debt and small holdings but rather by the absence of a great leader like Napoleon Bonaparte. The French peasantry incorrectly identified their problem as an absence of a Napoleon (Bonaparte) and the solution as a new Napoleon (Louis). They thus put their faith in the rectification of their situation in what Marx calls *idées napoléoniennes*. In short, French peasants were suffering deprivation, but they misidentified both the cause and the solution (Marx & Engels, 1978, pp. 594–617).

Determination and Free Will

Major concerns with the theory of historical materialism are worries about predetermination and free will. These have arisen as a concern not only due to Marx's position on what determines consciousness but also because many of his comments in the Preface lead some to conclude that the historical change that Marx describes is inevitable (Heilbroner, 1980). In this section, we will consider claims concerning the determination of consciousness and life chances and the predetermination of the future in Marx's writings.

As has just been discussed, the consciousness of people is determined by their world, and their world is not determined by their consciousness. German idealist concerns about the origin of ideas and Marx's critique are addressed in the chapter on ideology. At present, we should examine in an everyday sense what Marx thinks about how people can create their world through their decisions and their convictions.

To begin, can people create a world for themselves in any way they like, or are they bound by the social dynamics of their time? Marx's answer is yes, people are bound by the social dynamics of their time. These dynamics make people who they are, and people must operate within them or struggle against them to create their world.

In the chapter on class, it was explained that Marx develops an objective theory of class position. This means that people's life chances will be affected by their class position. This is the case whether they are aware of their class position or not. In addition, this is the case even if they are hostile toward the interests of their class. In all cases, people's life chances are determined by their class position.

For example, people who are objectively in the working class may be advocates for capitalist class interests. They could actively support policies that would benefit capitalists and criticize measures that would benefit members of their own class. The outcomes of their life are still shaped by their class position. As members of the working class, their employment and their wages are subject to the decisions of capitalists. They cannot create their own jobs or their own employment because they do not own sufficient amounts of the means of production to employ themselves. They could try to obtain funding to start a business, but their prospects of obtaining funding are shaped by their class position. It is difficult for workers to obtain funding for a business because they do not have sufficient collateral or sufficient business experience to be seen as a good risk (Burczak, 2006, p. 75). Last, they may receive a gift from a capitalist due to their support of capitalist interests, but this too is shaped by their class position. If they were not members of the working class, they wouldn't have to accept a gift to start their own business.

In the Preface, Marx states that people "enter into definite relations that are indispensable and independent of their will" (Marx & Engels, 1978, p. 4). This appears to be true for all practical purposes. This does not mean that people cannot work within the relations of production to attempt to build a world that they favor. People can struggle against the dominant relations of their time, they can join with them, or they can try to ignore them. No matter what people choose to do, their lives are shaped by their class position. Marx's comments at the beginning of *The 18th Brumaire* speak to this issue: "Men make their own history, but they do not make it just as they please; they do not make it under circumstances chosen by themselves, but under circumstances directly found, given and transmitted from the past" (Marx & Engels, 1978, p. 595). In a nutshell, human consciousness can shape the world through action, but it does not determine the world. People must use the world as it is to attempt their projects.

This brings us to considerations of predetermination and inevitability. Were the epochs of human society inevitable? Did capitalism have to come about? In the same vein, must socialism be the next stage of human society's development? The comments that Marx makes on such matters are more contradictory than those on other topics. On the one hand, he states in the Preface and earlier in *The Communist Manifesto*:

> Therefore mankind always sets itself only such tasks as it can solve; since, looking at the matter more closely, it will always be found that the task itself arises only when the material conditions for its solution already exist or are at least in the process of formation. (Marx & Engels, 1978, p. 5)

> We see then: the means of production and of exchange, on whose foundation the bourgeoisie built itself up, were generated in feudal society. At a certain stage in the development of these means of production and of exchange, the conditions under which feudal society produced and exchanged, the feudal organization of agriculture and manufacturing industry, in one word, the feudal relations of property become no longer compatible with the already developed productive forces; they became so many fetters. They had to be burst asunder; they were burst asunder. (Marx & Engels, 1978, p. 478)

On the other hand, Marx states in a letter to Ferdinand Lassalle in 1861:

> Darwin's book [*Origin of the Species*] is very important and it suits me well that it supports the class struggle in history from the point of view of natural science. One has, of course has to put up with the crude English method of discourse. Despite all deficiencies, it not only deals the death-blow to "teleology" in the natural sciences for the first time but also sets forth the rational meaning in an empirical way. (Marx & Engels, 1965, p. 115)

The Preface appears to find that the developments of society will occur. The ills of capitalism and our modern world—unemployment, poverty, alienation, and environmental decay, to name a few—are all solvable by humans. Humans made capitalism and they can unmake it. It is too strong a reading to say that all the solutions to all problems have already been solved. Where do the solutions exist, hidden somewhere in our minds? Rather, Marx's Preface comments are extremely optimistic. It's not that the solutions to humans' problems already exist but, instead, that we will find a solution to all of our problems. In addition, Marx's brief overview of the feudal relations of production fettering further development of the productive forces leads us to an *inevitable* transformation: "They *had* to burst asunder." In short, humans will solve their problems. Their problems won't destroy them.

In contrast, Marx's comments about the scientific achievement of Darwin's *The Origin of Species* in demonstrating that final causes (teleology) are unnecessary to explain the formation of life's processes stand in stark contrast to his apparently teleological comments from the Preface and the Manifesto. If Marx as a teleological thinker is too strong a reading and is in apparent contradiction to his general understanding of science, how should we take such comments? Can Marx maintain that social development is inevitable while also not utilizing teleology?

I would argue that Marx's comments in total concerning the potential for human society to solve its problems and survive into the future are too optimistic. G. A. Cohen (2000) notes that humans are somewhat rational and, when given the chance to improve their situation, they will do so (p. 153). This approximation of human potential for rationality and self-improvement is held by Marx also. This is a *general* approximation of human action and does not state that in all circumstances, human action will be rational or that self-improvement will be considered.

Two examples, one historical and one theoretical, will help demonstrate that humans may be irrational or unable to improve their situation in particular circumstances. First is the story of the Easter Islanders. The Easter Islanders constructed giant statues called the moai. The moai were constructed by competing tribes on Easter Island. They were objects of rank among the various tribes. It has been conjectured that giant palm trees were utilized to move the carved moai. The competition between the various tribes led to the deforestation of Easter Island. The results of this deforestation were that (1) birds that used to nest in the giant palms no longer came to Easter Island and (2) the islanders were no longer able to construct seagoing vessels, which were made out of the palm logs. The birds and deep-sea fish were food sources for the islanders. Eventually the Easter Islanders' population collapsed due to starvation and there was a period of survival cannibalism (Diamond, 2004).

This historical example can show an instance of humans not acting in a fashion that Marx would consider rational. That is, people may jeopardize their developmental potential and their material needs for other ends. The Easter Islanders' pursuit of rank superseded their own physical survival. Was it apparent to the Easter Islanders that their food sources were jeopardized? Did they realize that the material basis of their society was being destroyed? All in all, the cruel fate of the Easter Islanders stands in stark contrast to Marx's optimistic statement that humans only set themselves tasks that can be solved.

The second example is a theoretical one that builds on the first. David Laibman (2007) notes that the development of human society may be stopped by blockages of development, such as the slowdown in productive forces development indicative of Asiatic modes of production (p. 41). Laibman notes that the development of the productive forces also coincides with the development of destructive potential. Not only have humans progressively developed more destructive weapons, but also their impact on the biosphere has moved beyond the deforestation of Easter Island or the Alps. Thus, Laibman (2007) conjectures that humans may encounter an "ultimate blockage" to social development (p. 42). This means that "all the transitions are potential only" (p. 42).

With the possibility of the ultimate destruction of humans through atomic, chemical, or biological weapons or ecological collapse and the realization that humans are not always rational regarding their survival, it becomes apparent that Marx misjudged the inevitability of human social development. This means that communism is not inevitable. It does not mean that it is improbable. Can communism be made a greater possibility through human action? As Marx said, we do make our own world.

Conclusion

Marx's theory of historical materialism is partially a common way of looking at social development and is partially a very radical theory of social development. The conjecture that technological development and economic growth change social relations is commonly held by social scientists. The idea that stable social relations will one day become incompatible with a given technological form is partially accepted. For example, many people would agree that certain types of jobs and certain types of family formations have been changed by technological developments such as the automobile and birth control. To extend this conjecture to forecast that technological changes will bring about the end of classes due to unmet potential needs is unheard of in common discourse and is a minor discussion in most universities. The inevitability of such occurrences is held by almost no one.

Marx's optimism is not shared by many today. The Great Recession of 2007 to 2009 has been followed with a series of protests worldwide, some with more economic content than others. People have found that their needs for employment, housing, and education are being poorly provided. The renewed demand for need satisfaction following an economic crisis appears to conform to Marx's theory of historical materialism. But, as we all know, a theory's capacity to predict or explain a phenomenon does not mean that that theory is correct. For example, the geocentric model of our solar system was able to accurately predict the location of the planets and the sun. This was possible even if this theory held the Earth to be the center of our solar system.

Marx's theory of history has its obvious weaknesses. The conjecture that humans seek to improve their lives is at the heart of Marx's theory of social development and at the heart of his theory of revolution. Whether this apparently true observation can be developed into a workable theory of social evolution is still an open question.

Before we transition into a discussion of Marx's economics, a few questions for thought and discussion:

- What aspects of Marx's theory of historical materialism appear to still be valid?
- Is Marx's analysis of free will correct? Are we really bound by our society's limits?
- Is the primacy of the productive forces a reasonable conjecture for the development of human societies, or are social structures like class and caste more important?
- What role do artistic ideas have in the development of society according to Marx's theory of history?
- Are Marx's modes of production specific enough to describe the development of human societies?

6

Economics

M arx spent the greater part of his adult life studying and writing about the economic aspects of capitalism from the unique perspective of a social scientist suspicious of the capitalist *status quo*. Marx's mature work on economics, from the *Grundrisse* to *Capital* and many notebooks, spans 10 volumes in the *Collected Works of Marx and Engels*. *Capital* alone is three volumes comprising thousands of pages. Any chapter-length presentation of Marx's economics will be incomplete. I hope this chapter can serve as an introduction to many of the categories of analysis of Marx that he refined from classical economics or developed anew. Most of the presentations in this chapter will concentrate on the first volume of *Capital*, where many of the commonly discussed Marxian economic categories are located, at least in part. Marxian economics is famous not only for its presentation of exploitation with capitalist production but also for its theory of capitalist crisis. The well-known falling rate of profit theory of crisis is discussed in the third volume of *Capital*. This will be considered also. The chapter on further readings contains a discussion of more detailed presentations of Marx's economics and notable examinations and adaptations of his theory of crisis. Even though this chapter is a brief introduction to Marx's economics, I am hopeful that it will serve the needs of the large variety of readers that is this book's intended audience.

This chapter is structured to introduce Marx's economics in a manner that mirrors his own presentation in the first volume of *Capital*. The fundamental category that Marx utilizes to analyze capitalist production process is **value**. Understanding what is value and how the value of a commodity is determined lays the groundwork for Marx's critique of capitalism as a system in which all economic agents are treated equally. The equality of the marketplace is the supposed superiority of capitalism over feudalism and is also the supposed naturalism of capitalist relations. This was discussed earlier in this work in the section on Marx's critique of social contract theory. Marx shows that capitalism is not the equal treatment of all agents, which would be the natural and uncoerced state of affairs endorsed by the social contract theory. Rather, Marx uses the category of value to demonstrate that capitalism in all of its forms is based on exploitation and the coercion of *voluntarium imperfectum* (which is choice under dire necessity). In some forms of capitalism, direct force is used to make people labor, as Marx shows in the section of *Capital* on primitive accumulation.

This chapter will give an overview of the category of value and will then consider the category of surplus value. After this is done, many dependent categories will be discussed: exploitation, absolute surplus value, relative surplus value, and wages. Next, Marx demonstrates why unemployment is intrinsic to capitalism; this discussion is also dependent on the category of value. Then Marx's analysis of primitive accumulation and the creation of the modern proletariat are discussed. Finally, an overview of Marx's theory of crisis will be presented.

Value

The first volume of *Capital* begins with a discussion of economic commodities and value. A commodity is an object that "satisfies human wants of some sort or another" (Marx & Engels, 1978, p. 303). Commodities can be produced or found and bought and sold. They are physical items in some form. They exist as water stored in a tank or a river, as books on a shelf, as a song being sung, or as information inscribed on tape or in memory banks.

Economic value is different from moral value. Something's moral value is separate from its desirability or its exchangeability with other things. Marx's discussion is only of economic value and does not consider moral value as a category. From this point on in this chapter, the term *value* will be used as shorthand for the term *economic value*.

Marx finds that there are two types of value: **use value** and **exchange value**. Marx defines use value as the utility of a commodity. The utility of a commodity is determined by its physical qualities (Marx & Engels, 1978, p. 303). Water's use value, its utility, is its usefulness in ending thrust or generating power when it falls through a turbine, in cooling people off when it is collected in a pool, or the beauty it provides as a pond. Information is useful in allowing people to solve problems, make money, or be entertained when they read the data. In short, all things that are produced, found, bought, or sold are use values. That is, all commodities are use values.

All commodities are physical things according to Marx. Even ideas, which are information, must be contained in some physical substratum to be of use: either a brain, sound waves, paper, or arranged electrons. If a person's idea is never transcribed onto paper or spoken to another, it will be lost and will not be of use. If the idea is spoken, one can charge to hear the speaker or, if the idea is transcribed, one can charge to have a transcription. One could give away one's idea by speaking without charging or disseminating the transcription for free. No matter how something is disseminated, or whether one has to pay to obtain it, it is a physical thing and thus is a use value.

All commodities are use values, but not all use values are commodities. People can create useful items for themselves and others without them being bought or sold. When people prepare food for themselves and their friends, they create use values but not commodities. In addition, the basis of all use values is nature. Some products of nature—air, sun, water, plants, and so on—are useful without being products of labor. Of course, many natural products must be subject to labor to render them useful: Coal must be mined, water channeled, and grain ground. As Marx notes in *Capital* and in *Critique of the Gotha Program*, labor and nature are the sources of all wealth (Marx & Engels, 1978, pp. 309, 525).

The other type of value considered by Marx is **exchange value**. Exchange value is the proportion in which one commodity can be exchanged for another commodity. For example, take two commodities, a coat and a length of cloth. Marx notes that all commodities are equal to one another in the sense that one commodity can be exchanged for another commodity. This means that a coat is equal to a certain amount of cloth—one coat is equal to x amount of cloth, or the same notion, 1 coat = x amount of cloth. Thus, the exchange value of a commodity is "the proportion in which values in use of one sort are exchanged for those of another sort" (Marx & Engels, 1978, p. 304).

What makes commodities exchangeable values is not a physical quality. Items are not exchangeable because they have any natural similarity, geometric similarity, or chemical similarity. One coat does not exchange for x amount of cloth because they are both *made* of cotton. Nor does 1 coat exchange for x amount of cloth because they both contain the *same amount* of cotton. If a coat contains 2 kilograms of cotton and 10 meters of cloth also contains 2 kilograms of cotton, this does not determine their proportion of exchange. In particular, a cotton coat may be made of 2 kilograms of cotton, but it is exchanged for 20 meters of cotton, which weighs 4 kilograms (Marx & Engels, 1978, p. 304). This means that the coat is worth more than its weight in the material it is made of.

Marx also notes a commodities exchange value is not its use value in proportion to another commodity's use value. This means that 1 coat does not equal x amount of cloth because they have an equal amount of use value. People of course buy items because they satisfy some kind of want. Retailers buy clothes, coffee, and cars to sell them. In addition, manufacturers make clothes, coffee, and cars to sell them. Thus, the utility of the commodity that a retailer sells in her shop is different from the utility of those who buy her items. The retailer buys the coffee to sell it and the shopper buys the same coffee to satisfy a desire for a particular beverage (Marx & Engels, 1978, p. 305).

At this point, many readers may think that what all commodities have in common that renders them equivalent and exchangeable is a price denominated in money. This is of course true for our own economic world, in which the prices of various items are comparable. Marx will agree that all commodities are universally equivalent to each other when denominated in a single commodity. This commodity can be the money of a given region (Marx, 1990, p. 162). Interestingly, all commodities can be considered equal to any commodity. Thus, 10 meters of cloth can be equal to 1 coat, 10 kilograms of bricks, or 30 kilograms of coffee, or 10 meters of cloth can be equal to 10 kilograms of bricks which equals 30 kilograms of coffee which equals x amount of money.

People's relationship to commodities is by either their utility or what they can be exchanged for. What all commodities can be exchanged for in the modern world is money. The observation that all items can be exchanged for money is well founded. Nonetheless, Marx thinks that to simply equate all commodities to the exchange value in money misses the point that all commodities can be rendered as equal to any commodity, whether this commodity is considered money or not. Thus, we can have an equation of equivalent exchange values that is as large as all commodities produced in the world. One can construct a list of all commodities available and list all of them equivalent to a unit of money, such as the Japanese yen. The exact same list can again be listed as being equivalent to another unit of money, such as the Indian rupee. Alternatively, the same can be done again with gold, silver, copper, cloth, coffee, or bottled water. Accordingly, one can list the equivalent exchange value of cars and coffee to bottles of water. A particular model of car is equal to x bottles of water or a metric ton of coffee is equal to x bottles of water. Apparently, listing all commodities as equivalent to money is just more of the same. It still doesn't answer the question of what makes all commodities equal to one another.

If the value of one commodity changes, then its exchange value with all other commodities changes in proportion. If 1 coat was equal to 10 meters of cloth and then the value of the coat dropped by half, this would change the exchange values as such: 1 coat is equal to 5 meters of cloth. The coat is now worth less exchange value. In addition, a person cannot set the exchange value of a commodity according to whim. The exchange value of an item must be equivalent to the commodity it is exchanged against.

As can be seen, any commodities can be made equal to all other commodities according to their exchange value. In addition, all commodities' exchange values are determined according to some feature that sets their exchange values as being apart from their use values. Marx finds that the feature that all commodities have in common is that they are products of **labor power** (Marx & Engels, 1978, p. 305). Thus, what determines the exchange value of all commodities is the amount of labor power expended in the fabrication or procurement of them. For example, 1 coat is equal to 10 meters of cloth because they both take x amount of labor power to fabricate them. This means one can render equivalent all commodities as exchange values according to the amount of labor power it took to make them. Accordingly, 1 day of labor power would be equal to all commodities that take 1 day of equivalent laboring to be fabricated, or 1 day of labor power is fractionally equivalent to all other commodities. For example, if it takes 2 days to make a coat and 1 day to weave 30 meters of cloth, then half of a coat is equal to 30 meters of cloth, or 60 meters of cloth is equal to 1 coat.

If the amount of expended labor power determines the exchange value of commodities, what about things that have exchange value but are not products of human labor: timber, water, and minerals, for example? For such commodities, their exchange value is determined according to the amount of labor power expended in their extraction or procurement (Marx & Engels, 1978, p. 307). The exchange value of water is the amount of labor that must be expended for it to be brought to its point of consumption. The exchange value of water at its point of origin, let us say a mountain lake, has no exchange value since one can simply drink from the source at ease. A town several kilometers away from the source of its water supply requires that certain amounts of labor power be expended to bring it to the point of consumption. The total exchange value of a liter of water is equal to the congealed amount of labor power that was required to lay the pipes, install the pumps, treat the water, maintain the infrastructure, and run the system. The same applies to all other commodities of this type such as firewood. You can collect fallen wood in your yard by expending your own labor. The exchange value of firewood brought to your home is equal to the total amount of **necessary labor** expended in cutting the wood and transporting it to your home.

Simply, the labor theory of value hypothesizes that the value of commodities is determined by the amount of labor time that is expended for their fabrication and/or procurement. This is why people can't change the exchangeable values of commodities at will. If people are interested in exchanging as much as possible, then items will exchange at their values (Marx often just uses the term *value* when discussing exchange values). People will not sell their commodities for less than their embodied labor power, nor will people buy commodities for more than their embodied labor power. Items exchanging at their values are the norm for the vast majority of commodities. The outlier cases will be considered in what follows. The labor theory of value needs to clarify two points to make it more cogent: the same kind of commodities that are made with different amounts of embodied labor power and the exchange of commodities produced with different amounts of skill.

Socially Necessary Labor Time

What if two commodities of the same kind, a wool coat of a particular quality, embody different amounts of labor time. Coat A takes 2 days to make and coat B takes 4 days to make. No one who is rational would purchase coat B for twice the exchange value of coat A. Rather, if coat A represented the average amount of expended labor for wool coats, then coat B would sell at the same exchange value. As Marx described this phenomenon, "We see then that that which determines the magnitude of the value of any article is the amount of labour socially necessary, or the labour-time socially necessary for its production" (Marx & Engels, 1978, p. 306). It is common in Marxian economic literature to describe this average exchange value of a commodity as **SNLT**, or socially necessary labor time. Thus the **price** of a commodity is equal to its SNLT, or commodity x = SNLT.

Commodities exchanging at their SNLT means that some will exchange above or below the actual amount of embodied labor that fabricated and/or procured them. Using the wool coat example, those who produce coat B at 4 days of labor power will only receive exchange value that is equal to the SNLT of wool coats, which is 2 days. Thus, the workers who make coat B work 4 days and receive only 2 days of exchange value. The result of this will be the dying out of the way of making coat B and an increase in use of the means to make coat A. As can be seen, items exchanging for the SNLT will result in the decay of less productive industries in a given commodity and the emergence of more productive industries. Marx finds that this is the nature of capitalism (Marx & Engels, 1978, p. 476).

Types of Labor

Does the skill level required to make a commodity affect the amount of exchange value an item is worth? Marx finds that it does. Skilled labor is only a multiple of what Marx calls **simple labor**, which can be understood as unskilled labor. Marx considers all labor power as simple/unskilled labor for theoretical simplicity (Marx & Engels, 1978, pp. 310–311).

In addition to simple labor being the baseline for the calculation of exchange values, Marx also utilizes a distinction between **useful labor** and **abstract labor** (Marx & Engels, 1978, pp. 305, 310–311, 315). Useful labor, also called **concrete labor**, is a particular kind of labor that makes a particular kind of use value. The labor of a carpenter makes useful items out of wood. This is useful labor since it makes a use value. A worker in a car factory performs useful labor in the construction of a car, such as attaching the doors to the car. If the carpenter or the car factory worker stopped laboring without completing the use value, then their labor would not be useful since no use values were completed. One cannot exchange the useful labor of the carpenter for that of the car factory worker, since the useful labor is different. One kind of useful labor is not commensurable with another kind of useful labor.

Abstract labor is the necessary exertion of labor power designated in time elapsed. All expenditure of human labor power can be measured as abstract labor. For example, the labor of a carpenter and a car factory worker can be compared and commensurate as amounts of abstract labor. The commodities produced by the carpenter and the car factory worker can be compared as equivalent not as use values but as exchange values. The characteristic that allows these commodities to be compared is the amount of expended abstract labor each commodity embodies. A wooden bookshelf and a car can be compared as factional equivalents by the amount of congealed abstract labor time that was necessary for each to be fabricated. The same could be done with mined iron ore and health care services.

In addition, the skill levels of various labor can be reduced to their simple/unskilled equivalents as well. This means that all exchange values can be represented as equivalent according to the amount of simple abstract labor that they variously embody. For example, the skilled useful labor of a midwife could be rendered equivalent to any other commodity if their skilled labor is reduced to abstract simple labor power.

All exchange values are use values, but not all use values are exchange values. Marx notes that use values are "the material depositories of exchange-value" (Marx & Engels, 1978, p. 304). For a commodity to be an exchange value, it must also be a use value. People would not voluntarily exchange for something they did not find useful. Capitalists seek to make and sell commodities that people wish to exchange their money for. This means that they must find use values people wish to purchase. Capitalists don't particularly care what the use value is. They only care that it will be exchanged for. Not all use values are exchange values, since many use values are produced for personal consumption, such as homemade meals that are not exchanged. When people make their own use values, it is called self-servicing.

The Value of Money

It has been shown that the exchange value of a commodity is not determined by the perceived utility of the commodity or any natural characteristic of the commodity. Neither can a commodity's value simply be reducible to its price in money. Rather, as was shown, the money price of a commodity reflects the value of the commodity, which is the average socially necessary labor time expended to produce the commodity. Just like all commodities, money has a price and thus a value. How can the value of money be the embodiment of the socially necessary labor time it takes to produce money? The value of a single paper piece of currency is not worth the amount of labor that it took to produce that single piece of currency. In addition, it is obvious that the amount of labor that is required to make a currency note that is denominated as a hundred or a thousand times the value of a single unit of currency is not the embodiment of a hundred or a thousand times more expended labor power. In addition, most transactions do not even use actual currency notes; people use checks or electronic transfers of funds. The exchange value of an electronic entry is not the same as the amount of currency it represents.

These problems about money can be met with Marx's answer to the value of money. In Marx's day, money was commonly denominated in precious metals, usually gold. Nations would issue paper currency, which represented a certain amount of gold. In addition, their metal coin currency, even if it contained gold, was not the same amount of gold that it represented. All metals, including the precious metal gold, have values because labor must be expended for their extraction, refinement, and transport. Accordingly, the value of x grams of gold is the socially necessary labor time that must be expended to yield x grams of gold: "But gold can serve as a measure of value only because it is itself a product of labor" (Marx, 1990, p. 192).

This means that 1 day of simple abstract labor power can be used to measure the values of all commodities. For example, 1 day of labor power equals x grams of gold, x meters of cloth, x number of cars, x tons of coffee, and so on. In short, the value of money is the amount of labor it takes to produce x amount of the metal currency. This would be the case if any commodity were the unity of currency: silver, steel, wheat, and so forth (Marx, 1990, p. 190).

Does Marx's theory of commodity money apply today to modern nations' fiat money systems? A fiat money system is one in which a nation's currency is not legally redeemable for a precious metal. This means that if one owns a debt denominated in a fiat currency, one cannot demand that the debtor pay the debt in gold or silver. The United States, until August 15, 1971, had the dollar pegged to the price of gold at $35.00 an ounce. During this period of time, people, in particular foreign banks, could redeem their dollars for gold. Since this time, the United States has not been legally obligated to convert its currency into any other currency or any other commodity. If people, whether domestic or foreign, hold dollars, they can spend them or sell them on currency markets for other kinds of currency.

The upshot of the post–1971 monetary world is simply that money is not strictly a representation of an amount of a precious metal. Does this mean the labor theory of value does not hold? A comment by Marx on fiat money (a valueless symbol) replacing gold can help answer this question:

> Finally, one may ask why gold is capable of being replaced by valueless symbols of itself. As we have already seen, it is capable of being replaced in this way only if its function as coin or circulating medium can be singled out or rendered independent. . . . The presentation of the exchange value of a commodity as an independent entity is here only a transient aspect of the process. The commodity is immediately replaced again by another commodity. Hence in this process which continually makes money pass from hand to hand, it only needs to lead a symbolic existence. Its functional existence so to speak absorbs its material existence . . . One thing is necessary, however: the symbol of money must have its own objective social validity. The paper acquires this by its forced currency. The state's compulsion can only be of any effect within that internal sphere of circulation which is circumscribed by the boundaries of a given community, but it is also only within that sphere that money is completely absorbed in its function as medium of circulation, and is therefore able to receive, in the form of paper money, a purely functional mode of existence in which it is externally separated from its metallic substance. (Marx, 1990, pp. 225–226)

Marx's comment can be analyzed as such: (1) all money, whether metal or paper, is a symbolic representation of exchange value; (2) money presents the exchange value of a commodity; and (3) all money can represent the exchange value of an item if it is a socially accepted symbol of exchange value in a given area. Point 1 can easily apply to all money-like forms such as checks and electronic tallies. The importance of point 2 is that money is a symbol for exchange value. It is not equivalent to a certain amount of exchange value because it is the embodiment of a certain amount of expended labor power. This is unlike commodity money, such as gold. Point 3 stresses the social nature of fiat money. For a mere symbol to be accepted as a stand-in for an equivalent amount of expended labor power, it must be socially accepted in a given area. A competent person will only accept a symbol as money that he can use for exchanges in the future.

In a nutshell, fiat money, which is a valueless symbol in itself, is a mere stand-in for a commodity of actual value. If this is the case, then the exchange of commodities for money is exchanges of commodities for an equivalent amount of value symbolized in the accepted currency for the transaction. The upshot of the quoted passage is that items will exchange at their value. Marx's definition for price can apply to any money or money-like thing, whether a precious metal or not:

> Price is the money-name of the labour objectified in a commodity. Hence the expression of the equivalence of a commodity with the quantity of money whose name is that commodity's price is a tautology, just as the expression of the relative value of a commodity is an expression of the equivalence of two commodities. (Marx, 1990, pp. 195–196)

All commodities are in equivalence with all other commodities always. Money is simply a stand-in for a singular denomination of all exchange values.

Do Commodities Exchange at Their Labor Values?

It is interesting to note the contemporary statistical studies on whether commodities exchanged for their embodied labor values have found that commodities do exchange close to their labor values. Shaikh has found that "almost 92% of the changes in calculated prices of production are explained by changes in calculated values" (Shaikh, 1984, p. 74). The result of Shaikh's research means that commodities exchange close to their embodied labor values. The other 8% of price changes is due to the fluctuations of supply and demand. In addition, other researchers, Cockshott, Cottrell, and Michaelson (1995), have found that the labor theory of value can be empirically demonstrated with national accounts data.

With Shaikh's results in mind, the prices of items that obviously do not trade at their socially necessary labor time values need to be considered. Examples of such items are artistic works and historical artifacts. If one can buy an exact reproduction of Van Gogh's *Starry Night* for about $350.00 (this price was found on an art reproduction website), why would the original fetch tens of millions of dollars? The reason is, of course, that some items, when brought to market, will not exchange for their embodied labor values.

The price of items will be bid up or down depending on the demand for them. Since the overwhelming majority of commodities are interchangeable and do not have any historical or artistic significance, they will exchange at their values, according to Marx and the more recent empirical Marxist research.

Surplus Value and Exploitation

After Marx discussed value and money, he moved on to analyze a fundamental concept of his political economy, **surplus value**. Before undertaking a technical presentation of Marx's analysis of surplus value, let us make a brief consideration of what it is in general. Surplus value can be understood as the value that exceeds the invested value of a business venture when the venture has been completed. For example, suppose a merchant purchases $100.00 worth of commodities in one region and sells them in a different region for $150.00. At the end of her venture, the merchant has $150.00, which exceeds the invested value by $50.00 ($150.00 – $100.00 = $50.00). Thus, the surplus value obtained through the merchant's venture is $50.00. We commonly call the return on business venture "profit." The common definition of profit is the amount that remains after costs are subtracted from revenue. Profit and surplus value are not identical in Marx's political economy, as will be shown below.

In Chapter 4 of the first volume of *Capital*, Marx introduces some symbolic notation to help demonstrate the origin of surplus value (Marx & Engels, 1978, pp. 329–336). The notation is

C = Commodity

M = Money

M′ = M + ΔM = The original amount of money plus an additional amount of money

Marx utilizes this notation to demonstrate the circulation of commodities. Circulation is the movement of commodities throughout the economy, which is facilitated via exchange. For example, a person sells wood for money and then uses this money to buy bread. Marx would abstractly represent this example in the notation as C-M-C (commodity-money-commodity). In expanded form, this means C(wood)-M(money)-C(bread). A slightly different circulation example would be using money to purchase bread and then selling this bread for money. In Marx's notation, this would be M-C-M: M(money)-C(bread)-M(money).

The reason Marx introduces this notation is to show that a demonstration of the circulation of exchange relations is only the transfer of equivalents. Using money to buy a commodity only to sell the bread for the same amount of money is not only a pointless activity; it is not what business activity is about. When business is conducted, the point is to make more money than one invested. The point of business is to gain surplus value. Thus, to conceptualize a business venture as M-C-M does not describe the phenomenon of capitalism in which wealth increases. Rather, it is accurate to describe the business activities of capitalism as M-C-M′ where $M′ = M + \Delta M$. Money is exchanged for commodities and those commodities are sold for an amount of money greater than the original investment.

If exchange is supposed to be an exchange of equivalents, then where does the additional amount of money come from? That is, where does the surplus value come from? An obvious candidate for an origin of surplus value is through theft. Thieves can gain more through their thefts than it costs them in effort. Thus, they achieve surplus value by taking other people's commodities. Capitalism has had periods during which theft and plunder have provided an important way to gain surplus value—for example, the theft of precious items by piracy, pillage, or enslavement (Mandel, 1962, p. 103). This is not the means that Marx finds to be the main locus for gaining of surplus value. Additionally, no new value is created through theft. The value is only forcefully transferred from one person to another.

In addition, if one doesn't know the value of the items for sale, then one can be tricked or coerced into paying a higher price. This can be most commonly achieved in trading situations in which the buyers are disconnected from regular markets or after a natural disaster. The gaining of surplus value from selling in poorly informed markets or supply-deficient markets is temporary. These markets usually will bring in more merchants who are attracted by the higher than average surplus value. Eventually prices will drop due to increased supply (Mandel, 1962, p. 84). Once again, no new value is created when commodities are sold in poorly informed or supply-constrained markets.

The gaining of surplus value through theft, supply constraints, or lack of information is not the hallmark of the idealized capitalism that Marx assumes in his economic models. Rather, economic growth, which is an increase in value as opposed to a mere transfer of value, is indicative of capitalism. If items mainly exchange at their value and theft and special markets are not the main drivers of capitalist growth, where does surplus value come from?

Marx's answer to the origin of surplus value is his theory of exploitation. Surplus value is the result of exploitation of workers in the production process. According to the moral standards of capitalism, the exploitation of workers in the production process is not theft (Marx, 1990, pp. 680, 759). Marx would stress that the exploitation of workers in the production process is legal and moral within capitalism; this does not mean it is advantageous to workers. Capitalists gain at the expense of workers through the extraction of surplus value in the production process. Capitalists' accruing wealth allows them to be more powerful than workers politically. In addition, exploitation prevents workers from starting their own businesses. Marx concludes that exploitation is a disadvantage for workers, even if it is not seen as illegal or immoral by the standards of capitalism.

In order to understand how surplus value is produced through the exploitation of workers in the production process, two questions must first be answered: What is the production process? How is exploitation possible when workers are paid the full value of their labor power?

The **production process** is by which the current value of production inputs is preserved and new value is created through laboring. Surplus value is created in the production process, which allows for capitalists to enjoy more money at the end of the circulation of commodities, which is represented as M-C-M'. Since within idealized capitalism of Marx's models the majority of surplus value is due to the creation of new value within the production process and not through theft, poor information, or supply constraints, the origin of M' (i.e., more money than was originally invested) needs to be demonstrated. Marx introduces some new notation in order to explain how new value and surplus value are created in the production process (Marx, 1981, pp. 109–118):

P = Production process

L = Labor power

MP = Means of production

C' = C + ΔC = The original value of the commodities plus the newly created value

Utilizing the new notation, the production process can be simply demonstrated as:

$$M\text{-}C\text{-}P\text{-}C'\text{-}M'$$

This can be read as money (M) is used to purchase commodities (C) that are used in the production process (P), which results in commodities of a greater value (C') that can be sold for their equivalent value in money (M').

The expanded version of the production process allows one to see how new value and surplus value are created. The expanded version is:

$$M\text{-}C\text{-}P(L \text{ and } MP)\text{-}C'(C + \Delta C)\text{-}M'(M + \Delta M).$$

This expanded version can be can be read as money (M) is used to purchase the commodities (C) of labor power (L) and means of production (MP) that are used in the production process (P), which result in commodities of a greater value ($C' = C + \Delta C$) that can be sold for their equivalent value in money ($M' = M + \Delta M$).

As can be seen, the origin of surplus value occurs in the production process when labor is combined with the means of production. Value is created in the production process. Concrete labor is combined with particular raw materials and tools, and machines are used to create a product of higher value. For example, 8 hours (of value) of labor power combined with the value equivalent of 10 hours of raw timber and 2 hours of electricity are used to create wood boards whose value is equal to 20 hours of value. The application of labor power and energy to raw materials creates a higher-value product. The higher value is due to the additional expenditure of labor power and means of production in the fabrication of a new commodity. As has been previously discussed, a commodity is exchangeable in the equivalent of socially necessary labor time it takes to fabricate a product. Thus, wood boards are equal to 20 hours of value because they embody 20 hours of expended labor, 8 hours of direct labor and 12 hours of labor embodied in the harvested raw timber and the transmitted electricity.

The wood board example does not yet demonstrate the origin of surplus value, since all of the values listed are equivalent: 20 hours of value go into the production process and 20 hours of value come out. True, an item of higher value emerges, but it is equivalent to the value of the inputs. If capitalists invest their **capital** to achieve a return worth greater value, how does it happen? Where one must look to understand where surplus value comes from is the vantage point of the capitalist and what exactly the capitalist buys when she buys labor power.

Labor power is a very special commodity when it comes to the creation of value. From the perspective of exchange, when a capitalist buys labor power, it is like every other commodity. All commodities exchange at their values, and their values are equivalent to the socially necessary labor times for their production. What is the value of labor power? It is its cost of production in hours of embodied labor power:

> The value of labour-power is determined, as in the case of every other com-
> modity, by the labour-time necessary for the production, and consequently also
> the reproduction of this specific article. . . . in other words, the value of labour-
> power is the value of the means of subsistence necessary for the maintenance
> of its owner. (Marx, 1990, p. 274)

The cost of the production of labor power is the cost of purchasing the
subsistence for the bearer of labor power to live. The commodities comprising subsistence can have a large range: from food and shelter to pensions
and vacations. No matter what the level of subsistence, it is always in an
amount of value. When a capitalist purchases the labor power of a worker,
the price she pays is the cost of production for the labor power. If a capitalist purchases 1 week of labor power, then the price is equivalent to the cost
of producing 1 week of labor power. The cost of labor power is equal to the
consumption of all the commodities required to produce a certain amount
of labor power. The cost of purchasing the food, shelter, transportation, and
whatever else is included in the subsistence for a worker and her dependents
is the cost of labor power for the capitalist.

The wage of a worker is equivalent to the subsistence of that worker for
the time purchased by the capitalist. The product produced by the worker is
worth a greater value than the cost of her labor. The origin of surplus value
is that the worker produces more value than the cost of her labor power. The
inputs and outputs of the production process are equivalent: If 20 hours of
value are expended in 8 hours of labor power and 12 hours of materials,
then the product is worth 20 hours of value. If the price of the subsistence
of a laborer is equivalent to 4 hours of value, then the total cost to the
capitalist is 16 hours of value. Thus, the capitalist pays for 16 hours of inputs
(4 hours for labor power and 12 hours for materials) and receives 20 hours
in revenues with a profit of 4 hours.

Surplus value is possible because the worker can produce value in
excess of her subsistence requirements. If a worker and her dependents
require commodities equal to 4 hours of labor per day, then the capitalist pays wages equivalent to 4 hours of labor for a day of work from the
laborer. If a day of work is 8 hours, then the capitalist receives 8 hours
of value for the price of 4 hours of value. Marx describes the process
as such:

> Therefore, the value of labour-power, and the value which that labour-power
> creates in the labour-process, are two entirely different magnitudes; and this
> difference of the two values was what the capitalist had in view, when he was
> purchasing the labour-power. (Marx & Engels, 1978, p. 357)

When a laborer works for a capitalist, she produces an amount of value that is worth more in value than the cost of reproducing her labor power.

Marx utilizes new notation to demonstrate the rate of surplus value and the profit rate.

His notion is as follows (Marx, 1990, p. 320):

v = variable capital

c = constant capital

s = surplus value

These terms need to be defined. First, **variable capital** is the portion of capital that is invested in labor power; in other words, it is wages. Second, **constant capital** is the portion of capital that is invested in the means of production, including raw materials, equipment, depreciation, fuel, energy, and the like. Last, **surplus value** is the portion of newly created value by workers, which accrues to the capitalist. Variable capital is *variable* because the amount spent on wages can change. The amount spent on wages can go up if labor power is scarce and/or if worker militancy and its political success are high. Alternatively, it can go down if labor power is plentiful and/or if worker militancy and its political success are low. Thus, workers can try to increase their wages and capitalists can try to decrease wages. In particular, if capitalists can lower wages, they can increase surplus value, as will be shown. Constant capital is *constant* since the amount spent on the means of production Marx finds to be set in the short to medium run. Constant capital could be reduced through productive improvements and the discovery of new mineral and fuel sources. In general, Marx finds the important relationship is not between surplus value and constant capital but rather between surplus value and variable capital.

This is because only variable capital, labor power, can be exploited according to Marx. Constant capital is embodied labor power—dead labor, as Marx sometimes calls it—and it is nonconscious matter. It is socially acknowledged as having value, but it cannot create value. The variable capital portion of capital is labor power, people's ability to produce useful items. As conscious agents, people can preserve the value embodied in constant capital and create a product that embodies more value. This is why Marx calls variable capital living labor. Workers can create the same amount of value while receiving more or less wages, within the limits of survivability. This is why the surplus value and variable capital relationship is the origin of surplus value and the focal point of Marx's analysis of capitalism.

Marx utilizes the following equations to demonstrate the rate of surplus value and the rate of profit (Marx, 1990, p. 327):

$$\text{the rate of surplus value} = s/v$$

$$\text{the rate of profit} = s/(c + v)$$

To demonstrate the relationship between surplus value and variable capital, some numerical examples will help. In Table 6.1, the total amount of created value is held constant at 10 hours of value. The shares of surplus value and variable capital are altered. The altered values change the rate of surplus value. As one can see, the rate of surplus value increases as the variable capital share decreases and the surplus value share increases. This basic relationship is used by Marx to explain several features of capitalism, as will be shown in subsequent sections, including absolute surplus value, relative surplus value, and unemployment.

Table 6.1 demonstrates a basic mathematical relationship. The difference is directly related to an increase in the numerator and inversely related to increases in the denominator. This basic relationship is a model of Marx's hypothesis of the intrinsically antagonistic class relationship between capitalists and workers. At the level of control over distribution of total value created, it is in the interest of workers to have a higher share, and it is contrary to the interests of capitalists for workers to have a higher share. If capitalists wish to remain capitalists, they must exploit workers (Marx, 1990, p. 741). In addition, they are in competition with other capitalists, which is always the case, they must *increase* the exploitation of workers (Marx, 1990, p. 739). Marx outlines a series of common practices

Table 6.1

Total value, in hours of value	s, surplus value in hours of value	v, variable capital in hours of value	s/v, the rate of surplus value
10	1	9	1/9 = 11.11%
10	3	7	3/7 = 42.86%
10	5	5	5/5 = 100.00%
10	7	3	7/3 = 233.33%

capitalist engage in to increase the rate of surplus value extraction, which is the same as the rate of exploitation. We will examine these practices in the next section.

The rate of surplus value extraction is analyzed by Marx separate from the rate of profit, even though the rate of profit is what capitalists are interested in and what drives investment by capitalists. Why Marx analyzes the rate of surplus value separately is to demonstrate that the source of any surplus on an investment has its origin not in the total amount of capital invested, c + v, which is constant and variable capital. Rather, the source of capitalist profits is the exploitation of living labor power and not the exploitation of the means of production. Only living labor power can create more value than its cost of production. The value of the means of production can only be preserved in the production process by the actions of actual laborers. Thus, the ratio of surplus value to variable capital is the important ratio to capitalists, since this is where their means of subsistence is derived.

In the short run, the amount of constant capital must be held constant since changes to plant and equipment are long-term investments. The only variable that can be altered in the short run is variable capital. There are of course productivity increases that allow for a reduction in the cost of constant capital in the long run. After cost saving through productivity increases has run its course, the only means available to capitalists to increase the rate of surplus value is to increase exploitation. Table 6.2 provides an example in which constant capital is unchanged. In addition, the rate of profit is calculated (s/(c + v)).

As can be seen in Table 6.2, in the short run, where constant capital is unchanged, the only way to increase surplus value extraction and thereby

Table 6.2

Total value, in hours of value	s	c	v	Rate of Surplus Value s/v	Rate of Profit $s/(c + v)$
10	1	5	4	1/4 = 25.00%	1/9 = 11.11%
10	2	5	3	2/3 = 66.66%	1/4 = 25.00%
10	3	5	2	3/2 = 150.00%	3/7 = 42.86%
10	4	5	1	4/1 = 400.00%	2/3 = 66.66%

increase the rate of profit is to increase the rate of exploitation. This means, of course, an intensification of the class struggle by capitalists attempting to lower the wages of laborers.

Any readers who are interested in empirical estimates of the rate of surplus value should see Moseley (2000, p. 63) and Shaikh and Tonak (1994, p. 128). These authors provide an extensive discussion on how the rate of surplus value can be estimated using conventional economic data sets, which do not utilize Marxian categories of analysis.

Absolute and Relative Surplus Value

If exploitation makes surplus value extraction possible and thereby is the source of capitalist profits, then increases in or at least maintenance of the rate of exploitation is in the interests of capitalists. Marx analyzed two general means to increase profitability within the production process. These are the absolute and relative means of surplus value extraction. There are other ways of increasing profitability that are not directly within the production process, such as keeping wages down through unemployment and the replacement of adult male workers with immigrants, children, and women through the use of biased wage legislation and mores (Marx & Engels, 1978, p. 404). Marx's theory of unemployment will be considered below.

Absolute Surplus Value

The ratio of surplus value to variable capital was discussed earlier. The rate of surplus value can be increased by decreasing the amount of capital, which is spent, on variable capital. In a nutshell, the rate of surplus value can be increased when the wages of workers decrease in the *ratio* of surplus value to variable capital. Declining wages with a simultaneous and proportionate declining surplus value will yield the same rate of surplus value extraction. In addition, decreasing the wages of workers explicitly can be difficult, particularly when the economy is in an expansion. If workers can find work elsewhere, they have little rational reason to stay at their current job for less pay. In addition, explicit reduction in workers' wages may be illegal (due to minimum wage laws, etc.). Capitalists are thus interested in finding ways of decreasing the amount of variable capital relative to surplus value. Marx identifies two means of doing so within the production process: absolute surplus value extraction and relative surplus value extraction.

Absolute surplus value extraction is a rather brute means of reducing the ratio of variable capital to surplus value. Absolute surplus value extraction is basically the lengthening of the working day while holding the amount spent on variable capital constant. The length of the working day can be expanded in two ways: (1) through more time spent working at the work site per day overall and (2) an increase in the time spent working through a reduction in breaks and meal times. Marx's analysis of absolute surplus value extraction is premised on workers receiving a day rate for wages. A day rate is payment for a day of work, not an hour of work. Of course, if a "day" of labor is not defined, then the possibility of workers laboring longer for the same pay becomes cogent.

If the working day is undefined by some kind of limit, such as 8 or 10 or 12 hours of work, then capitalists will be able to increase the rate of exploitation by diminishing the amount of variable capital in the ratio. For example, if the current day of work is 8 hours and the cost of labor power is 4 hours, then the rate of exploitation is 100%: 4 hours surplus value divided by 4 hours of variable capital. The day rate in wages is equal to 4 hours of value. If the capitalist extends the day of work to 10 hours and the cost of labor power stays the same, then the rate of exploitation has increased to 150%: 6 hours of surplus value divided by 4 hours of variable capital. Obviously, for people who receive a day rate (or, more commonly in contemporary capitalism, those who receive a yearly salary), there is the possibility of absolute surplus value extraction occurring (Marx & Engels, 1978, p. 361).

Marx documented numerous cases in industries in which there was no limit to the working day and the appalling conditions people labored in during the 19th century. These cases include children as young as 5 working 15 hours straight and a woman who died from overwork. She sometimes worked for 30 hours straight (Marx & Engels, 1978, pp. 367, 371).

Marx notes that absolute surplus value extraction does not have to be legal. Workers could be forced to start early and end late by their employers (Marx & Engels, 1978, p. 366). Workers may accede to this illegal activity in order to keep their jobs. These kinds of exploitative work practices have become common in contemporary China (Li, 2011; Weil, 2006, 2008).

The second means to achieving absolute surplus value extraction is a reduction of breaks and meal times during a regular work period. Obviously, making workers labor more and not paying them increases the value of surplus value. For example, if a worker is supposed to receive two 15-minute breaks per workday and is coerced into taking only 10 minutes per break, the worker is exploited an additional 10 minutes per day. With a 6-day workweek, this is 1 hour of additional exploitation a week and 52 hours a year. Once again, Marx notes this reduction in break time may be illegal (Marx & Engels, 1978, p. 366).

There are two limits to the extension of the working day: physical and moral (Marx & Engels, 1978, p. 362). The physical limits of the working day are the general requirements of sleeping and eating. The moral limits are determined by the "intellectual and social wants" of the worker (Marx & Engels, 1978, p. 362). If we take Marx's comments on the variability of wages in *Wages, Price and Profit* as a guide, then we can surmise that the moral limits of the working day are determined socially (Marx & Engels, 1968, p. 222). This means that a society becomes accustomed to a certain pace of work and leisure, with the length of the working day limited by such preferences. Different outcomes regarding work can be demonstrated by the number of average hours worked per year for different industrialized countries: France, 1,562; Germany, 1,419; Italy, 1,778; Sweden, 1,624; United Kingdom, 1,647; United States, 1,778 (OECD, 2011, Table G).

Relative Surplus Value

Absolute surplus value extraction is achieved by lengthening the working day while the necessary labor time is kept the same in the ratio of variable capital to surplus value. Relative surplus value extraction is achieved by reducing the necessary labor time in the ratio while the total workday is kept at the same length. This reduction in necessary labor time is achieved through productivity increases. That is, more use values are created in the same amount of time. This means that surplus value will rise because variable capital is reduced.

An example will help demonstrate the notion of relative surplus value extraction.

In Table 6.3, two production schemes are represented. The difference between scheme 1 and scheme 2 is that scheme 2 represents a productivity

Table 6.3

Scheme	Total items produced	Wages	Means of production	Price per item	Total revenue	Surplus value	Rate of surplus value
1	10	$50.00 per day	$10.00	$10.00	$100.00	$40.00	$40/$50 = 80%
2	20	$50.00 per day	$20.00	$10.00	$200.00	$130.00	$130/$50 = 260%

increase. The change in productivity is simplified for ease of exposition, with the only change in technology being an increase in the cost of means of production, which is relative to the cost of materials. In both schemes, the cost of materials per item produced is $1.00. It takes 1 hour to produce one item with the technology of scheme 1. In addition, in scheme 1, the value produced by 1 hour of labor is worth $9.00. This means that if a worker labors for 10 hours, she produces $90.00 worth of value with the technology of scheme 1. Since the constant capital cost per item is $1.00 and the value added is $9.00, the price per item is $10.00. If 10 items are produced in 10 hours, this is $100.00 worth of value. Subtracted from this $100.00 worth of value is the going day wage of $50.00 and $10.00 for means of production (10 items produced at $1.00 materials cost per item). After these costs are subtracted, there is $40.00 of profit remaining. The necessary labor time is equivalent to $50.00 and the **surplus labor time** is equivalent to $40.00, which is a rate of surplus value of 80%. Thus, in scheme 1, the worker produces their subsistence after fabricating five items. Of the remaining five items that they create, one covers the costs of materials and four can be sold for surplus value.

The technology in scheme 2 doubles the output so two items can be produced in 1 hour. The material cost is the same, $1.00 per item. The amount of value added with scheme 2 technology in 1 hour is doubled to $18.00. The total amount of value added is $180.00. The cost per item has stayed the same at $10.00. With the production of 20 items in 10 hours, total revenue is $200.00. From this $200.00 is subtracted $50.00 in wages and $20.00 in materials, leaving $130.00 in profit. The necessary labor time is still equivalent to $50.00, but the surplus labor time is now equivalent to $130.00, which is a rate of surplus value of 260%. Thus, in scheme 2, a worker produces their subsistence again after fabricating five items—that is, in 2.5 hours. Of the 15 remaining items, 2 cover the cost of materials and 13 can be sold for surplus value. The worker produces their subsistence twice as fast, but they still receive the same wage. This is why the rate of exploitation increases when workers do not gain from technological improvements in productivity.

With this example, it can be understood that if wages can be held constant while there are productivity increases, the rate of surplus value can be increased. Interestingly, in the United States, wages have tracked productivity throughout the postwar period until the early 1970s, when wages did not grow as fast as productivity (Baker, 2007). Shaikh noted that "real wages tend to grow more slowly than productivity, i.e. the rate of exploitation tends to rise" (Shaikh, 2010, p. 49). There has been a turnaround in profitability also since the early 1980s that Shaikh concludes was assisted by a reduction in the wage component of total income (Shaikh, 2010, p. 50). Labor's income share of total income has declined from 75.6% in 1973 to 70.9% in 2009, while capital's income share of total income has increased from 13.8% to 19.9% (Economic Policy Institute, 2012a).

Productivity increases can conceal the rate of exploitation, since from the perspective of the worker, they spend no more time at work. They are now effectively producing more value for capitalists and relatively less for themselves. It becomes apparent that workers need analytical tools to keep track of the rate of exploitation and, accordingly, the degrees of power in the class conflict between capitalists and workers. The more surplus value that capitalists control, the greater their ability to withstand strikes by their workers, the greater their ability to finance research that supports capitalist outcomes, and the more influence they can have in the media and over political candidates. The more wages workers receive, the greater their ability to perform similar activities: support strikers, fund proworker research, and support proworker candidates.

The example is very simple since there are no real changes that occur in production other than an increase in the output of the produced item. Marx, as was shown in the chapter on historical materialism, found that changes in technology bring about wider social changes. Two results that Marx found to be indicative of technological change within capitalism are increases in unemployment and a decrease in the rate of profit. These will be considered in greater detail next.

Relative surplus value extraction can be performed in two other ways that do not utilize changes in technology: (1) changing the intensity of production and (2) the use of piece wages. The intensity of production is the pace at which people must labor (Marx, 1990, p. 533; Marx & Engels, 1978, p. 407). This changing of the intensity of production can bring about relative surplus value extraction since a greater pace of work will produce more output in the same span of time, thereby yielding a greater revenue while wages remain the same. The result is the same as the example from Table 6.3: the necessary labor time is reduced. Intensification can occur in two ways, an increase in the number of articles produced and the taking on of additional tasks. The first kind of intensification is when people must work fast at a given set of tasks. For example, an autoworker must work faster if they must produce 6 cars in 8 hours instead of the former 5 cars. Another example is when a mail clerk must sort an amount of mail that was previously sorted by two people in the same amount of time. These examples could be extended to the number of patients a nurse must see in a shift or the number of classes a teacher must teach in a day or the number of people an executive assistant works for.

The second kind of intensification is when a worker takes on tasks that were once performed by another person or persons. For example, a secretary who must now also act as a receptionist has had their labor tasks intensified. One person must now perform the activities that were once performed by two people. This practice of reducing workforces and dividing the tasks that were performed by many people is common in economic downturns as firms shed employees. This is effectively a reduction in workers' wages since they perform more tasks in the same amount of time. Or, as Marx would put it, they perform their necessary labor in a shorter amount of time, which is an increase in exploitation.

Piece wages are another means to extract relative surplus value. Piece wages are when workers are paid by the number of items they produce, the number of patients they see, the number of students they teach, and so on. If people are paid by the piece, there is a tendency to speed up their own work. Capitalists can extract more surplus value by increasing the complexity of the piece to be produced or by utilizing standards for production speed (Marx, 1990, p. 694). If the item that must be produced is more complex but is still considered one piece, then the amount of time spent on the item increases and accordingly wages fall. In addition, if workers must produce more pieces in the same amount of time, this is also a reduction in wages, since workers are working harder for the same amount of pay.

Marx was a strong critic of the pace of manufacturing along with his critique of relative surplus value extraction. His comments in *Capital* are similar to his pronouncements in *The Communist Manifesto* almost 20 years earlier:

> Some crippling of body and mind is inseparable even from division of labour in society as a whole. Since, however, manufacture carries this social separation of branches of labour much further, and also, by its peculiar division, attacks the individual at the very roots of his life, it is the first to afford the materials for, and to give a start to, industrial pathology. (Marx & Engels, 1978, p. 399)

Accumulation and Unemployment

An obvious and commonly discussed characteristic of capitalism is the high level of economic growth that has occurred since the beginning of industrialization in the late 18th century compared to earlier phases of human history (Jones, 2002, p. 12; Maddison, 2010, Table 2). Marx notes that the preferences of capitalists are a motive force of this growth. After capitalists have satisfied their initial desire for wealth, they are driven to maintain their position:

At the historical dawn of the capitalist mode of production—and every capitalist upstart has to go through this historical stage individually—avarice, and the drive for self-enrichment, are the passions which are entirely predominant . . . Moreover, the capitalist gets rich, not, like the miser, in proportion to his personal labour and restricted consumption, but at the same rate as he squeezes out labour-power from others, and compels the worker to renounce all the enjoyments of life. Thus, although the expenditure of the capitalist never possesses the *bona fide* character of the dashing feudal lord's prodigality, but, on the contrary, is always restrained by the sordid avarice and anxious calculation lurking in the background, this expenditure nevertheless grows with his accumulation, without the one necessarily restricting the other. (Marx, 1990, p. 741)

Capitalists drive growth by extracting surplus value. Growth occurs not only through making workers labor longer or more intensively but also by increasing productivity through technical change. As was shown, Marx was well aware that the preferences of capitalists for a continual increase in the amount of surplus value they gain causes capitalists to seek technical changes that will bring about relative surplus value extraction. In the common understanding of capitalism as well as in Marx's analysis, capitalism is synonymous with growth and rapid technical change.

Marx finds that another common conception of capitalism, the understanding that it produces a growth of employment, is not entirely correct. Marx found that growth within capitalism does not bring with it a corresponding growth of employment and that the growth with capitalism actually requires unemployment (Marx & Engels, 1978, p. 428). In short, there is a tendency for capitalist economies to have a continuous portion of their populations in unemployment, but the unemployed are not necessarily chronically unemployed. This means that capitalism does not lead to full employment, with full employment being defined as when all people who desire to be employed can find employment. Marx's term for the unemployed population is the *reserve army* or the *reserve army of the unemployed*.

Marx's comments on unemployment are structured within his response to Thomas Robert Malthus, the major theorist on overpopulation of the poor and the unemployed in the early 19th century. Malthus's theory of overpopulation is that the poor, due to lascivious attitudes toward sexual intercourse, will tend toward overpopulation if their wages are too high. Eventually a period of high wages would bring about an exhaustion of the food supply and starvation would result. The size of the working population was thus regulated by the limits of food. The outcome of Malthus's theory was that the poverty of workers was inevitable due to their natural proclivity toward overpopulation (Hunt, 1992, pp. 78–96). Malthus's predictions about a limited food supply have not been correct; poverty and hunger are distributional issues and not issues of absolute scarcity (Foley, 2006, pp. 45–61; Sen, 1999, pp. 160–188).

Marx found that the impoverishment of workers is not due to overpopulation but rather is due to exploitation and unemployment:

> But in fact, it is capitalistic accumulation itself that constantly produces, and produces in direct ratio of its own energy and extent, a relatively redundant population of labourers, *i.e.,* a population of greater extent than suffices for the average needs of the self-expansion of capital, and therefore a surplus-population. (Marx & Engels, 1978, p. 422)

Marx attempts to demonstrate that this passage is correct by showing that (1) growth within capitalism does not bring with it a corresponding growth of employment and (2) growth with capitalism actually requires unemployment. Marx provides some interesting empirical examples that won't be considered here (Marx, 1990, pp. 791, 803).

First, Marx finds that the dynamic for technological change within capitalism brings about unemployment (Marx & Engels, 1978, pp. 422, 425). Capitalists seek techniques that will increase the rate of surplus value extraction by reducing the share of variable capital in the ratio of surplus value to variable capital. The share of variable capital can be reduced by absolute and relative surplus value extraction as discussed. In addition, the share of variable capital can be reduced by reducing the number of workers through the increased use of automation. Capitalists will seek technological advancements, which allow them productivity increases and allow them to reduce their workforces. Thus, there is a tendency within capitalist economies to replace workers with machinery and not a tendency toward full employment.

Not only does capitalism have a tendency toward labor-saving technological innovation, but capitalism is also always seeking new markets and new products, which are not simply replacements to previous ones. The mass entertainment industry is a new industry and not simply a replacement for free time, nor is the automobile just a replacement for mass rail transit and the horse-drawn buggy. In order for a new industry to arise, there must be, among other factors, a workforce available to produce the new good or service. In order for people to replace their home-cooked meals with restaurant food, there must be workers available to prepare and serve those new products. In order for cars to become devices for short- to medium-range personal transport, workers must be available to build the parts, assemble the vehicles, build and maintain the roads, service the vehicles, and regulate their use. These available workers are those who are unemployed or are not part of the formal nonsubsistence farming workforce (the details of the different groups Marx identifies as unemployed are forthcoming).

In order for capitalism to grow, Marx finds that there must be unemployed people to staff the new industries (Marx & Engels, 1978, p. 423). To understand the structural phenomenon of unemployment for capitalist growth, it must be stressed that Marx is not saying that capitalism produces unemployed workers. Rather, Marx notes that capitalism requires an unemployed workforce for the growth dynamics of capitalism to operate as a *precondition*. This means that the unemployed must exist before capitalism expands. Interestingly, Marx's comments on primitive accumulation note the need for an unemployed workforce (willing or unwilling) for capitalism to begin.

Unemployment provides an additional condition for capitalism to operate according to the preferences of capitalists: It controls the growth of wages. "Taking them as a whole, the general movements of wages are exclusively regulated by the expansion and contraction of the industrial reserve army" (Marx & Engels, 1978, p. 426). As has been discussed, the main determinant of wages is the cost of the reproduction of labor power for workers and the care of their dependents. All commodities are subject to the fluctuation of supply and demand. The price of a commodity will increase if demand for that commodity increases, and its price will decrease if demand decreases. To prevent cost increases, the expansion of the supply of a commodity will help dampen upward price movements. If there are unemployed workers, there is an excess supply of the commodity of labor power. An unemployed population helps to keep the cost of wages in check by competition for scarce jobs between workers (Marx, 1990, p. 689).

Marx notes that there are obvious benefits for capitalists if they do not attempt to employ the reserve army. If wage growth increases as fast or less than the growth of the economy, then capitalists' share of surplus value should stay the same or increase, all else held equal. If the unemployed became employed, wages would increase since there would no longer be an excess supply of labor power. Marx is thus not surprised that capitalists and apologetic social scientists are generally hostile toward any assistance to the unemployed (Marx & Engels, 1978, p. 428).

Marx identifies three main groups among the unemployed and one additional group he calls paupers. The three main groups are called (1) the floating, (2) the latent, and (3) the stagnant (Marx & Engels, 1978, p. 429).

The floating reserve army of the unemployed are mainly people who have been previously employed. In Marx's own time, these workers were mainly males who were employed as children but were no longer employable since adults earn higher wages than children. Members of the floating reserve army may become employed again for a time (Marx, 1990, p. 794).

The latent reserve armies are those people who are currently employed in agriculture. In the industrializing phases of capitalism, when large numbers of people were employed in agriculture, these workers could migrate to cities as their rural employment opportunities became replaced by mechanization (Marx, 1990, p. 796). In industrialized countries, the latent reserve army composed of recently unemployed agriculture workers is rather small (Heilbroner & Galbraith, 1990, p. 597). There is a large number of people who are still employed in agriculture in industrializing countries.

The stagnant reserve army of the unemployed is those "with extremely irregular employment." This population is available for "special branches of capitalist exploitation," in particular manufacturing done within people's homes (Marx, 1990, p. 796). The stagnant reserve army appears as workers in the informal sector within modern economies. In the informal sector, people are employed sporadically at substandard wages with few or no benefits.

Finally, Marx describes a group of chronically unemployed people who he describes as paupers. Paupers are made up of three groups: (1) those who can work, (2) "orphans and pauper children," and (3) "the demoralized, the ragged, and those unable to work" (Marx, 1990, p. 797; Marx & Engels, 1978, p. 429). Some paupers are people in desperate circumstances who could work, but no work is available for them. This includes groups one and two and perhaps the demoralized and the ragged of group three. The remainder, those unable to work, are included by Marx seemingly to demonstrate that "along with the surplus population, pauperism forms a condition of capitalist production, and of the capitalist development of wealth" (Marx, 1990, p. 797).

Other than some members of the third group of paupers, there are, according to Marx's reasoning, a large number of people who have become unemployed or have never been employed due to the dynamics of capitalist accumulation. Thus, the dynamics of capitalism produce enough unemployment to prevent accumulation from being inhibited and to control the growth of wages.

Unemployment has become a chronic problem in many industrialized countries, particularly given the economic downturn following the global real estate bubble. The employment-to-population ratio decreased in several industrialized countries from 2007 to 2010 (OECD, 2011, p. 239). The employment of those under 25 and over 55 is particularly poor (OECD, 2011, pp. 242–244). The International Labor Organization finds that there is a need for 600 million jobs to be created in the next decade, and this doesn't address the under-US$2-a-day poverty of 900 million workers (ILO, 2012, p. 9). Production has become very productive since Marx's day. The propensity for industry to employ new workers has greatly declined (Mehrotra & Delamonica, 2007, p. 76).

There have been some recent attempts to provide empirical estimates of Marx's conception of unemployment. Deepankar Basu has developed estimates of the reserve army in the United States utilizing Bureau of Labor Statistics data (Basu, 2013). An estimate of global unemployment utilizing Marxian categories has found that the maximum size of the reserve army may be 2.4 billion people. This is a striking number when the number of people in active formal employment is 1.4 billion people (Foster, McChesney, & Jonna, 2011b, p. 20).

In review, Marx's analysis of the phenomenon of unemployment is that the profit-seeking behavior of capitalists produces unemployment, and capitalism requires unemployment to grow and to meet the preferences of capitalists. As will be discussed next, Marx finds that capitalism requires a kind of unemployed workforce to set in motion the dynamics of **capital accumulation.**

Primitive Accumulation

A common notion is that capitalism has its origins in thrift. Individuals who had a preference for future over present consumption invested their income and became the first capitalists. This notion is partially true. In order for people to become and stay capitalists, they must not consume their wealth; they must invest it in a production process. If they do not, they will not have command over the surplus value extracted via exploitation. Capitalists must save and invest so they can continually enjoy the consumption levels they prefer (Marx, 1990, pp. 739–741).

Marx thinks that the thrift story is one sided. Capitalist accumulation takes not only savings to invest but also workers to employ who have no other means of support (Marx, 1990, p. 874). Thrift only describes that there must be a surplus available that can be invested. This surplus could be achieved through thrift. Where do the free workers come from? If capitalism had its origin in the decline of feudalism, why were serfs or recently freed serfs without employment? Freed serfs still needed to work and their former lords still needed labor to be provided on their lands, so what happened to these employment opportunities?

Marx finds that the origin of capitalism and the answer to the question "where did free workers come from?" are to be found in the particular economic history of the 15th and 16th centuries and the rise of the wool industry (Marx, 1990, p. 878). The rise of the wool industry required that more sheep be available for sheering. In order to feed these sheep, land that was currently being farmed for food to feed humans and land that was held in common was converted into privately held grazing land (Marx, 1990, pp. 877–878). These two types of lands, tillage and common land, both supported the freed serfs, which were by this time in England peasants who either worked their own land and/or worked the land of landlords. Peasants gained their subsistence by working the lands of landlords and/or farming on their own and using the products of the commons. These peasants were suddenly without their means of subsistence when they were no longer needed to farm landlords' fields or could no longer gain access to the commons.

Marx finds the enclosure of common lands to be theft of the peasants' property (Marx, 1990, p. 876, footnote 2). These lands were fields and forests in which peasants could harvest food and fuel. They were owners of these lands, as were all other people. The conversion of these lands from common property to private property was performed without compensation and without the support of the peasants. Essentially, peasants were forced from lands that they held common property rights in. Marx recounts an example of common land seizure from the 19th century in Scotland by the Duchess of Sutherland:

> Between 1814 and 1820 these 15,000 inhabitants, about 3,000 families, were systematically hunted and rooted out. All their villages were destroyed and burnt, all their fields turned into pasturage. British soldiers enforced this mass of evictions, and came to blows with the inhabitants. One old woman was burnt to death in the flames of the hut she refused to leave. It was in this manner that this fine lady [the Duchess] appropriated 794,000 acres of land which had belonged to the clan from time immemorial. (Marx, 1990, p. 891)

Primitive accumulation is an ongoing process within capitalism. This ongoing primitive accumulation is twofold. First, the dynamic process of capitalism brings more and more people into the working class. Even if people are not directly removed from common land, they enter the working class by the disappearing of work opportunities in rural areas (Amin, 2004; Bryceson, 2009; Magdoff, 2013). The loss of petite bourgeois businesses and the proletarianization of some capitalists are also means of primitive accumulation. All of these factors increase the size of the working class, making increased rates of exploitation possible according to Marx's theory of unemployment. Second, parts of the natural world are becoming owned by private interests. In particular, seed types and genomes are able to be owned (Peekhaus, 2011). Marxists are interested in these occurrences because actual species can now be private property as opposed to the common property of everyone of the world, an occurrence similar to the enclosure of common lands. This private ownership of species allows capitalists to extract surplus value from anyone who grows a particular plant, increasing their range of profitability. Similar problems also arise from the privatization of water sources (Gündüz, 2011).

Capitalist Crises

A capitalist crisis is when the growth of the economy stops or slows down. This stopping or slowing of growth results in a withdrawal of investment by capitalists, insolvency of firms and banks, rising unemployment, declining income, and increasing poverty. A crisis is a major impediment to workers' lives since their means of subsistence is gained through the selling of their labor power. If they cannot sell their labor power, they must depend on the charity of others for support, whether public or private.

Marx discusses capitalist crises in many locations in his writings. In the third volume of *Capital*, Marx provides a detailed presentation of the causes of crises and the order of their dynamics. There is a large set of work that debates what exactly Marx's crises theory is and an even larger set of work that is influenced by Marx's writings on crisis. This section will consider Marx's statements alone and will not consider in any detail the literature that has developed around his statements.

In this section, the cause of capitalist crises, a fall in the rate of profit, will be discussed first. Next, the dynamics of crisis will be discussed. Third will be a presentation of the aftermath of a crisis. Last will be a discussion of Marx's statements on the political economy of crises within capitalism.

Marx finds the fall in the rate of profit to be a cause of economic crises. He notes that the rate of profit could fall for many reasons, but Marx is exclusively concerned with a fall in profit due to technical change (Marx, 1991, p. 319). The reason Marx is concerned with technical change as the cause of the fall in the rate of profit and economic crises is that technical change is intrinsic to the accumulation dynamics of capitalism. If capitalism exists, then there will be technical change, and if there is technical change within capitalism, this will result in economic crises. Thus, to end economic crises, one's society must transition into another mode of production. Marx does not find technical change itself to be a cause of falling profits and crises. Rather, Marx finds technical change within capitalism to be destabilizing to people's lives. Marx thinks that technical change in another mode of production, let's say within communism, is not destabilizing (Marx, 1991, p. 366).

The type of technical change that Marx thinks affects the fall in the rate of profit is what he calls a rise in the **organic composition of capital**. The organic composition of capital is the ratio of constant to variable capital, represented as

$$\text{The organic composition of capital} = c/v$$

According to the organic composition of capital equation, the organic composition rises if the value of constant capital increases while variable capital is unchanged. This equation is an abstract model of the tendency within capitalism toward the unrelenting implementation of technical change. As has been discussed previously, capitalists are always seeking new production methods to increase surplus value and to develop new products to outcompete other capitalists. Marx finds that technical change usually results in capital deepening where the value of constant capital increases.

A fall in the rate of profit will occur when the organic composition of capital increases. This can be demonstrated with Marx's rate of profit equation, which is

$$\text{Rate of profit} = s/(c + v)$$

Marx found that if the rate of surplus value is unchanged and constant capital increases, then the rate of profit will fall (Marx, 1991, p. 317). Table 6.4 demonstrates this phenomenon.

Marx finds that technical change and a rise in the organic composition of capital coincides with two dynamics of accumulation called the **centralization of capital** and the **concentration of capital**. As capitalists compete, they institute technical change, which results in an increase in the total capital advanced due to higher value constant capital being used in the production process. This growth of the value controlled by individual capitalists is the concentration of capital. Due to competition and the higher entry costs brought about by technical change, there is a decline in the number of capitals in a given industry. This is the centralization of capital, ownership of a particular industry by a smaller number of firms. Both centralization

Table 6.4

c, constant capital	s, surplus value	v, variable capital	Rate of surplus value	Rate of profit
5	5	5	5/5 = 100%	5/(5 + 5) = 50%
10	5	5	5/5 = 100%	5/(5 + 10) = 33.33%
15	5	5	5/5 = 100%	5/(5 + 15) = 25%
20	5	5	5/5 = 100%	5/(5 + 20) = 20%
25	5	5	5/5 = 100%	5/(5 + 25) = 16.66%

and concentration can occur at the same time, which yields a few large firms in the overall economy. Simply put, competition between capitalists causes investment in capital equipment, which results in the centralization and concentration of capital— fewer firms that own a lot of capital. If we accept Marx's assumption that the rate of surplus value is held constant, then an increase in the organic composition of capital will result in a falling rate of profit.

The result of a falling profit rate is an overproduction of commodities and the underemployment of workers (Marx, 1991, pp. 352, 359). Overproduction is when the commodities that are produced find no one to buy them. A falling rate of profit results in overproduction because these conditions make new investment unattractive to capitalists. Workers are underemployed during overproduction because there is more than enough product already. It is unprofitable to employ additional workers under these conditions. Marx notes in his *Theories of Surplus Value* that there is no natural tendency within capitalism for all commodities that are supplied to be met with adequate demand (Marx & Engels, 1978, pp. 444–456). This notion, anticipated by Marx, forms the basis for J. M. Keynes's theory of a demand-constrained economy.

On the one hand, capitalists cannot purchase the overproduced goods because they are driven toward accumulation (Marx, 1991, pp. 352–353). They must be to be capitalists (Marx, 1990, p. 741). A capitalist who consumes rather than invests may help overproduction be overcome, but they do so at their own expense. If some capitalists consume while others do not or consume less, the former capitalists may doom themselves to being outcompeted by the latter ones. This may occur because the former spends and the latter accumulates, thus making the latter wealthier and strengthening their position as a capitalist.

On the other hand, capitalists cannot fill the gap by making more factories. Their current factories already have excess capacity since they are at overproduction. In addition, the profit rate has already fallen, making new investments unappealing. It would be contrary to the rational preferences of capitalists to do so.

In addition, Marx finds that workers can't be paid more to consume the overproduced items, which currently have no buyers. This is not only contrary to the antagonistic class relationships of capitalism but would also involve a lowering of the rate of surplus value and further erosion of the profit rate (Marx, 1991, pp. 352, 366).

Faced with an overaccumulation of capital and an overproduction of commodities, a whole new and destructive form of competition ensues in which firms employ price cutting (Marx, 1991, p. 363). This price reduction spurs consumption, further production, a rise in wages, and another fall in the profit rate (Marx, 1991, p. 365). Competition accelerates with further price cutting, and businesses that can accept a lower profit rate run their competitors out of business (Marx, 1991, p. 331).

Finally, competition via price cutting becomes ruinous and price cutting causes payment obligations to break down, and the formal crisis begins when firms become insolvent and the production process stagnates (Marx, 1991, p. 363).

In review, the dynamics of capitalist competition bring about an increase in the organic composition of capital, which causes the rate of profit to fall (if the rate of surplus value is unchanged). Additionally, the dynamics of capitalist completion cause fewer but larger firms to develop due to competition and increased entry cost due to technical change. Overproduction is the result of such overaccumulation of capital. This overproduction cannot be solved by increased consumption by capitalists or by increased investment. Competition intensifies with the use of price cutting. Payment obligations break down and an economic contraction occurs. A crisis is in full swing, with the resulting rise in unemployment and lack of investment.

Marx realized that economic crisis is the solution to the falling rate of profit. The drop in prices and economic stagnation causes capital to become devalued because of price cutting, wages decline due to unemployment, and new, less costly, and more productive machinery is implemented (Marx, 1991, p. 363). All of these occurrences raise the rate of profit. The first and last effects decrease the organic composition of capital, and the second effect increases the rate of surplus value extraction. The cheapening of constant and variable capital due to an economic crisis allows accumulation to begin again. An improvement in the rate of profit will attract new investors and growth will resume.

Marx finds that capitalism will always move through such cycles of growth and contraction (Marx, 1991, p. 364). The whole process of growth and contraction according to Marx's comments is endogenous to the dynamics of capitalism. This means that growth, crisis, and growth again are intrinsic to the capitalist social system. The motivation of capitalists is to remain capitalist. They do so by seeking profit through accumulating surplus value and driving their competitors out of business. During the growth phase of a boom-and-bust cycle, capitalists accumulate surplus value by making technological improvements. These improvements will reduce the cost of variable capital and increase the rate of surplus value. In the medium run, technological improvements lead to a declining rate of profit. If capitalists can't further increase the rate of surplus value extraction due to overaccumulation of capital and overproduction, they will try to run their competitors out of business via price cutting. They thus seek a greater share of profit by eliminating competition and gaining a larger market share. This price cutting will cause an economic contraction in which the costs of variable capital and constant capital drop. Capitalists seeking profit will invest in this new, lower-cost environment.

The whole movement of growth and contraction can be described via the motivations of capitalists. What of the motivations of workers? As has been discussed, Marx finds that workers have everything to gain from moving out of capitalism and into communism. Marx doesn't think that there can be reformed capitalism (Marx & Engels, 1978, pp. 491–499). Marx's analysis of capitalism is based on class antagonisms. What is bad for workers is good for capitalists. Exploitation and unemployment are beneficial to capitalists. If a crisis allows exploitation to increase via falling wages and unemployment, this is what capitalists want. To improve capitalism through higher wages, income transfers, unemployment insurance, public benefits, and perhaps state employment will make labor more expensive and will lower capitalist profits. Thus, there is only one solution for workers: communism.

It is common for people to find that Marx's writings on crisis are deterministic—that since capitalism produces its own gravediggers, communism will organically grow out of it. A final collapse of capitalist accumulation will occur at the end of one crisis and there will be no more growth. Marx finds that there is no economic barrier to capitalism. Rather, what is a limit to capitalism is a political and social barrier. As capitalists accumulate, they develop more and more productive technology. At the same time, workers do not get to fully and continually take advantage of these advances while they are continually subject to exploitation, overwork, meaningless work, bouts of poverty, and unemployment. As was discussed in the chapter on historical materialism, humans seek to improve their lives and fulfill needs that can be fulfilled but are currently unfulfilled. The development of the productive forces allows for new needs to be met, but the class relations of capitalism prevent them from being met. Capitalism will be replaced with communism, but not automatically. It will be replaced because workers will realize that it is their best option.

The *true barrier* to capitalist production is *capital itself.* It is that capital and its self-valorization appear as the starting and finishing point, as the motive and purpose of production; production is production only for *capital,* and not the reverse, i.e. the means of production are not simply means for a steadily expanding pattern of life for the *society* of producers. (Marx, 1991, p. 358)

Conclusion

Marx developed a comprehensive and coherent economic analysis of capitalism. The main achievement of his work is to argue that capitalism is neither universally beneficial to all social actors nor is it a stable system of development tending toward equilibrium. Standard measures of economic detriment such as unemployment, poverty, and inequality are readily available means of showing that capitalism does not benefit all people. Marx's theory of exploitation delves deeper than these measures by conjecturing that the very operation of capitalism requires the conditions of inequality. This inequality of negotiation between workers and capitalists results in exploitation in which workers become less financially powerful while their laboring makes capitalists more powerful. Capitalism is not just a failure of distribution resulting in unemployment, poverty, and inequality. It is also, according to Marx's analysis, an economic system whose operation is biased in favor of capitalists gaining over workers.

The microbehaviors of capitalists are a pursuit of profit through the exploitation of workers. The macrophenomena resulting from these behaviors are rapid technical change, a tendency toward persistent unemployment, and ruinous crises. Unemployment and economic crises are endogenous to the operation of capitalism. There is no steady path of accumulation, according to Marx's analysis, without substantially altering the structural features of capitalism. To raise wages, maintain full employment, and minimize economic fluctuations would require that the capitalist preferences for profit seeking and unlimited accumulation be curtailed. This would require capitalists not to be capitalists, an occurrence Marx thinks would be impossible.

Before this chapter comes to a close, here are a few questions for thought:

- Is Marx's understanding of unemployment still applicable?
- Can one understand the recessions and depressions of the 20th and 21st centuries according to Marx's theory of crisis?
- Can one eliminate unemployment within capitalism?
- Are employment contracts and working conditions within capitalism unjust?
- Can one have capitalism without exploitation?
- Is the labor theory of value a correct approximation of prices?

7
Ideology

A definition and explanation of ideology and ideologists before discussing Marx's own analysis of ideology will aid in the presentation that follows. **Ideology** is a set of ideas and beliefs that explain, sanction, and justify the current social structure of positions, outcomes, and authority. An ideology can thus protect a current social structure from critiques that question whether the social structure is just, natural, exploitative, beneficial, or the only possible social structure. **Ideologists** are people who create, disseminate, or use the set of ideas and beliefs that form an ideology. Some analyses of ideology find that what separates ideological from nonideological ideas and beliefs is that an ideological set is false. For example, if someone holds an idea that capitalist class relationships are the natural social structure of human societies and this idea can be demonstrated as false, then this idea is ideological.

This brief discussion is not an exhaustive presentation of ideology. It is sufficient to present Marx's own analysis of ideology. Marx started to develop a theory of ideology in some of his earliest writings. Some of the most important contributions appear in works he cowrote with Engels, *The German Ideology* and *The Communist Manifesto*. Marx's critique of ideology is an important part of his theory of society since it helps one understand why exploitative class societies are able to reproduce themselves with the willing participation of the exploited classes. As has been previously discussed, Marx finds that the class antagonisms of a given society will eventually rupture in spite of an ideology that usually inhibits revolutionary impulses and reasoning. Thus, a study of the success and failure of ideology will supposedly allow a social scientist to understand what the strong and weak moments in a society's history are in respect to revolutionary transformations. Studying these moments will allow one to understand and explain why long-lived social structures, like feudalism or ancient slave societies, have been superseded by other social systems.

In particular, Marx is interested in showing that ideology is possible due to a flawed understanding of the origin of ideas. In *The German Ideology*, Marx and Engels provide a criticism of what he understands as the Hegelian-influenced theory of where people's ideas come from. His understanding of the Hegelian idea theory and his critique are described in detail in what follows. Simply, Marx shows that our ideas are due to external stimuli and do not originate in our minds. If this is the case, then people could receive false information from others or mistakenly develop ideas about the world external to our minds with the help of their imaginations. If we can have mistaken ideas about the external world, then ideology is possible.

If ideology is possible, Marx then provides a materialist explanation for the rise of ideology based on his theory of historical materialism. As discussed in the chapter on historical materialism, development of the productive forces and population growth allow for the division of labor (specialization) to appear. Once this occurs, ideological specialists are possible. These ideological specialists are people who devote their working lives to the production and dissemination of ideology.

A theory of ideology helps explains some important features of a class-divided society. First, ideology is a means to alleviate the antagonisms that exist between classes whose relationship is based on exploitation. Second, it can complement weak class alliances or be a temporary replacement for them. Third, ideology provides social scientific, religious, or juridical justification for a social system through the development and dissemination of theories that purport to demonstrate the naturalness, eternalness, or justness of the social system.

Marx finds that ideology can be demonstrated to be false through scientific critique. It is common for Marx to point out the untenable assumptions and conclusions that orthodox social scientists use. Marx provides an alternative explanation of the phenomena under examination, which he finds to be more accurate and which does not explicitly cater to the interest of the dominant class.

It is important to point out that Marx's conception of ideology as false and supportive of the current exploitive class structure is not the only definition of ideology. As already noted, this chapter is not an exhaustive treatment of ideology. Rather, this chapter is used to elaborate Marx's theory of ideology. But other theories of ideology exist that hold that an ideological set of ideas and beliefs is neither by definition false nor supportive of the current exploitive class structure. Therborn (1980) provides an outline of a theory of ideology that hypothesizes that a set of ideas and beliefs can be ideological that are not false and not supportive of exploitation. Readers who are interested in other perspectives on ideology should take a look at Therborn's work.

In this chapter, the first section will present Marx's materialist theory of ideology. This section will include an overview of his theory of ideas and his explanation for the rise of ideologists. The second section will consider Marx's critique of the ideology of capitalism, in particular the notion that capitalism is natural and just. Special attention will be paid to ideology's impact on class consciousness. The third section will be devoted to the ideological phenomena of commodity fetishism, wages, and exploitation. The fourth section will discuss the limits to ideology and the possibility of debunking ideology.

The Materialist Basis of Ideology and the Rise of Ideologists

Marx's theory of ideology develops out of his critique of the Hegelian theory of ideas. Hegel's theory of ideas is an idealist theory. Idealism claims that some ideas we have about the world are not empirically derived. Rather, these ideas are innate to the structure of our minds. What in particular bothers Marx about this theory is that its current adherents (the Young Hegelians of the 1840s) wanted to confront the social and political problems of Europe as problems of the mind (Marx & Engels, 1978, pp. 147–148, 494). If people could only understand the truth of their being, then their suffering and their problems would be alleviated. Marx thinks this view is not only wrong but harmful since it makes people ignore the material factors that cause poverty, overwork, inequality, and preventable disease (Marx & Engels, 1978, p. 171).

There appears to be a grain of truth to the Young Hegelian position. If people are unaware of the possibilities of their world, they may be unable to understand their situation as wanting and in need of improvement. Marx's analysis of the Young Hegelians is not against informing people of different possibilities for living. Rather, Marx finds the Young Hegelians to be obsessed with how to correctly think of something and not the actual rectification of the problem: "It has not occurred to any of these philosophers to inquire into the connection of German philosophy with German reality, the relation of their criticism to their own material surroundings" (Marx & Engels, 1978, p. 149).

Marx's own theory of ideas contains a politically revolutionary potential, as opposed to the metaphysical and religious revolutionary potential of the Young Hegelians. Marx, along with Engels, hypothesizes that people's ideas are ultimately derived from external stimuli: "Consciousness is, therefore, from the very beginning a social product, and remains so as long as men exist at all" (Marx & Engels, 1978, p. 158).

The origin of human consciousness, of the contents of the mind, is the external world. The external world for humans is not just the experiences of a lone individual. Humans are born into societies and are raised in societies (Marx & Engels, 1978, p. 223). Humans' conception of the world is learned through what sensory stimuli they receive, and the stimuli they receive are from the society they are raised and live within (Marx & Engels, 1978, p. 154).

How does ideology fit into Marx's theory of ideas? Marx defines ideology as "in all ideology men and their circumstances appear upside-down as in a *camera obscura*" (Marx & Engels, 1978, p. 154). A camera obscura is a device, known for centuries before the invention of the photographic camera, in which an image of an object is projected through a pinhole onto a surface. The object appears inverted when it is projected. Ideology is thus an idea or belief about the world, but it is not accurate. Indeed, the keynote of ideology, according to Marx, is that the idea or belief is supposedly not a conjecture about the world. Rather, ideologies are ideas and beliefs about the world that supposedly reveal the true essence of the world. But they actually don't. They are not theories meant to be proven or disproven. Ideological ideas and beliefs state the world as true without empirical evidence. Ideology is by definition an idea designated as eternally true. These ideas are supposedly above critique and revision (Marx & Engels, 1978, pp. 154–155).

Ideology and those who create it, ideologists, are possible due to the development of the productive forces:

> The division of labour, which we have already seen above as one of the chief forces of history up till now, manifests itself also in the ruling class as the division of mental and material labour, so that inside this class one part appears as the thinkers of the class (its active, conceptive ideologists, who make the perfecting of the illusion of the class about itself their chief source of livelihood), while the others' attitude to these ideas and illusion is more passive and receptive, because they are in reality the active members of this class and have less time to make up illusions and ideas about themselves. (Marx & Engels, 1978, p. 173)

Ideology is a product of ideologists, and they both are made possible by development of the productive forces. If a society is able to have a division of labor and a set of people who no longer have to produce material subsistence, then ideologists are possible. Once this happens, there can be a group of people who devote their lives to the construction of philosophy, theology, legal theory, social thought, and metaphysics.

Marx definitely thinks that ideology has a ruling-class bias. Thus, the content of ideology is not only unproven, but it explicitly supports the ruling class. Ideology performs this function mainly by developing and disseminating ideas about the social system of the time, which supposedly explains it as a natural, timeless, and just system. These ideological ideas often include notions about how the position of the ruling class is just and how its control of the surplus is also just. Examples of this will be reviewed next.

Marx conjectured that the first ideologists were priests (Marx & Engels, 1978, p. 159). Who else are ideologists today? In addition, are all ideologists capitalists? People who devote their lives to creating and disseminating ideology that is supportive of capitalism and capitalists' claim over surplus value are usually paid intellectual workers. Thus, they are not usually capitalists. They must sell their labor power to gain subsistence. The term *intellectual* is used in a very broad sense here to designate anyone who does not perform manual labor. Thus, ideologists can include teachers, social scientists, the judiciary, clerics, journalists, media workers, writers, and functionaries. All of these groups can create and disseminate ideas and beliefs about our society, which is supportive of capitalism with little or no empirical corroboration. These people hold a position of credentialed authority in which they are seen as experts, highly trained, or, at least, knowledgeable of the matter at hand. Their opinions can thus appear as correct analysis of our social world. Whether their statements are ideological is a matter of fact checking and analysis of their social theories.

Are all intellectual workers supportive of the ruling class and thus ideologists? Seemingly no, as discussed in the chapter on class. Some intellectual workers realize that capitalism is detrimental to the interests of wage workers (Marx & Engels, 1978, p. 481). Intellectual workers are not by definition ideologists. There are sociologists, economists, theologians, journalists, natural scientists, and jurists who produce theories that can be empirically verified. Of course, work that can be empirically verified does not have to be critical of capitalism. In addition, work that is critical of capitalism isn't always backed by empirical observations. Nonetheless, Marx definitely finds that supporters of capitalism usually only see the facts they want to see.

Marx thought that since the ruling class owns a sizable share of the means of production, it is in a unique position to control which theories are well financed for research and which ideas are disseminated on a mass scale (Marx & Engels, 1978, pp. 172–173). Even in an age with publicly supported universities, the wealth of capitalists can still attempt to make its ideas the ruling ideas of the age. Capitalists can finance research projects that are supportive of accumulation and dissemination misinformation on environmental issues (Farley, 2012). They can start new universities and finance departments that are conducive to surplus value extraction, such as biotech, instead of those that have little profitability, such as public health. Capitalists can finance think tanks and support procapitalist researchers. Whether capitalist-controlled media will allow anticapitalist opinions to appear on the air or in print is a legitimate question to consider. In addition, will anticapitalist social scientists be allowed to voice their opinions within privately held firms? Marx hypothesizes that capitalist control over the means of production allows for the regulation of which ideas are widely disseminated.

Marx's theory of ideology developed in *The German Ideology* may appear rather obvious to contemporary readers. Marx was writing during the rise of empirical social theory and the collection of social data. Today there are vast amounts of data, which are the basis for social scientific work. Nonetheless, Marx's critique of ideologists and ideology still is cogent today, since there can still be social scientists who hold to theories that have no empirical verification. For those interested in such critiques, see Hahnel (2002) and Hunt (1992).

Capitalism as Natural, Moral, and Just

As noted, the hallmarks of an ideological idea or belief are that it is not empirically verified and that it is designated as a timeless, natural, and just institution of our social world. If an institution is timeless, it can't be changed. If an institution is natural and if we change to a different institution, then the natural institution will reemerge. If an institution is just, then we shouldn't change it. Within capitalism, the notable institutions that are considered timeless, natural, and just are the market and private property. Thus, an attempt to change to a social system that does not have markets and private property either will be impossible, will ultimately change back, or will be an unjust violation.

In *The Communist Manifesto*, Marx describes the capitalist defense of private property as

> The selfish misconception that induces you to transform into eternal laws of nature and of reason, the social forms springing from your present mode of production and from of property—historical relations that rise and disappear in the progress of production—this misconception you share with every ruling

class that has preceded you. What you see clearly in the case of ancient property, what you admit in the case of feudal property, you are of course forbidden to admit in the case of your own bourgeois form of property. (Marx & Engels, 1978, p. 487)

Capitalists and their ideological defenders claim that capitalism is the result of eternal laws of nature. Marx finds that these defenders of capitalism have to explain why human societies have not been organized along capitalist lines since the rise of humans to the 18th century. To Marx's eyes, these noncapitalist modes of production appear as refutations to the claim that capitalism is a natural and timeless social formation. In addition, according to Marx's analysis in *Capital*, people did not freely join capitalism. They were expropriated from their common property and forced into work (Marx, 1990, pp. 873–904).

Beyond the defenders' notions of the origins of capitalism, Marx's own research on the history of property relations demonstrated to him that humans have had many different forms of property over their social evolution (Marx, 1965). This lead Marx to conclude that private property is not a natural form of property. Rather, Marx finds that humans require access to the natural world and its products in order to survive and develop their lives. This materialist outlook of Marx was considered in greater detail in previous chapters. It is important to stress that Marx does not find human property relationships to be fundamental to their social interactions. Rather, Marx found human productive relationships to be fundamental. Thus, when a person analyzes the history of humans, it should not be from an idealized standpoint of rights and duties but rather from the standpoint of humans' material abilities and requirements (Marx & Engels, 1978, pp. 155–156).

The upshot of Marx's analytical outlook and the result of his research is that property relations change when the productive abilities of humans change. Capitalist private property is no more a natural form of property than the ownership of slaves is. Thus, capitalists cannot defend private property as being naturally justified.

Following what has been established, ruling classes will define certain outcomes as just outcomes. Certain outcomes will be designated as not violating freedom or as being in agreement with law. Are freedom and law defined the same way throughout all time? Different societies have defined the freedom of different people in different ways.

For example, within capitalism, there are particular freedoms that people have. People are free to own property and free to sell their labor. These freedoms are unlike other modes of production in which property or labor can't be freely sold, such as within feudalism. Within feudalism, serfs had the right to the perpetual use of the lands granted to them and to the use of common land. They were not free to leave the service of the lord they were bonded to. In contrast, workers within capitalism have no allotment of land granted to them and no protected commons for their use. Workers are free to accept and cancel their work contracts. Serfs and free workers have different freedoms in regard to property that correspond to their respective modes of production.

Notions such as these lead Marx to find that freedom within capitalism is defined as capitalist freedoms alone: "By freedom is meant, under the present bourgeois conditions of production, free trade, free selling and buying" (Marx & Engels, 1978, p. 486). Freedom within capitalism is the right to use one's property as one sees fit. One can sell it, loan it out, use it in production, give it away, let it rot, or destroy it. In contrast—and this is where Marx's critique of capitalist property comes from—there could exist other freedoms that are not guaranteed within capitalism. For example, people are not guaranteed the right to minimal housing, nutrition, preventable health care, or education within capitalism. People are guaranteed they can dispense with their property as they see fit, but they are not guaranteed the basic services for their subsistence and development of their lives.

In addition, there are other freedoms that people do not have within capitalism, such as the freedom to use the property or the freedom to participate in decisions regarding the industrial development of one's nation. If one is not a capitalist, one doesn't have these freedoms. A noncapitalist is not at liberty to use property that is not his even if the property is currently not being used. Interestingly, Marx finds that people would have more freedom if property were publicly owned since they could always have a voice in the use and distribution of that property (Marx & Engels, 1978, pp. 485–486).

Marx's understanding of freedom is structured by his theory of historical materialism. People become advocates of certain kinds of outcomes because they believe they will meet their unmet needs. Capitalist private property facilitated the development of the productive forces. Private property also results in competition and crisis. This is turn leads to unemployment, poverty, and attempts to lower wages and limit social provision of goods and services. Humans will, according to Marx, realize that they must convert private property into public property to meet their needs for subsistence, economic security, and personal and social development. Marx finds that humans can develop fuller lives as society develops. This development of the capacity for human fulfillment is dependent on modes of production also developing (Marx & Engels, 1978, pp. 441, 491).

Marx also examines additional institutions that are commonly viewed as eternal and timeless, including law, the family, and morality (Marx, 1990, p. 759; Marx & Engels, 1978, pp. 187, 487). Common in Marx's critique of all these institutions is that the current law, family structure, and moral principles are defended as natural and eternal by a ruling class. Marx, in turn, attempts to show that the institutions are variable and determined according to the historical conditions of a society. An excellent example is Marx's critique of utility:

> The principle of utility was no discovery made by Bentham. He simply reproduced in his dull way what Helvétius and other Frenchmen had said with wit and ingenuity in the eighteenth century. To know what is useful for a dog, one must investigate the nature of dogs. This nature is itself deducible from the principle of utility. Applying this to man, he that would judge all human acts, movements, relations, etc. according to the principle of utility would first have to deal with human nature in general, and then with human nature as historically modified in each epoch. Bentham does not trouble himself with this. With the dryest naiveté he assumes that the modern petty bourgeois, especially the English petty bourgeois, is the normal man. Whatever is useful to this peculiar kind of normal man, and to his world, is useful in and for itself. He applies this yardstick to the past, the present and the future. (Marx, 1990, pp. 758–759, note 51)

In this passage, one can see that Marx is critiquing the notion of utility as an ideological notion. Before considering Marx's critique further, here are a few points of clarification. The definition of utility that Marx uses to describe why people desire to use values is different from the definition used by utilitarians such as Bentham. The utilitarians' definition of utility applies to the desirability of all things in the world, whereas Marx's definition describes the desirability of only use values. Marx's critique of utilitarians' definition of utility is that utilitarians find that people only seek utility and that they always seek the same sources of utility no matter what society they live in or which time they live in. The set of items humans universally desire in all societies at all times may be a very limited set. Humans may always desire food, shelter, and friendship. Will they always desire increasing amounts of wealth and greater amounts of status?

In Bentham's own time and our own, people desire wealth and status in increasing amounts, but is this because they do so by nature or because it is valued in their society and allows them to outdo others? Marx finds that people pursue wealth and status to preserve their economic security in a capitalist society. If people did not need to compete with others to maintain their subsistence, would they still privilege wealth? Marx definitely thinks they would not (Marx & Engels, 1978, pp. 491, 531).

In addition, identifying these values has definite use in meeting the desires of a particular segment of a populace. The values of this segment may not be the values of other segments of a populace. As shown in the quoted passage,

Marx finds Bentham's definition of utility to have a class bias. If class antagonisms exist, then the utility of such policies as the minimum wage, unemployment insurance, and social provisioning of services will be different for different classes. Workers would find the utility of these policies to be higher than what capitalists would find their utility to be.

In review, Marx's analysis of timeless moral concepts like utility always takes class interests into account. In general, any exposition of an idea or a belief that argues that this belief is natural and timeless usually conceals a ruling-class bias. As will be explored in the chapter on communism, Marx adheres to one of the standard goals of political philosophy, social unity. Marx finds that social unity is not an ideal that can be pursued in all societies. Rather, social unity can only occur when classes are overcome.

Ideology and Class Consciousness

In the chapter on class, the notion of class alliances was introduced. To review, a class alliance is when two or more classes are able to mediate their objectively antagonistic relationships. Class alliances can either be strong or weak. A strong class alliance is when members of a subordinate class are made members of the dominant class. For example, when middle-class executives are granted ownership in a firm, perhaps via a partnership, these individuals become capitalists. This is an effective means to ameliorate class antagonisms. Its effect is limited since all dominant classes live by exploiting subordinate classes. If all subordinate classes became members of the dominant class, then the dominant class would cease to exist.

A weak class alliance is when subordinate classes' wages and benefits are increased in order to lessen class antagonisms. For example, if workers seek to increase their economic security, this could be greatly advanced by achieving communism. A revolutionary solution to economic insecurity is a time-consuming process that would be vehemently opposed by capitalists. The institution of a welfare state could increase economic security, not as strongly as communism would but seemingly with less opposition by capitalists. Thus, capitalists have an incentive in a country with a strong and militant working class to form a weak class alliance. Increasing wages and instituting a social safety net may be costly, but it supposedly will lessen class antagonism (Briggs, 1961).

Class alliances have been reviewed since ideology is another means of lessening class antagonisms, which does necessarily involve any increase in the wages of a subordinate class or its admittance into the dominant class. An ideological idea or belief that the current class structure is the result of natural attributes alone or is eternally just can limit class antagonisms by diverting subordinate classes' attention from class antagonisms.

For example, suppose a country is suffering from unemployment. One ideological distraction from the inability of the capitalist economic system to maintain full employment is to blame the unemployment on other nations, particular races, immigrants, or moral depravity. All nations can provide full employment via fiscal spending, but to do so would lessen capitalist power by raising wages and lowering the disciplining effect unemployment has on workers. A nation can always employ its population in gainful activity (Minsky, 2013; Wray, 1998).

The notion that particular races or their perceived behaviors adversely affect employment is a nonspecific racist scare tactic that has no empirical foundation. Immigration may increase the supply of labor power, but this does not diminish the ability of a nation to fully employ all willing applicants through fiscal spending. Finally, moral depravity as a cause of unemployment appears fanciful if one is discussing involuntary unemployment. If a person is involuntarily unemployed, what is preventing their employment is the lack of jobs not their supposedly immoral actions.

The possibility that ideological notions concerning race, ethnicity, and nation can distract people from exploitation is demonstrated in Marx's internationalist position (Marx & Engels, 1978, p. 488). Internationalism is the position that the working classes of different nations have a common interest in a victory against capitalists. The ideologies of nationalism and racism prevent workers from forming a political bloc by replacing their true problem of class antagonism with the false problems of national superiority or racial paranoia.

An example of ideological distraction, which has been alluded to previously, is the case of the French peasantry in *The 18th Brumaire of Louis Bonaparte*. In this work, Marx identifies an ideological notion that prevented the French peasantry from perceiving their true class interests. At the time of the 1848 revolution in France, the peasantry was subsisting on small pieces of land that were uncompetitive. In order to provide for themselves, peasants mortgaged their land and took on excessive amounts of debt (Marx & Engels, 1978, pp. 610–611). Marx concludes that the peasants' economic insecurity would be best alleviated if the peasants became allies with workers (Marx & Engels, 1978, p. 612). The interests of the working class in achieving socialism are the same as those of the peasants who too can find no security within capitalism.

During the 1848 revolution, the peasants eventually sided with the anti-worker and procapitalist Louis Bonaparte. Why would the French peasants side with someone that advocated positions contrary to their class interests? Marx finds that the French peasants sided with Louis Bonaparte because they had faith that a man who was a namesake of Napoleon Bonaparte would solve their dire circumstances: "Historical tradition gave rise to the faith of the French peasants in the miracle that a man named Napoleon would bring all the glory back to them" (Marx & Engels, 1978, p. 608). The French peasants thus had an ideological notion that a Napoleon could solve their problems. That is, the French peasants had faith in a Napoleon as their eternal savior.

The peasants were the most numerous class in France at the time (Marx & Engels, 1978, p. 609). If they had sided with the workers during the revolution, there could have been a decisive victory for an anticapitalist movement. Accordingly, Marx is interested in why a class would act against its own objective interests. The main reason was that the French peasants had not formed themselves into a class. That is, they had no understanding of themselves as having similar economic interests. The reason Marx thinks the French peasants were unable to form themselves into a class is considered further in the section on the limits to ideology.

Two further manifestations of ideological illusion will be considered in greater detail: the fetishism of commodities and the just wage. Both of these ideological notions obscure the actuality of the phenomena they supposedly represent. Commodity fetishism hides the fact that the value of commodities is the result of the expenditure of human labor power. The just wage conceals the fact that exploitation occurs within capitalism. Each manifestation will be considered in turn.

Fetishism of Commodities

Marx's exposition on the value from and the origin of surplus value attempts to demonstrate that the underlying social dynamics of capitalism are hidden in the everyday exchanges of commodities and the sale of labor power. Marx found that people did not perceive commodities as products of labor, which exchange according to their socially necessary labor times. Rather, people commonly understood commodities as having a natural value that was intrinsic to their existence. Marx found this obfuscation of the true source of the value of commodities to conceal the exploitative nature of capitalism. Marx called this obfuscation fetishism (Marx & Engels, 1978, pp. 320–321).

The fetishism of commodities is a belief that the value of commodities is innate to these commodities. For example, why is a liter of water worth a certain amount or why is a coat worth a certain amount? As was discussed in the economics chapter, Marx argued that commodities exchange at their socially necessary labor time. Even though the reality of exchange is according to expended labor times, commodities are generally perceived as naturally having value. It must be stressed that this is not use value that people are perceiving. Rather, commodity fetishism is the perception that the exchange value of commodities is innate.

By the time Marx discusses commodity fetishism in *Capital*, he has already demonstrated that commodities exchange at their labor times. His reason for discussing commodity fetishism is to demonstrate that the reason commodities appear to have innate value is due to the production relations of capitalism. Marx examines three other productive forms to show that capitalism hides the true origin of value. The three forms of production Marx considers are the production of Robinson Crusoe, feudal production, and production by a community of free individuals (communism). In order to clarify, Crusoe production is production by a single person with no trade or contact with others. Feudal production is a class society in which serfs are obligated to perform labor for their lord. Production by a community of free individuals is when all members of a community own the total product produced and have a say in the distribution of this total product (Marx & Engels, 1978, pp. 324–326).

What these three noncapitalist forms of production have in common is that the expenditure of labor is measured in time. Crusoe keeps track of his various laboring activities by the amount of time expended. The labor that serfs must perform for their lord is a certain amount of time spent laboring per year. In communist production, decisions about what to produce are made according to required labor time. In addition, people are paid according to their total expended labor time within communism.

In contrast to these three noncapitalist forms of production, capitalist production does not make investment decisions in labor times, nor are people paid according to their total expended labor. Rather, decisions about investments and labor contracts are made with money as the means of calculation. Marx finds that the money form of value, in which value is measured in its equivalent in money and not in labor time, hides the expenditure of labor in the production of commodities and the determination of their value: "It is, however, just this ultimate money-form of the world of commodities that actually conceals, instead of disclosing, the social character of private labour, and the social relations between the individual producers" (Marx & Engels, 1978, p. 324).

Thus, commodity fetishism is possible because the valuation of items in money and not in their labor time makes commodities appear as if they have an innate value. The price tag on a commodity lists the cost of the item in dollars, yen, drachmas, or pounds, not in what actually determines the value of the commodity, which is expended labor time. Therefore, commodities seem to have exchange value because they naturally have exchange value. The same commodity, say a liter of water, is worth a different price depending on its extraction and transportation costs. The same liter of water has less value at the source than at the end of a faucet 20 kilometers away. Why? The transport of the water through the pipes is an expenditure of human labor power.

The effects of the fetishism of commodities are twofold: It hides the social character of production and it also hides exploitation. All commodities that have an exchangeable value are the product of human laboring. Fetishism, in concealing the expenditure of human labor, hides the fact that people have spent time in producing the goods we consume. They have given up their time so people can enjoy these items. Marx obviously wants people to think about how people spend their time and to think about whether their time is well spent. In his discussion of communism, Marx notes that the control over production will allow people greater control over their time, thus allowing people to develop their abilities and interests better than they could within capitalism (Marx & Engels, 1978, pp. 441, 490–491).

Fetishism, by concealing the expenditure of human labor, also hides the origin of surplus value in exploitation. If people receive money for laboring that is equal to the innate value of their contribution, there is no exploitation. If people receive money equivalent to the cost of the production of their labor power and not an amount equivalent to the amount of value they produced in the production process, they are exploited.

Fetishism of commodities is an ideological belief that helps legitimize capitalism. A commodity within capitalism appears to have innate value as opposed to the value that is the result of capitalist production. The commodities that are produced are seen as being valuable because they have innate value. An item that people choose to produce, which is the result of human labor power, has value. If people can choose how to spend their time laboring and what items should be produced, then this means that commodities are not naturally valued but are produced due to someone's conscious choice. The fetishism of commodities hides the possibility of people deciding how to invest their labor time in producing goods and services decided not by the capitalists interested in making profit but rather by a society seeking to meet its needs. This means that people could decide to work more or fewer hours, and in this time, they can decide to produce more items to be consumed publicly or personally. Ultimately, Marx thinks that communism allows people to decide how and what their society makes. Instead of passively being advertised, items are developed to allow capitalists to stay capitalists. The ideology of commodity fetishism prevents people from realizing that they can control production and that they do not have to accept their current scheme of production as natural.

Wages

As with the fetishism of commodities, Marx finds that wages also obscure the actual dynamics of capitalism. It has been noted before that Marx found the wage rate to be variable according to two factors, one physical and one social. The wages of all workers have a physical minimum that must be met or workers will not be able to purchase their means of subsistence. Of course, workers whose labor is arduous need higher wages to pay for their physically demanding tasks. Beyond the physical minimum, there is also the social factor, which is determined by "a traditional standard of life" (Marx & Engels, 1968, p. 222). Different standards of life explain why wages are different in different time periods and in different countries (Marx, 1990, p. 701).

At the root of the matter, the wage of a worker is determined by the value of labor power. The value of labor power is the cost of producing a unit of laboring, a day, a week, or a year, along with the subsistence of a worker's dependents (Marx & Engels, 1978, p. 404). Labor power can create more value than its cost of production. Thus, labor power can be exploited, which is the origin of surplus value.

In the marketplace for labor, workers sell their labor power for a set amount of time. If a worker takes a job for 8 hours of work, she is paid to perform the 8 hours of labor. The worker labors for 8 hours and receives her pay, let's say $80. Marx finds that the labor agreement between worker and capitalist (or their agents) obscures the exploitation that takes place in the production process. If the rate of surplus value is 100%, this means that the worker produces $160 worth of value in 8 hours. Of these 8 hours, 4 hours are necessary labor time and 4 hours are surplus labor time.

When the labor contract is made, the agreement between the worker and the capitalist or their agents is not a discussion of the ratio of necessary labor time to surplus labor time. A capitalist does not state in a job advertisement that "this job is for 8 hours and you will be paid only the equivalent of 4 hours of work." This hidden nature of exploitation leads Marx to find,

> We see, further the value of 3 shillings, which represents the paid portion of the working day. i.e. 6 hours of labour, appears as the value or prices of the whole working day of 12 hours, which thus includes 6 hours, which have not been paid for. The wage-form thus extinguishes every trace of the division of the working day into necessary labour and surplus labour, into paid labour and unpaid labour. All labour appears as paid labour. (Marx, 1990, p. 680)

Within capitalism, the labor contract hides exploitation, since exploitation does not occur in exchange but in the production process. During the exchange process of the labor contract negotiation, all quantities are rendered as equivalent: $80 in wages to equal to 8 hours of work. The hidden and exploitative aspects of capitalist production go unstated.

In contrast, in the feudal mode of production, the exploitation of serfs is readily apparent: "Under the *corvée* system it is different. There the labour of the serf for himself, and his compulsory labour for the lord of the land, are demarcated very clearly both in space and time" (Marx, 1990, p. 680). Within feudalism, the serf's labor for himself is distinct from the labor for his lord, since the serf's own labor is performed at particular times of the week or year and on particular pieces of land. When a serf is working his own lands, he is working for himself and his dependents. When the serf works for the lord, he is working on a different piece of land harvesting crops over which the lord has exclusive control.

The exploitation of a serf is thus explicit. He is working on the lord's lands and the lord gains all that the serf produces on these lands. The serf is not paid for this labor provided to the lord. Conversely, a worker within capitalism labors during a period for an amount of money agreed to in a work contract. The worker agrees to work for x unit of time for q amount of money. The worker is supposedly working for herself since she is supposedly paid for the whole time she is working.

The distinction between the appearance of exploitation within feudalism and capitalism is an important one in Marxian theory. All dominant classes are dependent on exploiting subordinate classes' labor according to Marx's conjecture. But, on the one hand, the exploitation of the serf is obvious since it occurs on lands from which the serf cannot derive benefit and during times that are not spent providing for the serf's subsistence. On the other hand, the exploitation of workers within capitalism is hidden because of the nature of the labor contract. Workers labor for their own subsistence and produce surplus value for capitalists at the same time and in the same place. It thus appears as if the worker is receiving the total amount of their produced value. Instead, every instant the worker labors, they produce their wages and surplus value for the capitalist. If all dominant classes live off of exploited labor, then capitalists do also. But within capitalism, the extraction of exploited labor is hidden and requires social analysis for it to be demonstrated.

Capitalist wages appear not as exploitation but as the neutral operation of the market. Of course, if workers had greater bargaining power—if capital was plentiful, for example—workers could bid their wages to the point where there would be no exploitation. Within capitalism, wages appear to be the result of two free agents bargaining as opposed to the serf dominated by the lord. The wage thus appears to be the result of freedom and not coercion: "Thus, in imagination, individuals seem freer under the dominance of the bourgeoisie than before, because their conditions of life seem accidental; in reality, of course, they are less free, because they are more subjected to the violence of things" (Marx & Engels, 1978, p. 199).

Wages are an ideological mystification of capitalism as a system in which free agents are able to transact without coercion. The reality is that wages are the result of coercion due to capitalist control over the means of production. Wages appear as an equal exchange: x amount of laboring for its equivalent in money. If wages are the result of an uneven playing field, then capitalism is a social system whose social outcomes favor capitalists. The ideological appearance of wages prevents social discontent by hiding the fact that capitalism is a social system in which the outcome is rigged for the benefit of capitalists.

The Limits of Ideology

Since ideology can be empirically challenged, what possible ways can it be demystified? Marx lists two ways that ideology can be demystified: scientific critique and class organization. Each way will be considered in turn.

The first way ideology can be demystified is through the application of scientific explanation to a given phenomenon. Since Marx was a social scientist, he applies empirical and logical analysis of economic and social phenomena to understand it in its reality. Many of these analyses have been reviewed already: the origin of surplus value, the nature of unemployment, primitive accumulation, and the relation of class. Marx attempts to demonstrate that the common understandings of many of the ideas or beliefs people have about capitalism are incorrect and have little or no empirical corroboration, thereby showing that these ideas or beliefs are ideological.

Marx finds that social scientific analysis allows people to attempt to understand what is beyond the appearance of a phenomenon: "all science would be superfluous if the form of appearance of things directly coincided with their essence" (Marx, 1991, p. 956). Following Marx's lead here, ideology can be understood as what is commonly offered as an explanation for a given phenomenon. This seems to be the case if ruling-class ideas are dominant in a given social system. One can thus take an ideological idea or belief as the appearance of a phenomenon.

An example of this is the idea that surplus value is remuneration to capitalists for their contribution in the production process. Social science would utilize observation and logical analysis to show that in reality, the essence, surplus value is not the result of capitalist contribution but is rather due to the exploitation of workers. This example is not to offer a proof of the origin of surplus value; it is only provided to show how Marx's own research could fit into one of his means of demystifying ideology. (See also Marx & Engels, 1978, p. 54.)

One can understand that Marx's research effort is an attempt to demystify the ideological notions that are supportive of capitalism. These notions claim that capitalism is a fair, noncoercive, and welfare-enhancing system. Marx attempts to show with his exposition on exploitation, primitive accumulation, unemployment, and economic crises that capitalism is not what its supporters claim it to be.

The second way ideology can be demystified is less direct than social scientific analysis but perhaps more effective. Marx notes in several locations that a class can become conscious of itself as a class when members of that class are located together in larger numbers and when mass communication becomes widespread (Marx & Engels, 1978, pp. 480–481, 608). Class formation is when members of a class realize that there are classes, they are part of the same class, they have similar interests due to being in a class, and that class interests are in antagonism with other classes' interests. When this class consciousness occurs, there is a realization that due to the antagonism between classes, the ideological claims about the mutually beneficial outcomes of capitalism appear fanciful. That is, how can a social system have mutually beneficial outcomes if the subsistence of one class is premised on the exploitation of another class? Marx's answer is that mutually beneficial outcomes and classes are mutually exclusive.

Conclusion

Marx's theory of ideology provides a materialist explanation for the origin of ideology and ideologists. Ideologies are beliefs and theories that are disseminated via physical means. People learn ideological notions through the reception of these transmissions and printings. Why people would learn notions that are ideological, which are false notions by definition, is that the dominant class has control over which ideas and beliefs are commonly disseminated. The might of the dominant class is a materialist might. Their control over the means of production is sanctified by the dominant legal and moral notions of the age. In addition, critiques and counternotions are limited in their dissemination due to the dominant classes' control over the means of production, which includes the transmission of information.

If the materialist theory of ideology is true, this means that ideology can be demystified through countertransmissions of information. The actual work of debunking ideological notions through countertheories and empirical evidence must be disseminated in order for dominant ideological notions to be demystified. The reason to debunk capitalist ideology is to demonstrate that capitalism is not the best of all possible worlds, nor is it the natural and just state of human social organization. The reason to critique capitalism and the reason for the working class to form into a revolutionary class is to move toward communism.

Dominant-class ideology and class alliances provide strong bulwarks against the development of revolutionary class consciousness without any need for the more coercive anticommunist tactics of imprisonment, blacklisting, or deportation. The movement toward communism is not a direct and linear process of uninterrupted class consciousness development. If the movement from one mode of production to another can be postponed through ideology, class alliances, and force, then there is no point in the future at which communism becomes inevitable, even if it is seen as desirable. Before we consider Marx's understanding of communism, here are a few questions for thought on ideology:

- Can empirical falsification be a definitive check on what is ideological and what is not?
- Is there a timeless conception of justice Marx uses to critique capitalism?
- Are capitalist social relations natural?
- Is Marx's theory of commodity fetishism true: Is the value of commodities determined by social convention?
- Is Marx correct that the dominant ideas of an age are ideas that support the dominant class?

8

Communism

M arx is famous, perhaps more than anything else, for his advocacy of communism. This fame was undoubtedly buoyed by the establishment of several nations that claimed to be communist regimes of the type Marx recommended. This chapter will not be a discussion of actually existing or formally existing communist states. Rather, this chapter will be an overview of Marx's comments on communism and an attempt to understand them systematically.

Before the chapter moves into the formal analysis, here is a note on some terminology. Marx commonly referred to his recommended postcapitalist society as communist as opposed to socialist. In *The Communist Manifesto*, many of the political movements Marx and Engels criticized are described as socialist. A few were called communist as well (Marx & Engels, 1978, p. 497). In *Socialism: Utopian and Scientific*, Engels discusses different kinds of socialism and advocates for a variety he calls scientific socialism. Thus, Marx and Engels did not use the terminology *communism* and *socialism* in a simply binary manner. With that said, Marx was fond of the term *communism*. Marx was a founder of the Communist League and wrote a manifesto of their political ideas, the famous *Manifesto of the Communist Party*. He obviously found the term *communism* to be a distinctive political position distinguishing a revolutionary anticapitalist position from the many reformist positions current in the 19th century. In addition, when he discusses some of his ideas about communism in *Critique of the Gotha Program*, he utilizes the same term. In this book, I have tried to be consistent and use only *communism* when discussing Marx's anticipated and hoped-for form of postcapitalist mode of production. Today *communism* is usually a term that people shy away from due to its association with the Soviet Union. This is not a book about the successes and failures of the Soviet Union. This is a book about Marx and his thoughts of himself as a communist.

This chapter will first provide a brief overview of why Marx was an advocate of communism. This section will be a review of Marx's critique of capitalism, which has spanned the previous chapters. This review is a condensed review of Marx's critique, so not all of the details of his analysis will appear. Second, a consideration of what communism is for Marx will be addressed. Finally, there will be a section that shows that Marx's vision of communism followed from his critique.

Marx's Critique of Capitalism

In order to understand why Marx was an advocate of communism, one must begin with his critique of capitalism. Communism is supposed to be an answer to the ills that result from the social dynamics of capitalism. Below is a list of the ills Marx identified as intrinsic to capitalism.

1. Capitalism prevents people from maximizing their prospects for economic security. The social dynamics of capitalism have produced rates of economic growth that have surpassed any previous social system's performance. The gains from this growth are not evenly shared. Inequality and poverty can increase while a nation or the world grows richer. Marx showed that capitalism could reduce people to abject poverty even if they are employed. Growth does not in itself ensure that people have a secure claim to economic security.

Wages within capitalism can grow along with a general increase in wealth, or they may stagnate or decline. Far more important for Marx's analysis is that wages are a site of class struggle. Real higher wages are, holding all else equal, a deduction from surplus value. It is thus in the interest of capitalists to control wage growth. The result of this is that the amount of total product workers have access to will always be circumscribed by the accumulation requirements of capitalists.

Therefore, there is a tendency not only for wage growth to be limited but also for an underprovisioning of social services: education, public health, unemployment insurance, and social insurance (pensions and disability). Positive externalities can be achieved by the provisioning of basic social services, but their incubation time can be long (the length of education, for example). In addition, the enjoyments of their benefits are diffused; that is, the benefits of public health are enjoyed by all of society and not just by those who pay for them. Capitalists will avoid paying for these services while trying to enjoy their benefits by avoiding taxes and locating their factories in areas with low social spending.

What is called structural unemployment is intrinsic to the operation of capitalism according to Marx's analysis. Structural unemployment is when workers are rendered unemployed due to technical change. Marx found that there was no tendency to prolonged full employment since labor-saving technological innovation is a common occurrence. Labor-saving technological change is of course desirable, but if there is no intervention to make sure that the dislocated workers are provided new employment, the gains achieved from labor-saving technologies cannot be enjoyed by all society's members. The unemployed cannot afford to purchase the new goods and services technological change makes available. In addition, they can't enjoy the increased leisure time labor saving allows.

Additionally, Marx found that cyclical unemployment is also a problem within capitalism. Cyclical unemployment is when people are rendered unemployed due to economic contractions such as depressions and recessions. Marx theorized that competition among capitalists would result in an economic crisis due to a failing rate of profit. When these crises occur, workers become unemployed, either because the businesses they work for go out of business or their employers cut staffing levels due to a decline in orders. Marx thought that crises must occur for capitalism to stay dynamic through recovery of the rate of profit. Thus, cyclical unemployment is an intrinsic feature to capitalism.

Marx found that hunger, deplorable working conditions, dangerous housing, overcrowded cities, child labor, and the overwork of caregivers also occurred within the capitalism of his day. All of these features still exist in the world but not necessarily in all countries. The citizens of industrialized countries still suffer from hunger, overwork, overcrowding, and substandard housing among other ills (Magdoff & Magdoff, 2005). These problems, for Marx, represented squalor amid opulence.

2. Capitalism limits the prospects for the development of people's abilities and the possibility for them to work toward their lifelong projects. Marx found that the division of labor between mental and manual labor, which is between creation and execution, is exacerbated within capitalism due to the mechanization of the labor process. If people do not run their own businesses or have the correct training, they become relegated to uninteresting work. This problem is actually greater than it seems because people's chances of owning a business or gaining the training to do creative work is limited by inherited inequality and economic fluctuations of capitalism. If one is not lucky enough to be born into

a family with sufficient wealth to pay for a business or for training, then one's prospects are subject to the whims of market fluctuations. Will workers be able to save enough for their children's future if they become unemployed? The economic insecurity of capitalism can have long-lasting effects.

People of course have interests beyond their jobs. Many people live for their families and their hobbies. The time people get to devote to their non-work interests is limited by the demands of the labor market. Since capitalism does not naturally tend toward full employment, labor power is generally not a scarce commodity. Workers are thus at a disadvantage when negotiating the amount of time spent at work. Interestingly, overwork can coexist with unemployment for Marx since labor-saving technical change can reduce the workforce and have the production process speed up and continue longer.

Private ownership of the means of production prevents all applicants from utilizing its capabilities. If people wish to take their chances in starting a business or even producing for themselves, they cannot do so unless they already own some means of production or are a good credit risk. Private property becomes owned by those who can best compete with other capitalists. This process of competition can reduce the number of people who have a voice in the use of the means of production. Thus, the freedom to own private property reduces the number of people who can freely use the productive resources of society.

3. Capitalism prevents social unity from fully developing due to class antagonisms. Social unity is when the individuals of a social unit—local, national, regional, or global—see each other as members of a political community; they are interested in the society functioning correctly and are interested in all members of their society doing well. Class antagonisms, mainly due to exploitation in Marx's work, prevent the achievement of social unity since the well-being of some members is always at the expense of other members. This antagonism can be interclass and intraclass and national or international in scope.

Interclass antagonisms are the famous conflict over surplus extraction between dominant and subordinate classes. Capitalists seek to increase exploitation to increase surplus extraction, while workers seek to decrease exploitation to control more surplus for themselves or to decrease the time spent working. Class alliances and ideological notions can either temper or distract classes from their antagonisms. Marx finds that class antagonisms are objective and can only be truly ameliorated by the end of class distinctions. Social unity is impossible, according to Marx, when classes exist due to the objective antagonism arising from surplus extraction.

Intraclass antagonisms are the lesser-known conflict among members of the same class. Capitalist class members can be in competition to maintain or increase their market share, the result of which can be the dropping of some members of the capitalist class into the middle and working classes. Workers are in competition with each other for scarce jobs, good jobs, or skill attainment. Intraclass antagonism does not assist in the development of social unity among class members. The competition for jobs and skills makes people see their fellow class members as impediments to their own and their children's success.

Thus, with both intraclass and interclass antagonisms, people do not become interested in the well-being of others or the proper functioning of society since it is not a benefit to their own advancement. Due to competition for market share, investment, and job development, antagonisms can develop between the various classes of different geographical regions within a nation or internationally. The people of a given region seeking investment enter into competition with the classes of people in other regions. This results in what is called "a race to the bottom" in which there is a degradation in wages, tax rates, working conditions, and pollution controls in an effort to attract investment. A competitive investment environment thus could lead to economic growth while wages, social spending, and environmental quality decline.

4. Capitalism limits people from having a truly democratic society. For Marx, a democratic society includes not only political democracy but also economic democracy. Universal suffrage was not widely achieved in Marx's time, and he was an advocate for its expansion. Marx was also a critic of the despotic power of the state used for ruling-class goals (Marx & Engels, 1978, pp. 490, 538). Marx does not think the state can be a neutral arbiter between classes. He thought that in a class society, the state would be captured by ruling-class interests.

Beyond the control of the state in political matters, the majority of people are cut off from participation in national and regional investment decisions and participation in management decisions at their place of work. The rate, location, and kind of investments affect people's life prospects in numerous ways. The pace of investment can affect not only the speed at which people's incomes grow but also the impact of investment on the environment, the development of cities, and the time spent at work. People have preferences for all of these matters and are excluded from making decisions about them due to private control of the means of production.

Investment can be lopsided regionally or in time. A nation could have strong growth in one region and contraction in another, and needed jobs and investments may be held up due to limited demand during recessions.

Options to invest in underdeveloped or economically depressed areas are again subject to private decisions and the chance of the business cycle.

In capitalist economies, investment in goods and services production can be either privately or publicly provided. The decision to provide health care, education, retirement, transport, and utilities as a private or public venture is limited not only by notions about the limits of government spending but also by private moneyed interests. A class society in which the state has been captured by ruling-class interests may find the creation of a public venture difficult to achieve even if it has the potential for universal and/or lower-cost service (Mehrotra & Delamonica, 2007).

Decisions of what to produce can be adversely affected by the market process. In particular, people may make suboptimal decisions when confronted only with competitively determined goods and services. If products are solely marketed for individual consumption with no consideration of how to coordinate these decisions, then people may end up with the under-provisioning of other goods and services. The classic example is the consumption of cars. Cars are sold to people individually, but the effects of car ownership are shared across all of society. Each person seeks to maximize their own well-being by buying a car, but eventually the overcrowding of streets and scarcity of parking spaces ensues. The result is people spending more time in their cars traveling and finding parking. The speed and convenience of a personal car becomes canceled out when the good is overconsumed for a society as a whole. This kind of coordination problem exists for housing, health care, and education (Hahnel, 2002).

5. Capitalism is destructive to the environment. Marx definitely found that dynamics of capitalist accumulation would place surplus value extraction before environmental concerns (Marx, 1990, p. 638; Marx, 1991, p. 949). A whole field of environmentalism has developed around Marx's critique of capitalism, which is called ecological Marxism. The next chapter will be devoted to this new application of Marx's work to the problem of environmental decay.

What Is Communism?

The critique of capitalism will be returned to soon. First will come an outline of what appear to be the key elements of Marx's vision of communism. These elements are:

A. Nationalization of the privately controlled means of production (Marx & Engels, 1978, p. 490). The conversion of private property into pubic property is the heart of Marx's understanding of communism. He and Engels even say in *The Communist Manifesto* that "the theory of the Communists may be summed up in a single sentence: Abolition of private property" (Marx & Engels, 1978, p. 484).

Since Marx's call to abolish private property has become a hated and feared idea, what he means by this must be considered. In particular, the abolition of private property has developed connotations that people own no personal effects and/or that Marx thought people should live in poverty. The latter idea will be considered first.

Marx was always against a communism of poverty. He finds that people who advocate a postcapitalist society in which living is meager are responding to envy due to wealth inequalities and a general rejection of the development of civilization (Marx & Engels, 1978, p. 83). Marx's own position was that the full developmental powers of technological, science, and human ingenuity could be utilized to provide for the well-being of humans (Marx & Engels, 1978, pp. 490, 531). Marx is obviously interested in people having lives in which their needs and desires are met as opposed to denied. Whether this advocacy of development is environmentally sound will be considered in the next chapter.

Now the first common belief about the abolition of private property can be considered. To refresh our memories, this belief is that if private property is abolished then people will own nothing. All their personal effects will be owned by everyone. They would own no clothes, no books, no keepsakes, no furniture, and no personal means of transport and have no space to themselves. This idea about the abolition of private property is particularly distasteful since it means that people can't live the lives they wish to live. Effectively, people can't assemble a life with the necessary material components. For example, how can one develop a passion for making art when anyone can walk into your home and claim your artistic materials? Seemingly, you could take them back. This does not allow people to live very stable lives. In addition, this is not a reasonably cogent determination of what a person owns.

What Marx means by the abolition of private property needs to be determined. Marx argues that there is a distinction between private property and personal property. Private property is property that is used as capital. This means that private property is the means of production utilized to produce items for sale. Private property is thereby property owned by capitalists that is used as a bargaining tool to force workers into exploitative conditions. In Marx's terminology, private property is thus not the personal effects of people. It is materials used for production and exploitation.

Property, which includes the personal effects of people, is called personal property. This means that all the items that people use to gain their subsistence and to live fulfilling lives are not to be converted into public property: "When, therefore, capital is converted into common property, into the property of all members of society, personal property is not thereby transformed into social property" (Marx & Engels, 1978, p. 485).

A good distinction between personal and private property is the distinction between consumption and production for sale. If a person uses items to consume the product, this is personal property. For example, if you make a sandwich to feed yourself, then the sandwich and the items you used to make the sandwich are personal property. If you use items to make a product for sale, this is private property. For example, if you make sandwiches and sell them in a store, then these sandwiches and the items used to make them are private property. Other examples: A home used for rest and living is personal property whereas a home that is rented out is private property. A car used to drive to work is personal property, whereas a car used to chauffeur people for payment is private property.

This distinction between private property and personal property is unambiguous for people utilizing items for consumption and for the numerous people who use the means of production owned by another at their job. What about people who work for themselves or run small businesses? It would seem unappealing to many to have an individual's art business seized by a revolutionary communist government, and it seems out of proportion with Marx's comments regarding exploitation.

There is an interesting passage in The Communist Manifesto that helps clarify this problem: "Communism deprives no man of the power to appropriate the products of society; all that it does is to deprive him of the power to subjugate the labour of others by means of such appropriation" (Marx & Engels, 1978, p. 486). It appears from this statement that the ownership of property is restricted in cases where a person's ownership of the means of production results in exploitation. Simply, Marx finds that the property, which should be turned into public property, is property used to coerce people into wage contracts they would not choose if capital were not scarce.

With the quoted passage in mind, one can make a decision regarding the property of individuals who work for themselves and those who own small businesses. It seems that people who work for themselves will not have their means of production converted into public property. Their gains may seemingly be taxed away, since Marx advocates for a very progressive income tax in the transition to communism (Marx & Engels, 1978, p. 490). This means that people who become wealthy working for themselves and have no employees would not have their property seized, but their high income would be taxed away. Additionally, Marx notes in the Critique of the Gotha

Program that communism will have an egalitarian remuneration structure based on the amount of time spent laboring. How this applies to individuals who work for themselves is unclear.

People who own small businesses and have employees would have their business property converted into public property, since as owners of the business they extract surplus value from their employees. On one hand, many people don't want to have their business turned into a publicly owned venture. On the other hand, perhaps their employees don't want to be exploited. Perhaps they would rather have increased control over their economic lives. Marx thinks that ending exploitation is much more important since this allows all people to control their lives as opposed to a few.

In addition, it seems that Marx was against the seizure of peasants' property and thought their children should be allowed to inherit the lands. Marx makes a distinction between capitalists who own land and lease it to peasants and peasants who own and work their land. Once again, Marx determined what private property should be nationalized according to if the property allows for exploitation (Marx & Engels, 1978, p. 543).

Finally, Marx notes that "nine tenths" of the population owns no private property; thus, conversion of private property into public property would be an immense boon for the majority of the population (Marx & Engels, 1978, p. 486).

B. Democratic control over production, investment, and economic development (Marx & Engels, 1978, pp. 193, 326, 490). Marx notes that once communism has been established and classes have dissolved, all members of society (he doesn't say if this means only adults) will organize production: "When, in the course of development, class distinctions have disappeared, and all production has been concentrated in the hands of a vast association of the whole nation, the public power will lose its political character" (Marx & Engels, 1978, p. 490).

It appears from Marx's comments in *The Communist Manifesto* and *Critique of the Gotha Program* that members within communism will be able to determine what will be produced, how development will proceed, and what will be invested in (Marx & Engels, 1978, pp. 490, 528–529). Marx appears to be of the opinion, especially in the *Manifesto*, that at the transition point between capitalism and communism, a general increase in production is required. He was probably of this opinion due to the deprivation of workers during the 19th century, who were poorly fed, clothed, and housed. Some people in developed nations still suffer from basic needs deprivation. In the developing world, poverty is rather extreme when 1.1 billion people live on less than $1.00 a day (Mehrotra & Delamonica, 2007, p. 8).

Decisions regarding whether new lands will be cultivated, what production techniques will be used, and what new cities and towns will be constructed will be determined democratically. People will thus decide if land should be used or not and what intensity of production will be implemented in factories and on farms. Marx thought that overcrowding in cities was a major problem. In response, he advocated the relocation of some industry to less populated areas to reduce congestion and overcrowding (Marx & Engels, 1978, p. 490).

Marx thinks that society as a whole can decide how much of a surplus to produce and how it should be invested. Decisions regarding increased provision of social services, consumption, or investment in new production facilities can all be subject to democratic decision making (Marx & Engels, 1978, p. 529).

In general, the overall pace and direction of economic development will be controlled by the whole of a society. These decisions are not made by individual factories or persons.

C. Class will be abolished (Marx & Engels, 1978, pp. 490–491, 539). Marx found the possibility of rectifying the ills of capitalism within a capitalist democracy to be nil. Rather, he found that classes must be first overcome before people can have a functioning democracy (Marx & Engels, 1978, pp. 490–491). Additionally, Marx notes "that the first step in the revolution by the working class, is to raise the proletariat to the position of ruling class, to win the battle of democracy" (Marx & Engels, 1978, p. 490).

Marx thus conceives of democracy developmentally where capitalist democracy can allow workers to become the ruling class of a transitional society and then the policies implemented by the workers prepare the stage for a classless society. There appear to be three stages: (1) workers gaining control of the political institutions of a capitalist nation, (2) workers implementing policies to bring a transition to communism, and (3) a classless society resulting from the achievement of communism.

Capitalist democracy is a means for the workers to achieve power. The real institutionalization of democracy only occurs when classes have disappeared. Marx's comments hide a process not just of the end of class positions but also of the end of people holding class interests and expectations. The moment after the ruling workers nationalize private property, class positions have ended; people's inheritance of class interests and expectations continues.

For example, in order for capitalists to stay capitalists, they must desire to be capitalists. If they have no interest in maintaining their class position as capitalists, they will not take the necessary actions to accumulate sufficient amounts of capital. Eventually they will be outcompeted and enter into the noncapitalist classes. Those individuals who do have the interest to stay capitalists will take the necessary actions to do so. If the working class becomes the ruling class and nationalizes the means of production, these former capitalists will still apparently have capitalist interests. This means that even if class positions no longer exist, the former members of these classes may still have the desire to live as these classes did (Marx & Engels, 1978, p. 530).

In order for class antagonisms to end, not only do classes themselves have to end, but there apparently must be a period of transition in which people become accustomed to the new society in which people have a right to make claims upon others for their development and begin to see each other as cosupportive of all of their development (Marx & Engels, 1978, p. 197). Marx thinks that communism will develop a social union by the elimination of classes and the eventual breakdown of old class interests.

D. Universal education and training without fees charged to students and their families who enroll in public schools (Marx & Engels, 1978, p. 490). Universal primary and secondary education became standard in Europe and in the United States by the end of the 19th century. There appears to be no reason why all education at all levels can't be financed via taxes and not fees. The intentions behind universal non–fee-financed education seem in line with Marx's position that people should be able to freely develop their interests and abilities.

Interestingly, Marx had a desire to make education more practical: "Combination of education with industrial production" (Marx & Engels, 1978, p. 490). This combination of education and practical training would help overcome the division between mental and manual labor and might help reduce class antagonisms. If people grow up working and learning with all professions, they may develop a greater acceptance of people's different social positions.

Marx's progressive attitude toward universal education contains a caveat regarding the influence of the state and church. Marx thinks religion and the state should not influence the curriculum. The state can regulate the operation of school but should not advocate allegiance to the state. Marx, in his characteristic dislike of religion as ideological distraction, doesn't want the "witchery of religion" to influence what people learn in school (Marx & Engels, 1978, pp. 539–540).

E. Control by individuals regarding decisions concerning type of work and the amount of work (Marx & Engels, 1978, p. 160). Beyond economic and political democracy, which Marx argues will give people within communism the ability to control the pace and kind of investment, Marx also thinks that communism will allow people a greater control over what kind of labor they will perform:

> For as soon as the distribution of labour comes into being, each man has a particular, exclusive sphere of activity, which is forced upon him and from which he cannot escape. He is a hunter, a fisherman, a shepherd, or a critical critic, and must remain so if he does not want to lose his means of livelihood; while in communist society, where nobody has one exclusive sphere of activity but each can become accomplished in any branch he wishes, society regulates the general production and thus makes it possible for me to do one thing today and another tomorrow, to hunt in the morning, fish in the afternoon, rear cattle in the evening, criticize after dinner, just as I have a mind, without ever becoming hunter, fisherman, shepherd or critic. (Marx & Engels, 1978, p. 160)

At first blush this passage has a ridiculous vision of the future, which seems impossible even under the most advantageous circumstances. Also, people can't become adept at all pursuits, so people must practice some skills regularly. Even though Marx and Engels's poetic nature may have gotten the best of them in this passage, there is the notion that within communism, people can study what they wish and have time available outside of work to pursue other activities.

One of Marx's mature statements attests to the hope that productivity improvements will allow for great amounts of free time:

> Freedom in this field [of physical necessity] can only consist in socialized man, the associated producers, rationally regulating their interchange with Nature, bringing it under their common control, instead of being ruled by it as by the blind forces of Nature; . . . Beyond it begins that development of human energy which is an end in itself, the true realm of freedom, which, however, can blossom forth only with the realm of necessity as its basis. The shortening of the working day is its basic prerequisite. (Marx & Engels, 1978, p. 441)

Marx's hope for more free time is not far fetched since many nations spend less time at work than they did 30 years ago (Economic Policy Institute, 2012b). Marx thus thinks that communism will allow people greater control over the economies they live in and their individual lives.

F. Full employment, the requirement of work, and the provision of social insurance and health insurance (Marx & Engels, 1978, pp. 326, 490, 528). As has just been shown, on one hand Marx is an advocate of people spending less time at work if they wish and more time in a variety of pursuits. On the other hand, Marx not only wants work available for everyone, but he also thinks all people should work who can work.

Before a consideration of the obligation to work, here is a look at Marx's comments on full employment and a social safety net. In *The Communist Manifesto*, Marx advocates the creation of "industrial armies, especially for agriculture" during the transition to communism (Marx & Engels, 1978, p. 490). These industrial armies are public employment. Why would special public employment be necessary when the means of production has just been nationalized? Can't people be employed in the industries just nationalized? Marx doesn't elaborate, but since he was generally worried about capitalism not producing enough jobs and output for everyone, there may be a large number of unemployed after the transition. The capacity for existing industries to absorb these people may be limited; thus, new public enterprises may be required.

In addition, Marx realizes that some people may be unable to work, and thus they should receive support. This would include sickness and injury payments and seemingly also retirement pensions (Marx & Engels, 1978, pp. 528–529).

Once communism starts to develop, Marx undoubtedly thought that all people seeking jobs would find them. Marx's comments on the obligation to work are different than arguing for jobs for all who seek employment. In the *Manifesto*, Marx recommends "equal liability to all to labour" (Marx & Engels, 1978, p. 490). It is unclear whether all people must labor or there is no other means of support for them, such as a basic income grant. The first possibility may have been instituted as a means to facilitate the elimination of classes. If capitalists have no private property, there exists a very progressive income tax, and because there is no inheritance, seemingly, former capitalists would have to work to support themselves.

The second reading of equal liability to labor is when those who can work receive no transfer payments. Marx gives no reason why this should be the case. Of course, Marx is interested in empowering workers and improving their bargaining situation. If people received income transfers and/or unemployment payments, this would improve their bargaining position to gain more desirable work. Even if there is full employment, people may wish to take their time in finding work that suits them best. This would be in alignment with Marx's comments about people being able to become accomplished in any branch of work they wish.

It is important to stress that Marx's vision of communism provides full employment, access to the means of production, disability payments, sickness transfers, (seemingly) retirement transfers, and free schooling. This means that a person can find work or education and training if they wish or will receive income if they cannot work.

The two remaining situations that are not explicitly discussed are income for people performing child care or elder care and those who do not wish to work. Not discussing transfer payments for care work is an oversight by

Marx, which coincides with the spirit of his work. This leaves only support payments for adults without young children or aged people to care for who can work but do not wish to. Should they receive income support? Perhaps, as previously mentioned, a job search transfer payment with a time limit (How long? Six weeks? One year? Two years?). Why should they receive an unlimited transfer payment? The apparent Marxian answer is that work, which is meaningful, is a great good in a person's life and should be facilitated by society. It appears to be Marx's idea that society should seek to fulfill people's desire for meaningful work instead of merely keeping them alive.

It is common to understand work to be something of a necessary harm. Marx thinks that work is part of human nature. The reason people find their jobs undesirable is exploitation and the absence of workplace democracy. Additionally, people must keep undesirable jobs since involuntary unemployment is the usual circumstance within capitalism. Also, if the social safety net is inadequate, sick or infirm people need to keep jobs for income. All of these factors make the world of work undesirable for many within capitalism. Thus, it is unsurprising that many have a low opinion of work. But useful and enjoyable work is desirable for the worker and the rest of society. If work can be made more desirable and expressive of people's interests, then this would be a good outcome for all.

G. Egalitarian remuneration during the first phase of communism and unequal remuneration by choice during a higher phase of communism (Marx & Engels, 1978, p. 531). In *Critique of the Gotha Program*, Marx makes some fascinating statements about what people will be paid during two phases in communism. These phases are called the "first phase" and "a higher phase of communist society" by Marx (Marx & Engels, 1978, p. 531). The first phase is when communism "*emerges* from capitalist society" (Marx & Engels, 1978, p. 529). The higher phase is when the division of labor has ended, labor has become life's prime want, and there appears to be economic abundance (Marx & Engels, 1978, p. 530).

During the first phase of communism, people will receive payments that are equal to their expenditure of labor (Marx & Engels, 1978, p. 530). Marx makes no account of skilled or unskilled labor altering the payment. Marx doesn't mention it, but if people's schooling and training are paid for by taxation, then they would have to receive a premium in their wages to cover the education cost. He does note that intensity of laboring can be determined (Marx & Engels, 1978, p. 530). A person's payment appears to be equivalent to how long they work and the intensity of the work. Some work that is designated as arduous would receive higher wages.

Marx is interested in noting that equal pay for equal work results in an inequality due to two reasons: natural abilities and a person's support of their dependents. First, natural ability can affect the equality of payment by reducing the amount of effort that is expended while working. For example, a person who is naturally strong may find difficult work to be less burdensome than a person of average strength does. Both people may work the same amount of time at the same job, but the naturally strong person has expended less effort. They thereby receive more payment than the average person since they have expended less effort for the same amount of means of consumption. There is not equal work for equal pay when people have different natural abilities.

Second, Marx notes that some people may have more dependents to support than others. For example, Steve has two children to support whereas Jan has no dependents. They both work at the same job for the same amount of time and receive the same quantity on their claim certificate for means of consumption. Jan is able to spend all of her pay on herself, whereas Steve has to support himself and his two dependents. Thus, the amount of consumption Jan spends on herself is greater than the amount of consumption that Steve spends on himself. This means that Jan is paid more according to Marx (Marx & Engels, 1978, p. 531).

Marx doesn't bring it up, but there may be an equality-preserving transfer from Jan to Steve. As was noted, those who are unable to work receive income transfers. A similar transfer paid to Steve to help him support his two children could render Jan's and Steve's consumption equal. People in this communist society already make deductions for those unable to work, so supporting children does not seem like a stretch.

Marx argued that during a higher phase of communism, people would not be paid an equal claim on the amount of labor they expended, and people could consume an amount greater than the amount they labored. This distributional idea is captured in the famous slogan, "from each according to his ability, to each according to his needs" (Marx & Engels, 1978, p. 531). As noted earlier, this higher phase of communism is when the division of labor has been eliminated, when there is economic abundance, and when people's prime interest has become their work. It is hard to see this kind of society actually arriving. It is much more interesting to perhaps think about a world in which people willingly allow others to consume more while they consume less. This is different from support payments for people unable to work; it is allowing some people who can work to consume more than they have produced.

Unequal consumption relative to one's labor contribution would be an overcoming of the strict equality of consumption based on contribution

Marx found to be part of capitalist ideology. In a higher-phase communist world (according to my interpretation of the slogan), some people would work more and some would consume more relative to their labor contribution and their consumptive extraction. But this inequality of outcomes is not exploitive since people are not coerced to labor and the means of production are owned as public property. Rather, the inequality of labor and consumption is driven not by exploitation but by the differences in people's personalities. Some people prefer to labor more and others prefer more consumption. Laboring more or consuming more than one's labor contribution would no longer be a source of conflict, nor would it generate feelings of poor self-esteem. Instead, people could participate in the production of society based on the aspects of their personality instead of social obligation or natural necessity. Higher-phase communism could be a society in which the requirement to labor becomes absent for people who are uninterested in working. Work would be performed by those who are interested in working and find it to be desirable.

This image of the future may be hard to imagine since our own social mores determine work, on the one hand, to be a necessary harm and, on the other hand, require that work be performed by all who have no other means of support (such as inherited wealth). Nonetheless, it is interesting to conceive of a social world in which people are not lazy who do not labor and those who do labor do so freely as an enhancement to their personality. Our world measures our worth by the pay we receive by laboring or by being lucky enough to inherit wealth. To be free of such strictures on our well-being might be liberating.

Why Does Communism Correct the Problems of Capitalism?

Now that Marx's vision of communism has been discussed, we must return to his critique of capitalism to show how communism solves the ills of capitalism.

The first ill of capitalism listed is that capitalism prevents people from maximizing their economic security. In particular, the following identified problems will be discussed: inequality, poverty, underfunding of social services, structural and cyclical unemployment, and overwork.

Inequality would be minimized by egalitarian pay, payment for those who can work, the nationalization of the means of production, and democratic control of economic development. Nationalization would eliminate class positions and thereby end capitalist control over surplus value. This would prevent some people from accumulating large incomes through profits. Within communism, the amount of surplus accumulated and the use of the surplus would be decided democratically. Accordingly, the surplus could be used for transfer payments to those who cannot work. Egalitarian pay scales would limit inequality. Democratic control of economic development and the provision of full employment could facilitate the creation of industry in areas with unemployment problems. This would provide incomes to the people in these areas and would thereby reduce inequality.

Poverty is caused by low income from work, being unable to work, or having no other means of income support. The provision of full employment and democracy of economic development would enable all who seek work to obtain it. In addition, people who couldn't work would receive transfer payments. These measures would apparently eliminate or seriously curtail one kind of poverty, which is called absolute poverty. Absolute poverty is when people do not have enough income or other means of support to meet their basic needs of food, shelter, and clothing. Providing work for all who seek it and transfer payments for those who cannot work would provide income and thus help reduce poverty. Democratic control over development would enable the population of a communist country to shift distribution from investment to consumption if wages were too low to provide for basic needs, or they could change the type of investment to increase the production of consumption goods if there is an insufficient supply.

The other kind of poverty is relative poverty. Relative poverty is when people can meet their basic needs but can't consume other goods that are common in their society. For example, a family suffers from relative poverty but not absolute poverty if it can afford food, shelter, and clothing but can't afford the standard items of its society such as the current standard of transportation, access to communication and media, contemporary appliances, access to cultural events, access to leisure activities, living in safe housing, access to the current standard of medical care, and access to contemporary standards of school and training. In addition, relative poverty has detrimental effects on people's health due to psychosocial feelings of worthlessness and failure (Wilkinson, 1994). Relative poverty would be extremely minimized by Marx's recommended egalitarian pay structure.

The underprovision of many goods and services is common within capitalism, in particular health care, schooling, and social insurance. Democratic control of economic development would allow decisions about how much of society's output and laboring should be devoted to such services to be discussed and debated nationally. There is no guarantee that democratic control of economic development would provide adequate levels of provision. The participants in the debate have changed dramatically away from antagonistic classes toward a populace that does not gain its subsistence through exploitation and that has very similar incomes. There would be no group interested in minimizing social provisioning due to a desire to limit wages and minimize taxes on capital income.

Conflict may arise between people who receive their income from work and those who do not, such as retirees, the infirm, students, and people who provide care to dependents. Since the work of the former provides the means to provision themselves and the latter, there may be disputes over provision when it comes out of the former's wages. Of course, if people who care for dependents do receive a wage, they would become part of the first group. In addition, students may be a favored group since the training and education they receive would allow the current workers a retirement in which greater provision is possible due to productivity increases.

Structural and cyclical unemployment would seemingly be eliminated within Marxian communism due to public full employment programs and democratic control of economic development. Even if communist societies suffer recessions (which was not the case for the Soviet Union; see Mandel, 1978b), cyclical unemployment could be absorbed by public full-employment schemes. The retirement of certain industries could be planned for with gradual employment losses and retraining to minimize the effects of structural unemployment.

Individual control over the amount of work people will have to do is an important part of Marx's vision of communism. Overwork could become nonexistent. In addition, social determination of provisioning could provide the chance for people to have increased guarantees of vacation time. Democratic control of economic development may have a bias toward reduced workweeks instead of increased investment since there would be no capitalist survival interest in increasing surplus extraction.

The second ill listed in the first section is that capitalism limits the prospects for the development of people's abilities and work toward their lifelong projects. The problem is manifested as the division between mental and manual labor, inability to use the means of production, inability to gain an education, and insufficient nonwork time.

Nationalization of the means of production and democratic control of economic development would enable people to implement changes in how work is performed in the firms they work for and nationally. At the firm level, all members of the business could participate in decisions regarding management, product development, business models, the pace of work, and the structure of the labor process. On one hand, at the regional and national levels, there can be participation regarding the direction, type, and pace of investments. On the other hand, there could also be an attempt to structure education to facilitate a development of mental and manual skills. If people can be educated in the development, engineering, management, and fabrication of goods and services, they can be active at several levels of a firm's business.

In addition, access and control over the means of production that cannot be taken away means that people can utilize the means of production to actualize their goals. Marx wants people to have access to the means of production, but exactly what this means is unclear outside of national planning goals. It is possible to conceive of individuals or groups petitioning national or local economic governance agencies to start new ventures. These small-scale firms don't seem out of alignment with Marx's vision. These ventures should be subject to egalitarian pay differentials and the general disinclination toward competition, which permeates Marx's vision of communism.

In addition, universal access to nonfee education would allow people, no matter their background, to gain education in areas that they are attracted to. People wouldn't be kept from education due to lack of funds or former class positions. The legacy of class may affect those who qualify for certain schools, since children from capitalist and professional families may have access to particular home situations that allow them to perform well on entrance exams and in academic environments. Open enrollment at some institutions may be required so that Marx's desire for people to attempt to become accomplished in any branch of learning they wish can be realized.

Finally, the control of economic development and the ability to control the amount of time one spends at work would greatly facilitate people's nonwork pursuits. People's goals may best be met in areas where they don't receive paid employment, such as sports, hobbies, travel, or time with their friends and family. Control over the amount of time spent at paid employment is the means to increase one's interest in these areas. Interestingly, Marx's notion about a higher phase of communism in which people provide labor with no expectation of equal pay may be a world in which people can develop their interests without concern for needing to work. Perhaps some people would be happy to devote themselves to developing and producing goods and services while some people will spend their time at nonwork activities. Could such a world exist in which some people work who find it to be their prime want in life and others spend all of their time in nonwork pursuits, and all these decisions are uncoerced?

The third problem listed in the first section is that capitalism prevents social unity from fully developing due to class antagonisms. The nationalization of the means of production will eliminate class positions. The mere elimination of class position does not end class interests that have been inherited or the aspirations of people to gain the advantages of a ruling class. How people's desires are achieved within communism is different from how they are achieved within capitalism. In communism, people must negotiate with others in democratic forums. If people want more pay, they need to request that their peers allow them to have it. If people want more authority at work, they must do the same.

Within capitalism, some groups can request more pay and authority from their peers: in Congress, partners in a firm, or in a co-op. Unions can attempt to use their bargaining power and solidarity to achieve more pay and authority at their jobs. Many people are subject to the decision-making power of their bosses. Others attain or inherit their position as business leaders and can make these decisions on their own.

Important to these distinctions is that there is a definite increase in equality with communism due to the end of class position. Power can of course be exercised in communist forums due to electoral majorities, through parliamentary alliances, or by knowledge and negotiating ability. Even if the smart, charismatic, and well organized will be dominant in a communist society, their achievements cannot become compounded as long as the means of production cannot be privatized, wealth accumulated, essential services become competitively priced, or entry into certain professions restricted by credentialing authorities.

In addition, the process of communist decision making definitely privileges cooperation due to these limits on the acquisition of power. Marx thinks that this process will help develop a sense of social unity. To refresh our memories, social unity is when the individuals of a social unit—local, national, regional, or global—see each other as members of a political community; they are interested in the society functioning correctly and are interested in all members of their society doing well. If people require others to agree to their plans, they must meet the interests of those people they are negotiating with. There is little to no chance of exiting the negotiations, since people do not own a sufficient amount of property to achieve many goals on their own within communism. These processes of negotiation must cater to the goals of others in order for people to achieve their goals. Apparently, Marx finds that if people can achieve their goals within communism, they will begin to prefer it as opposed to within capitalism, where Marx finds that class antagonisms will perpetually frustrate the achievement of people's goals and prevent a stable preference for the system, particularly for the members of the working class.

The fourth problem Marx found is that capitalism limits people from having a truly democratic society. The dearth of democracy is manifested by capture of the state by ruling-class interests, inability of people to participate in how their economy and firm develop, inability to reasonably plan the development of their lives, and lack of coordination, which results in market failure.

Most of these topics have already been discussed except for market failure, which will be discussed next. It is good to review that the nationalization of the means of production and the ability for people to democratically control development of the economy result in increased participation in a diversity of areas. The elimination of the material basis of class power allows for people to participate in the social, economic, and political processes that affect their lives. People can no longer be shut out from participation due to control of the means of production by capitalists.

Coordination problems resulting in market failure are when the rational choices of individuals result in suboptimal societywide effects. Coordination problems can occur in transportation, housing and urban development, and education. For example, if it is rational for people to try to move into an affluent town so their children can attend the excellent school system, the result will be people investing more of their resources in paying for rent and mortgage payments. Housing costs will rise and people will seek more income to compete for a limited number of available housing units. Other school districts will suffer underinvestment as a result, and their performance may fall farther behind. Overall, there is an inefficient use of resources in attempting to secure a limited number of spaces in the prized district. The resources could be spent more efficiently by improving existing schools and the lives of the families as opposed to bidding up the price of housing in a particular district.

This example demonstrates that democratic control over investment in a society can avoid such coordination problems. Democratic decisions regarding investments in schooling will avoid the suboptimal results due to competition. More importantly, viewing decisions as ones that must be made by a community reinforces the importance of strengthening the abilities of all society's members. Democratic control over such funding issues leads to the realization of the interdependent nature of people's lives. As Marx and Engels put the matter in *The Communist Manifesto*: "The free development of each is the condition for the free development of all" (Marx & Engels, 1978, p. 491).

Finally, the fifth ill discussed is that capitalism is destructive to the environment. This was not a major portion of Marx's analysis of capitalism, but he did make the case that capitalism is destructive to the environment due to capitalist accumulation. The next chapter has been devoted to this topic due to its contemporary importance.

Conclusion

Marx's vision of communism has been partially achieved through the establishment of welfare states of different types. Economic insecurity is not a phenomenon for all members of all advanced industrialized nations. The extent of the safety net is different for different countries. Even with the increased attack on the welfare state over the last decades, some Nordic countries have maintained full employment and have been close to eliminating poverty (Esping-Andersen, 1990; Goodin, Headey, Muggels, & Dirven, 1999). Conditions in developing countries are comparable to those in Marx's time, with poverty-level wages, unemployment, and grinding poverty still occurring (Mehrotra & Delamonica, 2007).

The centerpiece of Marx's vision of communism, public ownership and democratic control over production and investment decisions, has obviously not occurred in advanced capitalist nations. If a capitalist nation eliminated poverty, unemployment, overwork, and homelessness; abolished inequality; of opportunity; and met people's needs for social services, would public control over the means of production be required? Would this capitalism without some of the ills of capitalism be a desirable world? Marx found that the most important aspect of human life was the potential of individuals to objectify their plans. This very human activity of conception and implementation is absent in the reformed capitalism discussed. Do people wish to live amid plenty without the ability to set their plans in motion and participate in the development of a good society?

Before we turn to the next chapter, a few questions on Marx's vision of communism:

- Is Marx's critique of the problems of capitalism still pertinent?
- Will democratic control over investment decisions improve people's lives?
- Is Marx's vision of a postcapitalist society desirable?
- Should people be required to work?
- Is communism the only possible postcapitalist society?

9

Capitalism and the Environment

Marx has not been known for his environmental critique of capitalism. He hypothesized that the accumulation dynamics of capitalism would not be environmentally sustainable. Marx's comments on capitalism and the environment and his analysis of capitalist accumulation have influenced the development of what is now called ecological Marxism. Ecological Marxism is not actually new since Marx and Marxists other than contemporary ones realized that capitalist accumulation had environmental implications. Contemporary ecological Marxism has made an explicit attempt to show that Marx's theory of capitalist accumulation has environmental implications, and it has also deepened and widened the study of capitalism as a cause of environmental decay.

In short, Marx's theory of how capitalism causes environmental decay is as follows. Capitalists seek to extract surplus value in order to stay capitalists. In order to do so, capitalists will seek new markets, develop new commodities, and implement technological change. This process of surplus extraction and economic development is endless. Accumulation only brings about more accumulation within capitalism. The reason accumulation is endless is that competition among capitalists does not end. Either capitalists can always try to outsell other capitalists and run them out of business, or some capitalist will be destroyed and replaced by a new one if there is an economic crisis. To put the matter simply, the goal of capitalist accumulation is just more accumulation.

The effects of accumulation have been discussed already. To review, within capitalism, accumulation takes precedence over full employment, overwork, low wages, poverty, inequality, the provisioning of social services, overcrowding, democracy, optimal coordination, health, and hunger. The well-being of the majority of people within capitalism is secondary to the demands of accumulation.

The environmental results from this process of accumulation are of the same pattern as the general effects of accumulation. The overuse or exhaustion of resources, the extinction of species, the pollution of the biosphere, and the impact on the health and well-being of humans is secondary to accumulation.

Why this is the case is the same reason the well-being of the majority of people is secondary to accumulation. The interests of capitalists are short term in nature due to competition. An individual capitalist who is concerned about poverty and environmental degradation and changes their business practices to accommodate these problems is placing their survivability as capitalists as secondary to the well-being of people and the protection of the biosphere. The objectivity of capitalist class interests places accumulation before other goals. The medium- to long-term effects of capitalist accumulation are secondary in importance because they must be in order for capitalists to maintain their class position. To do otherwise is to risk being outcompeted.

First, this chapter will review the dynamics of capitalist accumulation. The focus of this review will be to examine how the goal of accumulation is further accumulation. Next will be a consideration of some of Marx's explicit environmental statements. Finally will come a brief consideration of whether communism can be environmentally sustainable.

The Endlessness of Capitalist Accumulation

In *Capital*, Marx describes how the accumulation of capital is limitless. The process of commodity production, circulation, and sale has no end except more production, circulation, and sale *ad infinitum*. Accumulation is limitless because the motivation of the capitalists is for perpetual accumulation:

> The simple circulation of commodities – selling in order to buy – is a means to a final goal that lies outside circulation, namely the appropriation of use-values, the satisfaction of needs. As against this, the circulation of money as capital is an end in itself, for the valorization of value takes place only within this constantly renewed movement. The movement of capital is therefore limitless. (Marx, 1990, p. 253)

> Use-values must therefore never be treated as the immediate aim of the capitalist; nor must the profit on any single transaction. His aim is rather the unceasing movement of profit making. This boundless drive for enrichment, this

passionate chase after value, is common to the capitalist and the miser; but while the miser is merely a capitalist gone mad, the capitalist is a rational miser. The ceaseless augmentation of value, which the miser seeks to attain by saving his money from circulation, is achieved by the more acute capitalist by means of throwing his money again and again into circulation. (Marx, 1990, pp. 254–255)

As noted previously, the reason a capitalist's accumulation goal is more accumulation is due to the particularities of production within capitalism. Surplus production is a common feature to human activity, and surplus extraction via exploitation is the determining activity of all class societies. Surplus accumulation in noncapitalist modes of production is the extraction of useful items that slaves or serfs produce for their slave masters or feudal lords. Within capitalism surplus value is extracted in the production process, and this surplus value can only be realized if it is sold. If the surplus value extracted by capitalists is not sold, they may go out of business since they will have less capital to reinvest. In addition, capitalists can't consume all of their revenue since this would also jeopardize their existence as capitalists. Capitalists occupy a very precarious position due to this continual process of accumulation. It is thus in their objective class interests to continually utilize their revenues from surplus value extraction for more surplus value extraction:

> Moreover, the development of capitalist production makes it necessary constantly to increase the amount of capital laid out in a given industrial undertaking, and competition subordinates every individual capitalist to the immanent laws of capitalist production, as external and coercive laws. It compels him to keep extending his capital, so as to preserve it, and he can only extend it by means of progressive accumulation. (Marx, 1990, p. 739)

Unlike previous ruling classes who not only had a propensity to consume their surplus product, the social systems they lived within also insulated their social position from challenge through the legal sanctioning of class. Lords were designated as lords through the granting of land and by birth. Slaves were forced into slavery or born to it. Some capitalists may be born into the capitalist class, but they can lose their wealth without the violation of any law.

The fury of capitalist accumulation and the churning of those who are members of the capitalist class make the constant accumulation of capital a rational preference for capitalists. The working class must also conform to the demands of capitalist production. Workers must acquiesce to the structure of capitalist accumulation to compete for scarce labor positions. If workers resist capitalist accumulation, they fight against what makes capitalism a unique mode of production.

One can't preserve capitalism while jettisoning its intrinsic structures. To stop accumulation or to restructure the adoption of new technologies while also stopping or slowing economic growth would be the end of capitalism. Such alteration would require the coordination of all members' actions. For example, imagine that a capitalist society decided to have a no-growth economy in which new technologies were still developed. In this society, new technologies would have to be selected by an authority: democratic, bureaucratic, technocratic, or oligarchic. The implementation of the new technology would designate how much of it could be used and how many of it could be produced. The use of other technologies would be affected in order to maintain zero economic growth. This regulation of what is produced is required to make sure that individual firms do not exceed the limits of production, which would restrict their economy to zero growth.

The example demonstrates that if accumulation is regulated, then fragmented capitalist decision making cannot be used. For example, in a capitalist society, the development of new technologies is individually decided by multiple firms. Each firm may choose to develop slightly different varieties of the technology in order to capture market share. New firms may enter the new market seeking profits. In addition, cost reductions in production techniques would spur increased production to sell the newly affordable item. The upshot of all this is that if accumulation decisions are left to individual capitalist firms, the rate of economic growth cannot be contained. Each firm is seeking to produce as many items as can be sold. Some firms will succeed and some will fail. Productive improvements will result in more production and further sales. When this dynamic is multiplied across all industries, the result is a range of firms seeking to realize their surplus value. The physical result is increased throughput of resources and positive economic growth. Capitalist societies are built around growth due to the particularities of capitalist class positions and their objective interests. Overall, individual firms will not limit production if there is a market opportunity for their commodities. To do otherwise within capitalism is counter to capitalist class interests. This will be an important factor in Marx's environmental critique.

Marx on Nature and Environmental Decay

As has been discussed, Marx's materialist understanding of action assumes that humans are organic beings embedded in a natural environment from which they gain their subsistence. This view was held by Marx from his earliest writings to his latest. Two passages demonstrate his position, one from the *1844 Manuscripts* and one from the *Critique of the Gotha Program* from 1875:

Nature is man's *inorganic body*—nature, that is, in so far as it is not itself the human body. Man *lives* on nature—means that nature is his *body*, with which he must remain in continuous intercourse if he is not to die. (Marx & Engels, 1978, p. 75)

Labour is *not the source* of all wealth. *Nature* is just as much the source of all use values (and it is surely of such that material wealth consists!) as labour, which itself is only the manifestation of a force of nature, human labour power. (Marx & Engels, 1978, p. 525)

Marx obviously thinks of humans as natural beings who live in nature and require it to survive. Does Marx think that humans can utilize nature in an unlimited manner? This view has been attributed to Marx, since he does state in *Critique of the Gotha Program* that in the higher phase of communism, "all the springs of cooperative wealth [will] flow more abundantly" (Marx & Engels, 1978, p. 531). As was quoted from the same document, wealth is labor and nature. Does the abundance that Marx thinks is part of higher-phase communism mean that nature can produce anything we wish in any amount?

If Marx did think this was possible, it would put him out of step with the current standard of environmental science in which there are conceivable limits not only to extractive resources but also to the capacity of the Earth to sustain life. Limitless abundance means limitless growth, and this is not a possibility given the limited resources and carrying capacity of the Earth.

Rather, Marx's conception of what constitutes abundance takes the ecological limits of the biosphere into account. Marx found that capitalism is detrimental not only to the economic and social prospects of workers but also to their environmental well-being. His conception of environmental limit is captured in a comment on capitalist agriculture:

But at the same time it creates the material conditions for a new and higher synthesis, a union of agriculture and industry on the basis of the forms that have developed during the period of their antagonistic isolation. Capitalist production collects the population together in great centers, and causes the urban population to achieve an ever-growing preponderance. This has two results. On the one hand it concentrates the historical motive power of society; on the other hand, it disturbs the metabolic interaction between man and the earth, i.e. it prevents the return to the soil of its constituent elements consumed by man in the form of food and clothing; hence it hinders the operation of the eternal natural condition for the lasting fertility of the soil. Thus it destroys at the same time the physical health of the urban worker, and the intellectual life of the rural worker. But by destroying the circumstances surrounding that metabolism, which originate in a merely natural and spontaneous fashion, it compels its systematic restoration as a regulative law of social production, and in a form adequate to the full development of the human race.... Moreover, all progress in capitalist agriculture is a progress in art, not only of robbing the worker, but of robbing the soil; all progress in increasing the fertility of the soil for a given time is a progress towards ruining the more long-lasting sources of that fertility. The more a country proceeds from large-scale industry as the background of its development, as in the case of the United States, the more rapid is this process of destruction. Capitalist production, therefore, only develops the techniques and the degree of combination of the social process of production by simultaneously undermining the original sources of all wealth—the soil and the worker. (Marx, 1990, pp. 637–638)

As can be seen in this passage, the limitlessness of accumulation is the driving force of exploitation and of environmental decay. The profitability of capitalist agriculture and industry takes precedence over the well-being of workers and the capacity of the soil to produce food.

A contemporary example of overuse of land resources and the breakdown in the metabolic cyclic include many agriculture and development issues. Contemporary agriculture imports chemical fertilizers to increase crop yield. But the quantities of fertilizers used cannot be absorbed by the earth, and chemical runoff flows into waterways. This runoff accumulates in ponds, lakes, and deltas. Some of the runoff collects in drinking water. Also, the increased amounts of fertilizer that collect in waterways spur the growth of algae. The increased growth of algae crowds out the growth of other marine life. This process is driven by capitalist accumulation.

Another example is the occurrence of urban and suburban sprawl. Developers seek farmland or unused lands to build residential housing. As this process proceeds, more and more land is taken up with human settlements. This increased building crowds out nonhuman species, endangers drinking water sources, and reduces open land for other purposes. In urban areas, large-scale buildings are constructed, which reduces the amount of sunlight and can result in the overcrowding of streets and public services. Once again, this process is driven by the developer's drive for profit taking precedence over other ends.

Marx's environmentalism is anthropocentric. He is concerned with the condition of the biosphere as it affects human beings. Further comments by Marx on large- and small-scale capitalist agriculture demonstrate this perspective:

In both forms [of agriculture], instead of a conscious and rational treatment of the land as permanent communal property, as the inalienable condition for the existence and reproduction of the chain of human generations, we have the exploitation and the squandering of the power of the earth. (Marx, 1991, p. 949)

Both quotes are concerned with the use of land for human beings. The first one comments on the fertility of the soil and the second discusses a rational perspective regarding the use of resources. Both quotes show that Marx utilizes an anthropocentric environmental perspective.

Marx's second comment on rational treatment of the biosphere needs to be explained in greater detail. First, a rational treatment needs to be evaluated. A rational action is an action that seeks to preserve the general conditions for action of all agents. For example, the rational use of a public park is to use the park in a manner that would allow all agents to use the park. This means that the rational treatment of the biosphere would mean that individuals perform actions that will not threaten the use of the biosphere for other people. For example, a person should not use an amount of water that will threaten the use of the water source for others.

Interestingly, Marx's discussion of rational treatment contains a time preference clause regarding the biosphere: "as the inalienable condition for the reproduction of the chain of human generations." The term *time preference* has many uses. I am using the term here to signify the set of representative agents people must take account of when treating a resource rationally. The size of the set of representative agents depends on two factors: Who are the included agents now and who will be included as agents in the future? The set of representative agents could be as small as oneself during the current moment or could include the entire human population and their future generations toward infinity.

The set of representative agents for which Marx thinks we can rationally have a time preference appears to be the entire human population and its future generations toward infinity. This is quite a large set of people, but Marx obviously finds that it would be irrational to have any other set of representative agents. To do so would require us to decide who is included in the set. Marx's comments can reasonably be interpreted to hold that the set of representative agents includes all possible future generations if rational treatment continues. This means that the pace and type of economic development must be sustainable on the longest time horizon possible.

From Marx's comments, we can infer a few standards regarding economic growth and environmental sustainability: (1) Economic growth should not take precedence over the well-being of humans. (2) Economic growth should not take precedence over maintaining the capacity of the biosphere to sustain human life. (3) Humans' use of resources and the capacity of the environment to absorb waste should take the current technological projections for sustainable use into account when forming our time preference.

Many people are concerned that an anthropocentric environmental perspective does not allow for the preservation of species and habitats. This is an obvious concern since an anthropocentric environmental standard takes human well-being as the decisive factor when making biosphere use decisions. An anthropocentric perspective does not regard the biosphere as an agent with rights, but it can be quite inclusive. The preservation of species and habitats can be achieved with an anthropocentric standard since the well-being of humans is dependent on the existence of biological diversity. In addition, with the extremely conservative time preference used by Marx, the preservation of species and habitats for the use, study, and enjoyment of future generations would be the rational result.

In review, Marx appears to place environmental sustainability for the well-being of all current people and possible future generations before economic growth. This is decisively at odds with his analysis of capitalism, which he finds places economic growth before environmental sustainability and the maintaining of well-being of current and future people.

Communism and Environmental Sustainability

The social dynamics of capitalism, according to Marx, prevent accumulation from being secondary to any other goal. The reason accumulation will always take precedence over all else is the class structure of capitalism. As long as capitalists wish to remain capitalists, they must outdo other capitalists. The result of this competition is a tendency toward endless growth.

It was discussed that Marx's environmental perspective decisively argues for environmental sustainability over economic growth. Does Marx's vision of communism conform to this position as well?

It was noted previously that Marx, in his comments on the higher phase of communism, thought that an abundant flow of wealth will occur (Marx & Engels, 1978, p. 531). It is difficult to surmise what level of production this corresponds to and if it corresponds to continual economic growth. What this boils down to is to ask if communism is compatible with environmental sustainability, in particular a no-growth economy.

Some other important statements regarding life within communism do not mention economic abundance. In *The German Ideology* and in the third volume of *Capital*, Marx's conception of a communist future is one in which productivity increases allow people not necessarily to consume more but rather to work less (Marx & Engels, 1978, pp. 160, 441). Marx thinks that people have a preference for developing their abilities. There is not an overt overture to continually increasing consumption. If this is true, then increased control over economic development, which communism is supposed to bring about, will allow people to pursue ability development as opposed to increased consumption.

Mandel has argued that the idea that communism as a world of increasing consumption is not only impossible but also undesirable:

> People cannot just consume an unlimited quantity of air trips, telephone conversations or television programmes within the space of one lifetime, where there is increasing concern for such questions as health, happiness and mental/psychological stability. An overdose of anything just kills. (Mandel, 1992, p. 206)

Rather, activities such as friendship, art, study, and sport are more meaningful when they are engaged in over many years. The "consumption" of such activities does not require increasing production of items and an intensification of resource extraction. The reduction of work time in communism would allow people such improvements in the quality of life as opposed to mere quantitative increase of consumption. Such a shift in human life may not be too hard to imagine. Many European people have "consumed" their productivity increase over the past decades in increased leisure as opposed to increased consumption (Economic Policy Institute, 2012b). Also, Keynes thought that people would prefer to consume their productivity increases as leisure in the 21st century (Keynes, 2010).

The motivations of capitalists have already been discussed regarding their preference for continual economic growth and accumulation. What about other classes? Do they have any reason to work longer hours other than being forced to by a threat of unemployment? First, if a country has a poor social safety net, people must save for their own medical care, education, and retirement. This is particularly the case if people find their employment to be precarious due to cyclical economic fluctuations. Second, people have a strong preference for their children to have desirable lives. If desirable positions in universities, professional schools, and companies are scarce, parents can attempt to assist their children in outdoing other children for these positions. Parents can send their children to elite primary schools, have them receive extra tutoring and join select clubs, and facilitate other activities to increase their chances of gaining entrance to the upper echelons of society. Inequality in social provisioning and a minimal social safety net can result in welfare-decreasing outcomes for society as more economic resources are devoted to gain access to scarce positions.

If people are guaranteed economic security, then the incentive to work longer hours to provide for oneself or one's children's future is greatly minimized. If communism can provide economic security, then noncapitalist preferences for more remuneration could be limited.

Thus, the possibility that economic activities can be coordinated within a communist society to maintain zero growth appears feasible with the absence of objective class interests that favor growth over human welfare. The real question is if humans truly have a preference for leisure over increased consumption of resource-intensive goods and services. Will the opportunity to work less and spend more time with one's friends and family, developing new passions and satisfying one's lifelong goals, be taken advantage of by people? Do people want to take long hikes with their friends, or would they prefer to have sumptuous vacations hours away by jet? Do people prefer to develop new hobbies, or would they rather have larger homes stocked with electronic devices and foods from around the world?

These are real questions for our age and real questions about capitalism and communism, in particular since capitalism is driven by increased consumption of vacations, jet trips, housing, electronic devices, and imported goods. Are people's appetites for increased consumption natural drives or preferences crafted by advertising? Will people, once free of the accumulation dynamics and competition of capitalism, decide differently than they do now? This may be the defining question of environmental sustainability for capitalism and communism. Galbraith (1958, 1967, 1973) and Hirsch (1976) considered these questions in greater depth.

The public and democratic organization of production that is indicative of Marx's vision of communism may be the only way to avoid the competitive dynamics that drive environmental degradation. The decentralized decision making of capitalist production drives growth and innovation. But it also drives increased throughput of resources in the production process. As capitalists compete, nationally and internationally, the world economy grows and uses more resources. If one or a few capitalist countries engage in a slow- or no-growth environmental plan, other countries may be able to outcompete them by engaging in resource-intensive growth. If all capitalist countries are to meet the challenges of environmental degradation, they must all participate in less resource-intensive growth. If environmental sustainability takes precedence over capitalist accumulation, this is in tension with capitalist preferences. Capitalists become successful by breaking with the current standards and finding new products and markets. Capitalism is driven not by conformity but by new avenues of profit. Holding all the world capitalists to a low- or no-growth standard appears contrary to the nature of how capitalists structure innovation. It seems that environmental sustainability can't be achieved within the decentralized decision-making structure of capitalism. Rule breaking is intrinsic to the capitalist development process.

It thus appears that capitalism may be difficult or even impossible to pair with environmental sustainability due to the way decisions are made within capitalism. A democratically planned world economy that regulates how a no-growth economy can, on the one hand, meet the needs of all people of the world and, on the other hand, facilitate innovation without the disruptive capitalist accumulation drive is a theoretically desirable option. It may be the case that a democratically planned economy that is environmentally sustainable is the only option for the future that does not depart from the Enlightenment hope for a better social world.

With these ideas in mind, this chapter closes with a few questions for thought:

- Is Marx correct that capitalist accumulation is limitless?
- Would people prefer more leisure to more consumption of commodities?
- Is environmental sustainability affected by different kinds of social systems?
- Is capitalist accumulation driven by the objective interests of capitalists?
- Is the democratic planning of production necessary to avoid environmental degradation?

10

Further Readings

T his chapter's purpose is to assist those interested in reading more about Marx's work and elaborations of Marx's ideas. The first section is on sources of Marx's work that are readily available. The second section is on interpretations and analysis of Marx's work. This section contains sources from the general to the specific. The last section is on journals that are devoted to discussing Marx's work or that present research influenced by Marx and debates about his work.

Marx's Writings

Marx wrote a tremendous amount during his lifetime. The most complete set of his and Engels's work that has been translated into English is the *Marx and Engels Collected Works*. This 50-volume set is published by International Publishers. The set does not contain all of Marx's work, but it contains significant components of his writings, spanning his entire life from young adulthood to his last years.

Many of Marx's writings have been posted on the website marxists.org. The content on this site can be searched, and Marx's writings are arranged by date. Marxists.org also contains the writing of numerous Marxist writers. It is a treasure trove of information related to Marx, Marxism, and other left-wing political movements.

The complete publication of Marx and Engels's work in German begin in the 1960s. The title of this compete series is *Marx-Engels-Gesamtausgabe* (MEGA). This work continues to this day and is being orchestrated by the

International Institute of Social History in Amsterdam. Information on this project can be found at http://www.iisg.nl/imes.

Two commonly used readers are Tucker's *The Marx-Engels Reader* (Marx & Engels, 1978) and McLellan's *Karl Marx: Selected Writings* (Marx, 2000). Both offer a wide selection of Marx's writings, with the exception of the Tucker volume containing some of Engels's significant solo writings while the McLellan contains a larger selection of Marx's writings. These works are commonly used in courses where Marx's ideas are introduced. However, they have their limitations, particularly concerning Marx's economic writings. A thorough study requires the full text of *Capital* and the related writings. Other than International Publishers' *Marx and Engels Collected Works*, Penguin Publishers does print all three volumes of *Capital* and the *Grundrisse*.

Analysis of Marx's Work

There are numerous books on Marx's work. Most of this work is on specific categories and topics that Marx discussed. This section is divided according to these categories and topics.

Alienation has become an important category for Marx scholars since the discovery and publication of the *1844 Manuscripts*. Wood (2004) is a good place to start. A nice short book on the topic is by Mandel and Novack (1970). Two rather important books on alienation are by Mészáros (1970) and Ollman (1976). Mészáros provides a history of the concept of alienation before Marx and a full analysis of the concept within Marx's writings and discusses the importance of the notion within our current societies. Ollman analyzes the concept of alienation along with Marx's understanding of human nature.

Class is a central category in Marx's work and one that can be empirically estimated. For those who are interested in the problems in Marx's class theory, reiterations of the category, and empirical estimations of class, the work by Wright (1985, 1996) is an excellent place to start. Other than empirical estimates of Marxian class categories, Wright provides an extension of Marxian class categories to encompass a distinction among capitalists, workers, and the middle class. Another useful estimate of Marxian class categories is by Wolff and Zacharias (2007). An accessible book that is deeply influenced by Marx's class analysis and is a class analysis of the United States is Zweig (2000). The class basis in determining the probability for people's life trajectories has been demonstrated, in a non–Marxist fashion, through generational income studies (Mishel, Bernstein, & Shierholz, 2009, p. 101).

A modern use of Marx's class formation analysis for the current political situation in China is found in Li (2011, pp. 38–51).

In the past few decades, the debate on Marx's theory of historical materialism has developed to a new level of sophistication. G. A. Cohen's *Karl Marx's Theory of History* (2000), originally published in 1978, provided a thorough reexamination of Marx's statements on historical materialism. Cohen is often described as developing a determinist reading of Marx's theory. The strength of the materialist reading has been questioned by several authors and fostered a new round of examination concerning the cogency of historical materialism. Two notable contributions to the literature are Wright, Levine, and Sober (1992) and Laibman (2007). Wright and colleagues and Laibman both consider if historical materialism can be a scientific theory. Both books develop new hypotheses concerning social development, which they think can be scientifically corroborated.

This volume had only a single chapter devoted to Marx's economics even though Marx's adult life was devoted to the study of the subject. A vast amount of material went unexamined in these pages. Readers interested in a general introduction to Marx's economics could start with Sweezy (1942) and Mandel (1962). Sweezy provides a great overview of the key categories of Marx's economic system. Mandel's presentation is more thorough and offers a wide-ranging Marxist analysis of economic development and economic categories. For those who are more mathematically inclined, Foley (1986) provides a thorough introduction to Marx's economics. Foley is mainly writing for intermediate-level economics students. His presentation offers comparisons between Marx's economics and neoclassical theory. Roemer (1988) offers a critique and expansion of Marx's ideas that is more in alignment with neoclassical theory. In addition, Roemer is interested in discussing Marx's economics in light of contemporary distributive justice literature. Harvey (1999) also provides a thorough treatment of Marx's economics. He has an extensive section on Marx's theory of rent, which was not touched on in this work. Foley (1986) and Mandel (1962) also discuss Marx's rent theory.

In addition, this volume did not address what many consider to be a major problem in Marx's economics, the transformation problem. The transformation problem is when the money prices of commodities differ from the amount of labor required to produce the commodities. This has been understood to be a major inconsistency in Marx's work, and many have thought this calls the labor theory of value into question. Sweezy (1942) and Foley (1986) both present the problem and discuss possible solutions. Hunt (1992) also gives an overview of solutions and places Marx's labor theory of value in the overall history of economics.

Marx's crisis theory has also been the subject of much debate and new research. Sweezy (1942), Shaikh (1978), and Foley (1986) contain good overviews of the debate. Sweezy expanded upon Marx's work and argues for a new interpretation of capitalist crisis (1942). He develops this theory later in Baran and Sweezy (1966). Mandel (1962) is critical of Sweezy's first presentation of the theory from 1942. His work also contains a presentation of Marx's crisis theory. Other notable contributions to the theory of capitalist crisis include Mandel (1978a, 1995), Laibman (1997), and Kotz, McDonough, and Reich (1994, 2010). Some Marxist analyses of the recession of 2008 are Shaikh (2010), Foster and Magdoff (2009), and the collection edited by Holt and Huato (2010).

Expansions of Marx's theory of ideology can be found in Mandel (1978a). For contemporary attempts to demonstrate the ideological nature of procapitalist social science, see Hahnel (2002) and Hunt (1992). Other theories of ideology are influenced by Marx's work but embrace the notion that ideology is not simply false theories and beliefs about the world. The works of Therborn (1980) and Marcuse (1964) both develop theories of ideology that consider ideology to be a pervasive understanding of the world. This is in contradistinction to Marx's theory of ideology, which understands ideology as the dominant explanation of social reality supported by control over the means of production. Marx found that ideology could be demystified through social scientific critique and class formation.

Ideology's purpose is to forestall the development of a revolutionary class consciousness and revolutionary action. Mandel (1994) has a long discussion of class consciousness and the role of a revolutionary party. Przeworski (1986) discusses how the transition to communism will need to be based on preferences beyond simply material security. Cohen (1985) develops an analytical model of why revolutionary action is the only recourse for proletarians.

Marx's vision of communism is discussed further by Engels in *Socialism: Utopian and Scientific* (Marx & Engels, 1978, pp. 683–718). Ollman (1979, pp. 48–98) provides a detailed examination of Marx's comments on communism. An interesting body of work has developed on the theory of socialism since Marx's life. The debate since the 1970s has become particularity rich. Schweickart (1996, 2002), Nove (1991), and Roemer (1994) have developed theories of socialism in which the market is used to determine prices as opposed to a planning authority. Planning theory has been advanced particularly by the work by Cockshott and Cottrell (1993). They have produced an interesting model involving the use of computers to calculate prices. Devine (2002) is especially interested in the capacity for socialist democratic planning to build social unity. The journal *Science and Society* has devoted a special issue to the questions related to the design of a socialist economy (Campbell, 2012). A work inspired by the socialist movement in Venezuela is Lebowitz (2006), which takes democratic involvement in the building of socialism as the keynote to developing a new nonantagonistic society. A contemporary restatement of the reasons for socialism has been made by Magdoff and Magdoff (2005).

Ecological Marxism has become a vibrant discipline over the past two decades. Burkett (1999) produced the seminal textual interpretation of Marx as an environmental thinker. Those seeking a deeper textual analysis of Marx's ecological view should start there. Foster (2000, 2005, 2008, 2009) has developed Ecological Marxism in new directions beyond Marx's own writings. He has shown that many of the main analyses of environmental degradation contain critiques of capitalism within them. Li (2008) has combined Ecological Marxism with World Systems Theory to demonstrate the limits of capitalist accumulation. An excellent overview of Ecological Marxism can be found in Wang and colleagues (2013). This article also discusses the impact of Ecological Marxism in China.

This volume did not discuss imperialism, but Marx notes in *The Communist Manifesto* and in *Capital* that pillage is a means for accumulation. Lenin (1987) developed the notion of imperialism, further hypothesizing that it is a stage of capitalist development. Post-World War II authors developed notions of imperialism in an age when colonies were coming to an end. An early and thorough contribution was by Baran (1957). He developed a theory of economic development in which nations that receive foreign investment can still fail to have general economic growth, the result being that these nations never entered into competition for finished products. Magdoff (1978) developed these notions further.

Marx does discuss the domination of women in his work, but his comments are not systematic. Marx and Engels do note a form of slavery that begins in the family in *The German Ideology*, written in 1845 to 1846 (Marx & Engels, 1978, p. 151). In 1884, Engels considered the development of property in relation to the domination of women based on Marx's notes in *The Origin of the Family, Private Property, and the State* (Marx & Engels, 1978, p. 734). A notable contemporary of Marx and Engels who developed a Marxist feminist position was Clara Zetkin. She was an advocate of universal suffrage and gender equality. A collection of her writings is available on the website Marxists.org. There has been much work on contemporary Marxist feminism. Martha Gimenez, Lisa Vogel, and Teresa Ebert have written extensively on Marxist feminism. Their work is an excellent place to begin. Also, the journal *Science & Society* published a special issue on Marxist feminism in January of 2005.

This book dealt with some of Marx's philosophical conceptions. Wood (2004) provides an excellent overview of Marx's more philosophically inclined work. His discussion of Marx's position on morality is very interesting. Bertell Ollman has written several books on Marx with particular focus on Marx's dialectical method. Ollman (2003) is a good place to begin. Gomberg (2007) has written a book that expands many of Marx's insights about the material basis of class antagonisms to engage with the problem of racial prejudice. Holt (2009) outlines how Marx's materialism was structured by his philosophy of nature. Holt (2011) discusses Marx's practical outlook in respect to Rawls and G. A. Cohen.

Journals Focusing on Marx's Work and Its Various Aspects

There are many journals published in English devoted to Marx's work or in which discussion of Marx and Marxism has a special place. Several are listed below in no particular order. Their associated websites are listed also. You should be able to access these journals through your university or public library systems. A few publish their articles directly for the public.

Science and Society: scienceandsociety.com

Historical Materialism: historicalmaterialism.org

Rethinking Marxism: rethinkingmarxism.org

Review of Radical Political Economics: rrp.sagepub.com

Critique: critiquejournal.net

New Left Review: newleftreview.org

Socialist Studies: socialiststudies.ca

Mediations: mediationsjournal.org

Capitalism, Nature, Socialism: cnsjournal.org

Monthly Review: monthlyreview.org

Radical Philosophy: radicalphilosophy.com

Conclusion

This book appears at an interesting time for our species and for its dominant mode of production, capitalism. The capacity for capitalist social relations to produce increasing well-being for the majority of the earth's population, for all practical purposes, is in doubt. Mass unemployment, increasing inequality, rising poverty, and ecological degradation are all problems that appear intractable within our current social relations. These problems are not of a world that lacks knowledge of solutions. Rather, our problems are of a political nature. The lack of political imagination and will, at least in the popular arena, has stymied solutions to our social-economic and ecological problems.

Marx was well aware that lack of vision and imagination would prevent people from proposing solutions that would overcome the limitation of their current social situation. In particular, our current outlook considers unemployment, poverty, and inequality to be at best voluntary and at worst necessary for economic growth. Is this true, or has our political imagination become locked into an intellectual framework that is apologetic as opposed to rigorous, scientific, and critical? Must we organize our social and economic lives in ways that prevent people from utilizing the means of production that lie idle? Is it desirable for individuals to have a right to horde wealth for unproductive purposes? I hope that this book helps to prompt people to ask if their current society has to be the way it is. Humans are naturally productive and inquisitive animals and have overcome the adverse circumstances of our past. Many of us alive today will see if human ingenuity can solve problems that are its own creation.

This book closes with a few final questions for thought, which are wider ranging and provocative than the previous sets:

- Why is the popular political and social scientific imagination and vision limited? Are the roots of this limitation ideological?
- Are mass unemployment, poverty, and inequality without solution? And are the benefits of unemployment, poverty, and inequality worth it to the majority of people?
- What justifies the current concentration in wealth and the control of industry in a few hands? And does this concentration add to or detract from the well-being of the majority of people?
- Are class relationships and profit seeking necessary for technological development? Or, to ask this question in another format, was capitalism necessary as Marx thought, or did the industrial and scientific revolutions occur in spite of capitalism?

Glossary

Abstract labor   Abstract labor is the necessary exertion of labor power designated in time elapsed. Abstract simple labor is used to calculate the exchange value of commodities.

Alienation   Alienation is when something is hostile, detrimental, or not accepting to a person. Marx thinks that people are alienated in capitalism in four ways: (1) People are alienated from the products of their labor; (2) people are alienated from the activity of labor; (3) people are alienated from their species being; and (4) people are alienated from other people (Marx & Engels, 1978, pp. 73–77).

Base   The base of a society is the relations of production.

Bourgeoisie   See *Capitalist*.

Capital   Simply, capital is the economic value of a business enterprise. Capital can take the form of money, physical machinery, land, buildings, raw materials, or finished goods.

Capital accumulation   Capital accumulation is the process by which capitalists attempt to increase and maintain their holdings of capital. The process of capital accumulation is carried out through primitive accumulation and exploitation. Capital accumulation helps preserve the class structure of capitalism by preventing workers/proletariat in any substantial numbers from leaving the conditions in which they must sell their labor power.

Capitalism   Historically, capitalism is a period beginning in the late European Renaissance (approximately the 16th and 17th centuries) and extending to today. Capitalism can be described as having the following characteristics: (1) People are free to sell their labor, (2) people can own private property, and (3) market transactions are the dominant form of economic transactions. In addition, Marx finds that capitalism is structured by a set of behaviors through which capitalists continually seek to expand their capital through the process of exploitation.

Capitalist, capitalist class   Capitalist is a class position within the capitalist mode of production. Individuals are capitalist if they own sufficient amounts of the means of production not to work for their own subsistence.

Centralization of capital   Centralization occurs when few capitals occupy a given industry.

Class consciousness   Class consciousness for Marx is when members of a class have a representation of their class position in society, how they are interrelated with other classes, what is beneficial and detrimental to them as members of their class, and how their own benefits and detriments as members of a class are achieved along with or at the expense of other members of their class or other classes.

Class formation   Class formation is when members of a given class become conscious of being members of a class and conduct political actions based on their class interests.

Class position   A class position is a structurally determined relationship to other classes. Marx's class theory determines class position based on what and what amount of productive forces a person owns.

Class, classes   Class and classes are organized by Marx according to structural class position. Structural class positions are determined by what and what amount of productive forces are owned by a given individual.

Common property   Common property is when all people have equal access to a given property without consent of others.

Concentration of capital   Growth of the value controlled by individual capitalists.

Concrete labor   *See* Useful labor.

Constant capital   Constant capital is the portion of capital that is invested in means of production, including raw materials, equipment, depreciation, fuel, energy, and the like.

Division of labor   The division of labor is when people specialize in particular trades and when the mental and manual labor of a society are performed by different people.

Exchange value   Exchange value is the proportion in which one commodity can be exchanged for another commodity. What determines the exchange value of all commodities is the amount of labor power expended in the fabrication, transport, and procurement of them.

Exploitation   In general, exploitation is when one person gains at the expense of another. Marx defines exploitation as when a person produces more value during the production process than she or he is paid for.

Fettering   In Marx's terminology, fettering is when the production relations of a given mode of production hinder further development of the productive forces. That is, the production relations fetter the development of the productive forces.

Feudal lord   *See* Lord.

Feudalism   Feudalism is a mode of production. It occurred after ancient slave societies and before capitalism. Its representative classes are lords and serfs. It also has the following characteristics: (1) Serfs could not freely sell their labor, (2) the majority of property was controlled by feudal lords or the church and was not commonly for sale, and (3) market transactions existed, but command transactions were common.

Forces of production   The forces of production have two components: the means of production and labor.

Foundation   *See* Base.

German Idealism, German Idealist   German Idealism is a philosophic movement that is known for its sophisticated analysis of human consciousness. Its most notable members include Immanuel Kant and G. W. F. Hegel.

Historical materialism   The theory of the development of human societies, which considers technological change and social organization as decisive causes.

Ideologists   Ideologists are people who create, disseminate, or use the set of ideas and beliefs that form an ideology.

Ideology   Ideology is a set of ideas and beliefs that explain, sanction, and justify the current social structure of positions, outcomes, and authority.

Independent producer class   The independent producer is a class position within the mode of production of capitalism. An individual is an independent producer if he or she owns enough of the means of production to provide for his or her own subsistence through laboring. Also called the petite bourgeoisie class.

Labor power   Labor power is the abstract activity exerted by workers that creates value. This value includes the wages that workers use to provide for their subsistence and the surplus value that capitalists control.

Lord, feudal lord   A lord is a class position within the mode of production of feudalism. An individual is a lord if he owns a sufficient amount of the means of production not to work for his own subsistence and also owns some of the labor power of serfs.

Lumpen proletariat   The lumpen proletariat is structurally members of the working class. However, due to their lack of class formation, they are usually the paid underlings of capitalists according to Marx's class analysis.

Materialism, materialist   A philosophic theory that considers that the entire existence of people and the universe is physical matter. This theory is often contrasted with various types of idealism or religious theories that find that there is more than just physical matter people and the universe are composed of. In particular, the idealism of the German Idealists, such as Kant and Hegel, thought that humans were essentially self-consciousness. Marx, in contrast, thought humans to be essentially physical beings with organic needs and social needs, the latter of which can change over time.

Means of production   The means of production are composed of the tools, machinery, buildings, spaces, and raw materials used in the production of goods.

Mode of production   The mode of production is the combined social, economic, and technological aspects of a society.

Necessary labor   This is the part of labor power expanded by the worker during the working day that is equivalent to the amount necessary for that worker's subsistence. This portion of the working day is provided to the worker in the form of wages.

Organic composition of capital   The organic composition of capital is the ratio of constant to variable capital.

Personal property   Personal property is the objects people consume to provide for their needs. This includes items such as shelter, clothing, food, personal transportation, tools for preparing food and clothing, and personal effects. Personal property is under the exclusive control of a person or persons. People must obtain permission from the owners of personal property to use it.

Petite bourgeoisie   Also called the *independent producer class.*

Price   Price is the value of a commodity in units of money.

Primitive accumulation   Primitive accumulation is the process by which people are divested of their property through force in order to be turned into workers or, in many instances in the development of capitalism, a slave labor force.

Private property   Private property is means of production that is utilized to produce commodities for sale under the exclusive control of a person or persons. People must obtain permission from the owners of the private property to use it.

Production process   The production process is the process through which the current value of production inputs are preserved and new value is created through laboring.

Productive forces   *See* Forces of production.

Proletarians   It is the same as the *working class.*

Public property   Public property is means of production that is utilized to produce commodities for sale or free distribution under the exclusive control of a political entity, such as a community, town, city, county, province, state, or nation. People must obtain permission from the owners of the public property to use it.

Relations of production   The relations of production, or production relations, are the class relationships of a given mode of production.

Serfs   A serf is a class position within the mode of production of feudalism. An individual is a serf if some of the person's labor power is owned by a lord and if that person has control over some of the means of production.

Simple labor   Simple labor is unskilled labor.

Slave   A slave is a class position within the slavery mode of production. An individual is a slave if a slave owner owns all of that person's labor power.

Slave owner   A slave owner is a class position within the slavery mode of production. An individual is a slave owner if he or she owns all the labor power of slaves and owns enough of the means of production not to work for his or her own subsistence.

Slavery   Slavery is a mode of production. Its representative classes are slaves and slave owners. It existed before feudalism.

SNLT   An acronym for socially necessary labor time.

Social contract   The social contract is a method of deciding on political arrangements. It is composed of arguments about what laws and form of society people would choose if they were in a situation in which they were not part of a society. The social contract method was developed by Hobbes (1994), Locke (2003), and Rousseau (1987). It has been utilized by modern political philosophers such as Rawls (1999), Nozick (1974), and Cohen (1995).

Species being   Species being is the ability of humans to use the natural world to satisfy their needs and to develop new needs.

Superstructure   The superstructure of a society is its legal and political institutions.

Surplus labor   This is the part of labor power expended by workers during the working day, which is beyond the amount necessary for workers' subsistence. This part of expended labor power is accumulated by the capitalist and is called surplus value.

Surplus value   Surplus value is the portion of value created by workers that accrues to capitalists. It is the result of exploitation within the production process.

Use value   Use value is the utility of a commodity. The utility of a commodity is the usefulness it provides.

Useful labor   Useful labor is the particular labor that makes useful items. This is in contradistinction to abstract labor. Useful labor is also called *concrete labor*.

Value   Value is the measure of exchange for all commodities. The value is determined by the average necessary labor time a commodity takes to produce.

Variable capital   The amount of capital used as wages.

Voluntarium imperfectum   Choice under dire necessity. Usually considered unjust since the choice is between an undesirable outcome and the loss of life, limb, or health for oneself and one's dependents. Choice under dire necessity obtains only if the outcomes of the choice can reasonably be improved. Reasonable improvement means that another person will not be subject to loss of life, limb, or health if the original party's choice is improved.

Worker   *See* Working class.

Working class   The working class is a class position within the mode of production of capitalism. Workers do not own enough of the means of production to provide for their own subsistence. Workers must sell their labor power to provide for their subsistence. The working class sells its labor power for wages. It is the same as the *proletarian class*.

References

Amin, S. (2004). *The liberal virus: Permanent war and the Americanization of the world*. New York: Monthly Review Press.

Baker, D. (2007). *The productivity to the paycheck gap: What the data show*. Washington, DC: Center for Economic and Policy Research. Retrieved from http:// www.cepr.net

Baran, P. A. (1957). *The political economy of growth*. New York and London: Modern Reader Paperbacks.

Baran, P. A., & Sweezy, P. M. (1966). *Monopoly capital: An essay on the American economic and social order*. New York: Monthly Review Press.

Barraclough, G., & Overy, R. (Eds.). (1999). *Hammond atlas of world history* (5th ed.). Maplewood, NJ: Hammond Incorporated.

Basu, D. (2013). The reserve army of labour in the postwar U.S. economy: Some stock and flow estimates. *Science & Society*, 77(2), 179–201.

Becker, G. S., & Rayo, L. (2010). Why Keynes underestimated consumption and overestimated leisure for the long run. In L. Precchi & G. Piga (Eds.), *Revisiting Keynes: Economic possibilities for our grandchildren* (pp. 179–184). Cambridge, MA, and London: MIT Press.

Blanchard, O. (2002). *Macroeconomics*. Upper Saddle River, NJ: Prentice Hall.

Briggs, Asa. (1961). The welfare state in historical perspective. *European Journal of Sociology*, 2. Reprinted in Christopher Pierson & Francis G. Castles (Eds.), *The Welfare State Reader* (2nd ed.). Cambridge, UK: Polity, 2006, 16–29.

Bryceson, D. F. (2009). Sub-Saharan Africa's vanishing peasantries and the specter of a global food crisis. *Monthly Review*, 61(3), 48–62.

Burczak, T. A. (2006). *Socialism after Hayek*. Ann Arbor: University of Michigan Press.

Burkett, P. (1999). *Marx and nature: A red and green perspective*. New York: St. Martin's Press.

Campbell, A. (Ed.). (2012). Designing socialism: Visions, projections, and models. *Science and Society*, 76(2), 140–276.

Cockshott, P., Cottrell, A., & Michaelson, G. (1995). Testing Marx: Some new results from UK data. *Capital and Class*, 19, 103.

Cockshott, W. P., & Cottrell, A. (1993). *Towards a new socialism*. Nottingham, UK: Spokesman.

Cohen, G. A. (1985). The structure of proletarian unfreedom. In J. Roemer (Ed.), *Analytical Marxism* (pp. 237–259). Cambridge, UK: Cambridge University Press.

Cohen, G. A. (1995). *Self-ownership, freedom and equality*. Cambridge, UK: Cambridge University Press.

Cohen, G. A. (2000). *Karl Marx's theory of history: A defense* (Expanded ed.). Princeton, NJ: Princeton University Press.

Descartes, R. (1984). *The philosophical writings of Descartes, volume II*. Cambridge, UK: Cambridge University Press.

Devine, P. (2002). Participatory planning through negotiated coordination. *Science and Society*, 66(1), 72–85.

Diamond, J. (1997). *Guns, germs and steel: The fates of human societies*. New York and London: W. W. Norton & Company.

Diamond, J. (2004, March 25). Twilight at Easter. In *The New York Review of Books* (Vol. LI, No. 5). New York: New York Review of Books.

Economic Policy Institute. (2012a). Share of market-based personal income by income type, 1959–2009. *The State of Working America*. Washington, DC: Economic Policy Institute. Retrieved May 24, 2012, from http://stateofworking america.org/chart/swa-income-table-2-9-share-market-based

Economic Policy Institute. (2012b). Average annual hours actually worked per worker, 1979–2009. *The State of Working America*. Washington, DC: Economic Policy Institute. Retrieved June 20, 2012, from http://stateofworkingamerica. org/files/pre-files/international_average_annual_hours_per_worker.pdf

Esping-Andersen, G. (1990). *The three worlds of welfare capitalism*. Princeton, NJ: Princeton University Press.

Farley, J. W. (2012). Petroleum and propaganda: The anatomy of the global warming denial industry. *Monthly Review*, 64(1), 40–53.

Feldstein, M. (1978). The private and social costs of unemployment. *American Economic Review*, 68(2), 155–158.

Foley, D. K. (1986). *Understanding capital: Marx's economic theory*. Cambridge, MA, and London: Harvard University Press.

Foley, D. K. (2006). *Adam's fallacy: A guide to economic theology*. Cambridge, MA, and London: Belknap Press of Harvard University Press.

Foster, J. B. (2000). *Marx's ecology: Materialism and nature*. New York: Monthly Review Press.

Foster, J. B. (2005). Organizing ecological revolution. *Monthly Review, 57*(5), 1–10.

Foster, J. B. (2008). Ecology and the transition from capitalism to socialism. *Monthly Review, 60*(6), 1–12.

Foster, J. B. (2009). *The ecological revolution: Making peace with the planet*. New York: Monthly Review Press.

Foster, J. B., & Magdoff, F. (2009). *The great financial crisis: Causes and consequences*. New York: Monthly Review Press.

Foster, J. B., McChesney, R. W., & Jonna, R. J. (2011b). The global reserve army of labor and the new imperialism. *Monthly Review*, 63(6), 1–31.

Freeman, R. B. (2010). Why do we work more than Keynes expected? In L. Precchi & G. Piga (Eds.), *Revisiting Keynes: Economic possibilities for our grandchildren* (pp. 135–142). Cambridge, MA, and London: MIT Press.

Galbraith, J. K. (1958). *The affluent society*. Boston and New York: Houghton Mifflin Company.

Galbraith, J. K. (1967). *The new industrial state*. Princeton NJ, and Oxford, UK: Princeton University Press.

Galbraith, J. K. (1973). *Economics and the public purpose*. Boston and New York: Houghton Mifflin Company.

Gilens, M. (1999). *Why Americans hate welfare: Race, media, and the politics of antipoverty policy*. Chicago and London: University of Chicago Press.

Gomberg, P. (2007). *How to make opportunity equal: Race and contributive justice*. Maden, MA: Blackwell.

Goodin, R., Headey, B., Muggels, R., & Dirven, H.-J. (1999). *The real worlds of welfare capitalism*. Cambridge, UK: Cambridge University Press.

Gündüz, Z. Y. (2011). Water—women's burdens and companies' profits. *Monthly Review*, 62(8), 43–52.

Hagan, J. (1994). Crime, inequality, and efficiency. In A. Glyn & D. Milband (Eds.), *Paying for inequality: The economic cost of social injustice*. London: IPPR and Rivers Oram Press.

Hahnel, R. (2002). *The ABC's of political economy: A modern approach*. London and Sterling, VA: Pluto Press.

Harvey, D. (1999). *The limits to capital* (New ed.). London and New York: Verso.

Heap, S. H., Hollis, M., Lyons, B., Sugden, R., & Weale, A. (1992). *The theory of choice: A critical guide*. Oxford, UK, and Cambridge, MA: Blackwell Publishing.

Hegel, G. W. F. (1977). *Hegel's phenomenology of spirit*. (A. V. Miller, Trans.). Oxford, UK: Oxford University Press. (Original work published 1807)

Hegel, G. W. F. (1991). *Elements of the philosophy of right*. (H. S. Nisbet, Trans.). Cambridge, UK: Cambridge University Press. (Original work published 1821)

Heilbroner, R. L. (1980). *Marxism for and against*. New York and London: W. W. Norton & Company.

Heilbroner, R. L., & Galbraith, J. K. (1990). *The economic problem* (9th ed.). Englewood Cliffs, NJ: Prentice Hall.

Hill, L. E. (1998). The institutional economics of poverty: An inquiry into the causes and effects of poverty. Remarks upon Receiving the Veblen-Commons Award. *Journal of Economic Issues*, XXXII(2), 279–285.

Hirsch, F. (1976). *The social limits to growth*. Cambridge, MA: Harvard University Press.

Hobbes, T. (1994). *Leviathan*. Indianapolis, IN: Hackett Publishing Company.

Holt, J. P. (2009). *Karl Marx's philosophy of nature, action, and society*. Newcastle upon Tyne, UK: Cambridge Scholars Publishing.

Holt, J. P. (2011). The limits of an egalitarian ethos: G. A. Cohen's critique of Rawalsian liberalism. *Science and Society*, 75(2), 236–261.

Holt, J. P., & Huato, J. (Eds.). (2010). Capitalism and crisis in the 21st century. *Science and Society*, 74(3), 285–449.

Hunt, E. K. (1992). *History of economic thought: A critical perspective* (2nd ed.). New York: Harper-Collins.

ILO. (2012). *Global employment trends 2012: Preventing a deeper jobs crisis*. Geneva, Switzerland: International Labor Office.

Jefferson, T. (2003). A summary view of the rights of British America: Set forth in some resolutions intended for the inspection of the present delegates of the people of Virginia, now in convention. In B. Blasdell (Ed.), The Communist Manifesto *and other revolutionary writings: Marx, Marat, Paine, Mao, Gandhi, and others* (pp. 41–55). Mineola, NY: Dover Publications. (Original work published 1774)

Jones, C. I. (2002). *Introduction to economic growth* (2nd ed.). New York and London: W. W. Norton and Company.

Keynes, J. M. (2010). *Economic possibilities for our grandchildren*. In L. Precchi & G. Piga (Eds.), *Revisiting Keynes: Economic possibilities for our grandchildren* (pp. 17–26). Cambridge, MA, and London: MIT Press.

Kindleberger, C P., & Aliber, R. (2005). *Manias, panics, and crashes: A history of financial crises* (5th ed.). Hoboken, NJ: John Wiley & Sons.

Kotz, D. M., McDonough, T., & Reich, M. (1994). *Social structures of accumulation: The political economy of growth and crisis*. Cambridge, UK: Cambridge University Press.

Kotz, D. M., McDonough, T., & Reich, M. (2010). *Contemporary capitalism and its crises: Social structure of accumulation theory for the 21st century*. Cambridge, UK: Cambridge University Press.

Laibman, D. (1997). *Capitalist macrodynamics: A systematic introduction*. Houndmills, Basingstoke, Hampshire, and London: MacMillan Press.

Laibman, D. (2007). *Deep history: A study in social evolution and human potential*. Albany: State University of New York Press.

Lebowitz, M. A. (2006). *Build it now: Socialism for the twenty first century*. New York: Monthly Review Press.

Lenin, V. I. (1987). *Essential works of Lenin*. New York: Dover Publications.

Li, M. (2008). *The rise of China and the demise of the capitalist world economy*. New York: Monthly Review Press.

Li, M. (2011). The rise of the working class in China. *Monthly Review*, 63(2), 38–51.

Locke, J. (2003). *Two treatises of government and a letter concerning toleration*. New Haven, CT, and London: Yale University Press.

Maddison, A. (2010). Statistics on world population, GDP and per capita GDP, 1-2008 AD. Retrieved March 11, 2012, from http://www.ggdc.net/MADDISON/oriindex.htm

Magdoff, F. (2013). 21st century land grabs: Accumulation by agricultural dispossession. *Monthly Review*, 65(6), 1–18.

Magdoff, H. (1978). *Imperialism.* New York: Monthly Review Press.

Magdoff, H., & Magdoff, F. (2005). Approaching socialism. *Monthly Review,* 57(3).

Malkin, E. (2005, June 13). In Mexico, a split between factory and workers. *New York Times.* Retrieved from http://www.nytimes.com/2005/06/12/world/americas/12iht-mexico.html

Mandel, E. (1962). *Marxist economic theory.* (B. Pearce, Trans.). London: Merlin Press.

Mandel, E. (1971). *The formation of the economic thought of Karl Marx* (B. Pearce, Trans.). New York: Monthly Review Press. (Original work published 1970)

Mandel, E. (1978a). *Late capitalism.* (J. De Bres, Trans.). London and New York: Verso. (Original work published 1972)

Mandel, E. (1978b). *The second slump: A Marxist analysis of recession in the seventies.* (J. Rothschild, Trans.). London: NLB. (Original work published 1977)

Mandel, E. (1992). *Power and money: A Marxist theory of bureaucracy.* London and New York: Verso.

Mandel, E. (1994). *Revolutionary Marxism and social reality in the 20th century.* Atlantic Highlands, NJ: Humanities Press.

Mandel, E. (1995). *Long waves of capitalist development: A Marxist interpretation.* London and New York: Verso.

Mandel, E. & Novack, G. (1970). *The Marxist theory of alienation.* New York: Pathfinder Press.

Marcuse, H. (1964). *One-dimensional man.* Boston: Beacon Press.

Maréchal, P.-S. (2003). Manifesto of the equals. In B. Blaisdell (Ed.), The Communist Manifesto *and other revolutionary writings: Marx, Marat, Paine, Mao, Gandhi, and others* (pp. 92–95). Mineola, NY: Dover Publications. (Original work published 1796)

Marx, K. (1965). *Pre-capitalist economic formations.* (J. Cohen, Trans.). New York: International Publishers. (Original work published 1939)

Marx, K. (1968). *Theories of surplus value. Part 2.* Moscow: Progress Publishers.

Marx, K. (1981). *Capital. Volume 2.* (D. Fernbach, Trans.). New York: Vintage Books. (Original work published 1885)

Marx, K. (1990). *Capital. Volume 1.* (B. Fowkes, Trans.). New York: Penguin Books. (Original work published 1867)

Marx, K. (1991). *Capital. Volume 3.* (D. Fernbach, Trans.). New York: Penguin Books. (Original work published 1894)

Marx, K. (1993). *Grundrisse.* (M. Nicolaus, Trans.). New York: Penguin Books.

Marx, K. (2000). *Karl Marx: Selected writings.* New York: Oxford University Press.

Marx, K., & Engels, F. (1965). *Selected correspondence.* (I. Lasker, Trans.). Moscow: Progress Publishers.

Marx, K., & Engels, F. (1968). *Karl Marx and Frederick Engels selected works, in one volume.* Moscow: Progress Publishers.

Marx, K., & Engels, F. (1975). *Marx and Engels collected works. Volume 1.* London: Lawrence & Wishart.

Marx, K., & Engels, F. (1978). *The Marx and Engels reader* (2nd ed.). New York: W. W. Norton and Company Inc.

Mehring, F. (1936). *Karl Marx: The story of his life.* (E. Fitzgerald, Trans.). London: Butler and Tanner. (Original work published 1918)

Mehrotra, S, & Delamonica, E. (2007). *Eliminating human poverty: Macroeconomic and social policies for equitable growth.* London and New York: Zed Books.

Mészáros, I. (1970). *Marx's theory of alienation.* London: Merlin Press.

Minsky, H. P. (2013). *Ending poverty: Jobs, not welfare.* Annandale-on-Hudson, NY: Levy Economic Institute.

Mishel, L., Bernstein, J., & Shierholz, H. (2009). Economic Policy Institute. *The State of Working America 2008/2009.* Ithaca, NY, and London: Cornell University Press.

Moseley, F. (2000). The rate of profit and stagnation in the U.S. economy. In R. Baiman, H. Boushey, & D. Saunders (Eds.), *Political economy and contemporary capitalism: Radical perspectives on economic theory and policy* (pp. 59–67). Armonk, NY, and London: M. E. Sharpe.

National Assembly of France. (2003). The declaration of the right of man and of the citizen. In B. Blaisdell (Ed.), The Communist Manifesto *and other revolutionary writings: Marx, Marat, Paine, Mao, Gandhi, and others* (pp. 85–89). Mineola, NY: Dover Publications. (Original work published 1789)

Neumann, F. (2009). *Behemoth: The structure and practice of national socialism, 1933–1944.* Chicago: Ivan R. Dee.

Nove, A. (1991). *The economics of feasible socialism, revisited* (2nd ed.). London: Harper-Collins.

Nozick, R. (1974). *Anarchy, state, and utopia.* New York: Basic Books.

OECD. (2011). *Statistical annex.* Paris: OECD.

Ollman, B. (1976). *Alienation: Marx's conception of man in capitalist society* (2nd ed.). Cambridge, UK: Cambridge University Press.

Ollman, B. (1979). *Social and sexual revolution: Essays on Marx and Reich.* Boston: South End Press.

Ollman, B. (2003). *Dance of the dialectic: Steps in Marx's method.* Urbana, IL, and Chicago: University of Chicago Press.

Oreopoulos, P., von Wachter, T., & Heisz, A. (2012). The short- and long-term effects of graduating in a recession. *American Economic Journal: Applied Economics, 4*(1), 1–29. Retrieved from http://dx.doi.org/10.1257/app.4.1.1

Peekhaus, W. (2011). Primitive accumulation and enclosure of the commons: Genetically engineered seeds and Canadian jurisprudence. *Science and Society, 75*(4), 529–554.

Philpott, J. (1994). The incidence and cost of unemployment. In A. Glyn & D. Milband (Eds.), *Paying for inequality: The economic cost of social injustice* (pp. 130–144). London: IPPR and Rivers Oram Press.

Plato. (1968). *The republic of Plato.* (A. Bloom, Trans.). New York: Basic Books.

Polanyi, K. (1944). *The great transformation: The political and economic origins of our time.* Boston: Beacon Press.

Przeworski, A. (1986). Material interests, class compromise, and the transition to socialism. In J. Roemer (Ed.), *Analytical Marxism* (pp. 162–188). Cambridge, UK: Cambridge University Press.

Rawls, J. (1999). *A theory of justice* (Rev. ed.). Cambridge, MA: Harvard University Press.

Reich, M. (1981). *Racial inequality: A political-economic analysis*. Princeton, NJ: Princeton University Press.

Robson, S., & Ward, A. (2012, December 10). The REAL toy story: Chinese factory workers forced to sleep among piles of doll parts as they churn out Christmas presents. *Daily Mail*. Retrieved from http://www.dailymail.co.uk/news/article-2245066/Real-Toy-Story-TheChinese-factory-workers-forced-sleep-factory-floors.html#ixzz2TxZgPi4y

Roemer, J. (1988). *Free to lose: An introduction to Marxist economic philosophy*. London: Radius, Century Hutchinson Ltd.

Roemer, J. (1994). *A future for socialism*. Cambridge, MA: Harvard University Press.

Rothstein, R. (2013). Racial segregation and Black student achievement. In D. Allen & B. Reich (Eds.), *Education, justice, and democracy* (pp. 173–198). Chicago and London: University of Chicago Press.

Rousseau, J. (1987). *The basic political writings*. Indianapolis, IN: Hackett Publishing Company.

Ryan, J. A. (1996). *Economic justice: Selections from* Distributive Justice *and* A Living Wage. Louisville, KY: Westminster John Knox Press.

Schweickart, D. (1996). *Against capitalism*. Boulder, CO: Westview Press.

Schweickart, D. (2002). *After capitalism*. Lanham, MD: Roman & Littlefield.

Sen, A. (1999). *Development as freedom*. New York: Anchor Books.

Service, E. R. (1975). *The origins of the state and civilization: The process of cultural evolution*. New York: W. W. Norton and Company Inc.

Shaikh, A. M. (1978). An introduction to the history of crisis theories. In Union of Radical Political Economics Staff (Ed.), *U.S. capitalism in crisis* (pp. 219–241). New York: U. R. P. E.

Shaikh, A. M. (1984). The transformation from Marx to Sraffa. In E. Mandel & A. Freeman (Eds.), *Ricardo, Marx, Sraffa, The Langston Memorial Volume*. London: Verso.

Shaikh, A. M. (2007). Globalization and the myths of free trade: History, theory, and empirical evidence. *Routledge frontiers of political economy*. New York: Routledge.

Shaikh, A. M. (2010). The First Great Depression of the 21st century. In L. Panitch, G. Albo, & V. Chibber (Eds.), *Socialist Register 2011: The crisis this time*. New York: Monthly Review Press.

Shaikh, A. M., & Tonak, E. A. (1994). *Measuring the wealth of nations: The political economy of national accounts*. Cambridge, UK: Cambridge University Press.

Shierholz, H. (2013). *Job openings and hiring dropped in December, and have not increased since early 2012*. Economic Policy Institute. Retrieved from http://www.epi.org/publication/job-seekers-ratio-february-2013

Staub, E. (2004). Basic human needs, altruism, and aggression. In A. G. Miller (Ed.), *The social psychology of good and evil* (pp. 51–84). New York and London: Guilford Press.

Sweezy, P. M. (1942). *The theory of capitalist development.* New York: Monthly Review Press.

Therborn, G. (1980). *The ideology of power and the power of ideology.* London and New York: Verso.

UN News Center. (2012, August 24). Safety conditions at South African mines have room for improvement, says UN expert. Retrieved from http://www.un.org/apps/news/story.asp/html/story.asp?NewsID=42736&Cr=South+Africa&Cr1=#.UxJ0W4WX7KA

U.S. Census Bureau. (2011). *Income, poverty, and health insurance coverage in the United States: 2010.* Washington, DC: U.S. Government Printing Office.

Veblen, T. (1994). *The theory of the leisure class.* New York: Dover Publications.

Wang, Z., Fan, M., D. Sun, H., & Li, L. (2013). What does ecological Marxism mean for China? Questions and challenges for John Bellamy Foster. *Monthly Review, 64*(9), 47–53.

Weil, R. (2006). Condition of the working classes in China. *Monthly Review, 58*(2), 25–48.

Weil, R. (2008). City of youth: Shenzhen, China. *Monthly Review, 60*(2), 32–49.

Wilkinson, R. (1994). Health, redistribution and growth. In A. Glyn & D. Milband (Eds.), *Paying for inequality: The economic cost of social injustice* (pp. 24–43). London: IPPR and Rivers Oram Press.

Wolff, E. N., & Zacharias, A. (2007). *Class structure and economic inequality* (Working Paper No. 487). Annandale-on-Hudson, NY: Levy Economics Institute.

Wood, A. W. (2004). *Karl Marx* (2nd ed.). New York and London: Routledge.

Wray, L. R. (1998). *Understanding modern money: The key to full employment and price stability.* Cheltenham, UK, and Northampton, MA: Edward Elgar.

Wright, E. O. (1985). *Classes.* London and New York: Verso.

Wright, E. O. (1986). What is middle about the middle class? In J. Roemer (Ed.), *Analytical Marxism* (pp. 114–140). Cambridge, UK: Cambridge University Press.

Wright, E. O. (1996). *Class counts: Comparative studies in class analysis.* Cambridge, UK: Cambridge University Press.

Wright, E. O., Levine, A., & Sober, E. (1992). *Reconstructing Marxism: Essays on explanation and the theory of history.* New York and London: Verso.

Zweig, M. (2000). *The working class majority: America's best kept secret.* Ithaca, NY, and London: Cornell University Press and ILR Press

Index

About the Author

Justin P. Holt currently teaches political philosophy at New York University. He completed his PhD in philosophy at the New School for Social Research. His first book, *Karl Marx's Philosophy of Nature, Action, and Society*, analyzed how Marx's understanding of nature shaped his social philosophy. He has also published numerous articles on socialism, G. A. Cohen, and John Rawls.

ⓈSAGE research**methods**

The essential online tool for researchers from the world's leading methods publisher

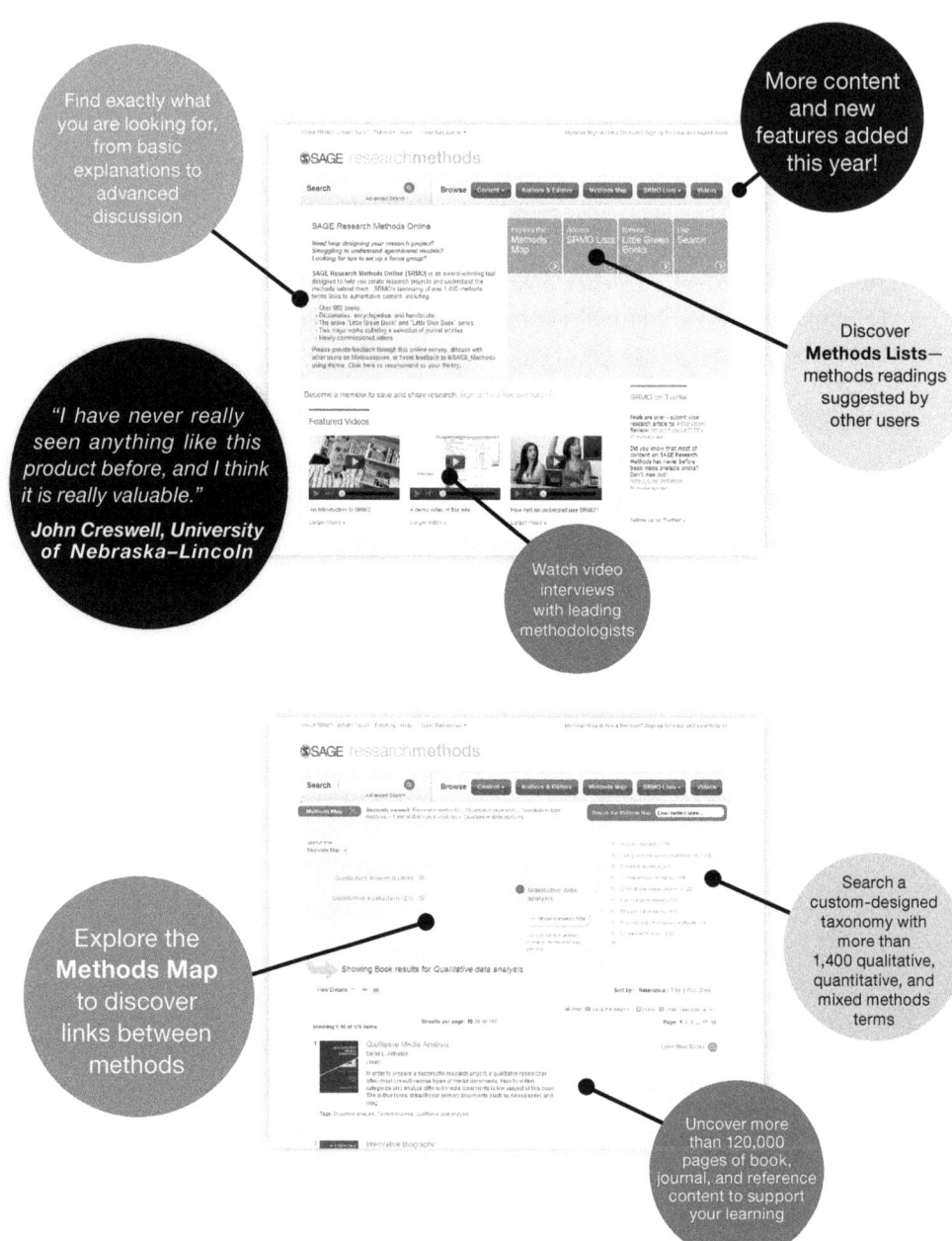

Find exactly what you are looking for, from basic explanations to advanced discussion

More content and new features added this year!

Discover **Methods Lists**— methods readings suggested by other users

"I have never really seen anything like this product before, and I think it is really valuable."

John Creswell, University of Nebraska–Lincoln

Watch video interviews with leading methodologists

Explore the **Methods Map** to discover links between methods

Search a custom-designed taxonomy with more than 1,400 qualitative, quantitative, and mixed methods terms

Uncover more than 120,000 pages of book, journal, and reference content to support your learning

Find out more at
www.sageresearchmethods.com

www.ingramcontent.com/pod-product-compliance
Ingram Content Group UK Ltd.
Pitfield, Milton Keynes, MK11 3LW, UK
UKHW021341180526
471099UK00008B/88

* 9 7 8 1 4 1 2 9 9 7 8 4 3 *